Priests

for the

Third Millennium

Bishop
Timothy M. Dolan

Our Sunday Visitor Publishing Division
Our Sunday Visitor, Inc.
Huntington, Indiana 46750

For Monsignor Adolph Matthew Schilly:
my pastor, mentor, friend, and brother priest
of the archdiocese of St. Louis
(1919-2000, R.I.P.)

Contents

Acknowledgments / 7

Foreword / 9

Introduction / 13

Part One: Living the Christian Life

1 / Faith / 17

2 / Hope / 29

3 / Love / 41

4 / Humility /53

5 / Fidelity / 67

6 / Obedience / 75

7 / Courtesy / 89

8 / Integrity / 99

9 / Prudence / 115

10 / Penance / 129

11 / Human Formation / 145

12 / Stewardship of the Spirit / 161

13 / Patience / 171

14 / Simplicity of Life / 185

15 / Joy / 199

Part Two: Living the Priestly Life

16 / The Eucharist in the Life of the Priest / 213

17 / Priestly Identity / 227

18 / Sacrament of Penance / 239

19 / The Liturgy of the Hours / 255

20 / Parish Priesthood / 267

21 / Priestly Zeal / 281

22 / Preaching / 295

23 / Celibacy and Chastity / 307

24 / Devotion to Our Lady / 323

Acknowledgments

My gratitude:

To the priests and seminarians of the Pontifical North American College, who listened patiently, reacted positively, and encouraged me mightily . . .

To the bishops of our board of governors, who urged — no, ordered! — me to have these conferences published . . .

To Lory Mondaini, my faithful secretary, who was able to make sense of my rambling thoughts and illegible penmanship . . .

To the Most Reverend Justin Rigali, my own archbishop, who has inspired and supported me in all my six years as rector, and as one of his priests.

Foreword

As archbishop of St. Louis it is a pleasure for me to present to the public this splendid volume written by Monsignor Timothy Dolan, entitled *Priests for the Third Millennium.*

Monsignor Dolan is a highly esteemed and zealous priest of the archdiocese of St. Louis who for the past six years has dedicated his ministry to the training of seminarians as rector of the North American College in Rome.

The present volume represents the fruit of his pastoral counsel to young men from the different dioceses of the United States studying for the priesthood in the See of Peter.

What was originally addressed to a limited audience of American seminarians as an incentive to assist them in their Christian lives and in the discernment of their priestly vocation becomes, through this publication, an encouragement to a much wider audience. The spirituality that Monsignor Dolan has shared with the seminarians is Christocentric. It presents Jesus Christ, true God and true Man, "the way, the truth, and the life," as the model of their Christian living, as well as of the priestly ministry to which they aspire.

Because of the important content of the material, its appeal goes beyond being relevant only for seminarians. So much of it will encourage and benefit those who have already been ordained and are living the priesthood, striving to serve God's people in holiness of life. A large part of the volume treats and bears witness to the universal call to holiness, as it is so insistently promoted by the Second Vatican Council.

A useful division is made in the presentation of the contents of the volume — "Part One: Living the Christian Life" and "Part Two: Living the Priestly Life." Hence the layperson — single or married — the Religious in consecrated life, the seminarian, and the priest can all profitably be sustained in their vocation by the reflections and insights of Monsignor Dolan.

From his opening treatment on *faith*, as it is expressed in the Apostles' Creed, to his concluding chapter on *devotion to Mary*, whom he presents as Mother of the Incarnate Word and Mother of us all, Monsignor Dolan faithfully teaches Catholic doctrine with his own customary and much admired enthusiasm and simplicity.

In treating the components of the Christian life, Monsignor Dolan not only dwells on *the theological virtues* but also aptly concentrates attention on *humility* and *obedience*. He gently reminds readers — young and old — that we must reject any neo-Pelagianism that incites us "to think that salvation depends on us" in the sense that we can win divine favor on our own merits.

With a great practical sense, he draws attention to the famous Litany of Humility of Cardinal Raphael Merry del Val, inviting us to pray: "From the desire of being preferred to others, deliver me, Jesus." "That others may be esteemed more than I, Jesus, grant me the grace to desire it." And once again how practical the insights of Monsignor Dolan, who links the success of obedient discipleship to *prayer!*

How refreshing it is to note the emphasis of a Christian humanism that extols the value of *courtesy, simplicity of life,* and *joy.* Monsignor Dolan's treatment of these issues will have a special effectiveness for all those acquainted with his own lifestyle and personal charisma.

In Part Two of *Priests for the Third Millennium,* there is no doubt that the image of *the Catholic priesthood* that Monsignor Dolan so aptly presents is that of the Second Vatican Council.

At the very center of the priesthood, as at the center of all Christian living, is *the Eucharist.* The author shows the unbreakable connection between the Eucharist and the whole priestly life and ministry. The daily celebration for the priest is the source of his joy and the inspiration of his service — all this in fidelity to Vatican II.

A particular contribution to the literature on *priestly identity* is Monsignor Dolan's inspirational treatment of the words of St. Maximilian Kolbe: "I am a Catholic priest." Whether he is speaking about the sacrament of penance, the liturgy of the hours, preaching, or so many other factors that make up the daily celibate life of the priest, Monsignor Dolan uplifts his readers with an exhilarating emphasis on true priestly identity—a life worth living, a life worth sharing, a life worth offering up to the Father through Christ and in the Holy Spirit.

In this book Monsignor Dolan truly offers to his readers a presentation of the Church's teaching that is pastoral, practical, and thoroughly Catholic. It will certainly renew in the hearts of many people the joy of being a Catholic.

✠ JUSTIN F. RIGALI, J.C.D.
ARCHBISHOP OF ST. LOUIS
MARCH 3, 2000
FEAST OF BLESSED KATHARINE DREXEL*

---

*Scheduled to be canonized in October of this year.

Introduction

Like my brother rectors at home, I try my best to take seriously the directive of the bishops of the United States, as found in their Program of Priestly Formation, to address my seminarians often each year on just what the Church expects of her priests. Again, like every other rector, I send those conferences to my board of governors. It is at their initiative that what follows, the conferences I have given my seminarians in Rome in my first five years as rector, 1994 through1999, are presented to you.

The North American College is the American seminary in Rome, where, at this writing, three hundred twenty-five priests and future priests, from two-thirds of the dioceses of the United States, are in formation, either at the seminary on the Janiculum Hill in the shadows of St. Peter's, at our graduate house, the venerable Casa Santa Maria, in the heart of historic Rome, or on our sabbatical program, the Institute for Continuing Theological Education of Priests. It is my privilege and joy to be rector of this historic college.

While the conferences were intended for seminarians, my hope is that they will also be found helpful by priests, and by anyone in a position of leadership or service in the Church. I have tried to edit them a bit to give them a much wider application, in the process trimming some of the more personal and in-house references from here in Rome.

Thank God, the formation our men receive here extends much beyond these conferences! In frequent spiritual direction, retreats and days of recollection, weekly sessions on topics essential for priestly life and ministry, and their own classes at the university, the men here, as at our own seminaries at home, are constantly presented with a realistic treatment of the noble demands of ordained life.

To live a faithful priestly life, we need all the help we can get! The Lord always comes through. If these simple chapters can contribute in some small way to the happiness, holiness, and fidelity of other priests, my efforts then have all been worth it, as I have then been able to encourage my brother priests, as

so many of them have encouraged me through my nearly quarter-century of priestly life.

Vergine Immacolata! Aiutateci!

("Immaculate Virgin! Help us!")

Part One

Living the Christian Life

1

Faith

(Scripture selection — John 20:19-29)

During my third parish assignment my pastor happened to be one of the auxiliary bishops of the archdiocese of St. Louis, George J. Gottwald. By that time Bishop Gottwald was nearing retirement, rather worn out from nearly fifty years as a priest and twenty-five as a bishop. He loved to linger at the table and speak of the Second Vatican Council, but he was less than enthusiastic in speaking about the other critical period in his life, the nine months he served as apostolic administrator of the archdiocese following the death of Cardinal Joseph Ritter in June, 1967.

Now, most of you were not even born then, but those years immediately following the council were climactic times: a lot of good, creative, vibrant, promising movement in the Church, all prompted by the genuine call for reform by the council; but, unfortunately, a lot of doubt, error, hurt, confusion, and downright silliness. At the height of all this, Bishop Gottwald, who had literally been a very effective but very plain country pastor who became an auxiliary bishop out of sheer obedience, was thrust into leadership.

One of his many crises was the seminary. One-fourth of the priest faculty left the priesthood, the student body was decimated by departures, and the theology being taught was anything but of the Church. The priests who remained on the faculty announced they wanted to join an ecumenical theologate, since, according to their interpretation of the council, it was useless to teach Catholic theology — since it probably no longer existed.

They demanded the presence of the apostolic administrator at what was really a "campus demonstration" in the early spring of 1968, there to present him with their list of demands, in front of the obligatory TV cameras.

Into this lion's den walked Bishop George Gottwald, shy, nervous, wishing he was still an unknown pastor in the Ozark hills of southern Missouri. The leader of the faculty and students informed the bishop that Kenrick Seminary might as well close, since the whole enterprise of priestly formation and Catholic theology was up for grabs. The bishop offered the comment that, even with the legitimate questioning and probing of the council, there were still clear, consistent truths that had to be taught any future priest.

"Hah!" snickered the faculty spokesman, "I dare you to tell me what we can possibly teach our students now that has not changed, that will not change, that can be stated with any amount of conviction at all! I dare you to tell me!"

The bishop's mouth went dry, he recalls, as all eyes were on him, as the microphones clicked on and cameras whirled for a sound bite, as they waited for him to take the dare! And what did he answer?

"I believe in God, the Father Almighty, Creator of heaven and earth; and in Jesus Christ, his only Son, our Lord: who was conceived by the Holy Ghost, born of the Virgin Mary; suffered under Pontius Pilate, was crucified, died, and was buried. He descended into hell; the third day he arose again from the dead; he ascended into heaven, sitteth at the right hand of God the Father Almighty; from thence he shall come to judge the living and the dead. I believe in the Holy Ghost, the Holy Catholic Church, the communion of saints, the forgiveness of sins, the resurrection of the body, and life everlasting. Amen."

The Apostles' Creed! A fundamental formula of faith expressed by the Church from near the beginning. This, my friends, was a man of *faith*: in the midst of doubt, ridicule, snickering, and confusion, he dared to state that there are certain truths that can always be counted upon because they come from God and not from us!

Faith. A steward carefully takes stock of what gifts, what treasures, what items he has at his disposal, realizing that he needs to draw upon them continually. We are stewards, and is there a more priceless gift in our interior storehouse than that of *faith*? Should we perhaps take stock?

"Faith," the Epistle to the Hebrews instructs us, "is the guarantee of the blessings that we hope for, the proof of the existence of the realities that at present remain unseen." Yes, in spite of the aimlessness, contradiction, and skepticism around us, our faith

18

allows us to cling to certain things with steadfastness: God exists! He loves us passionately! He has revealed truths to us! He has sent his Son as "the way, the truth, and the life" (John 14:6)! His Son has saved us by his death and resurrection, and is still alive, powerful, with us! Our hearts are steadfast in this faith! *Firmum est cor meum.*

Our faith assures us these propositions are true, based not on cold, clinical evidence, but on simple, childlike, humble faith in a Father who will never mislead us!

Faith of course has as its object not propositions and doctrines directly, but a *person*, namely Jesus the Christ. We believe in him, and thence flows our belief in what he and his Church have taught.

Many of you have sisters with children. If you're like me, you so love to watch your little nieces and nephews and see the *faith* they have in their mom. It's not rational but spontaneous, natural, part of their being. . . . The little child knows that . . .

- when I cry, she will come;
- when I am scared, she will hold me;
- when I am hungry, she'll feed me;
- when I'm lonely, I'll go to her.

Faith . . . and such is our faith in the Lord. Charles de Foucauld realized this when he wrote, "The moment I realized that God existed, I could not do otherwise than to live for him alone. . . . Faith strips the mask from the world and reveals God in everything. It makes nothing impossible and renders meaningless such words as anxiety, fear, and danger, so that the believer goes through life calmly and peacefully, with profound joy — like a child hand in hand with his mother."

How tragic it would be if we took this admittedly primitive aspect of our lives — *faith* — for granted! Hardly careful stewardship! I propose one of the reasons priests stumble and fall, or why they shrivel up into careless, crabby, comfortable, lazy bachelors, has little to do with vocation but everything to do with *faith*! As Bishop Sheen said, "The crisis in the priesthood is not one of identity but one of *faith*!"

A priest I admired immensely as a boy in the parish left the priesthood when I was here at the college. I was very upset. He sent me a letter I still read on occasion, in which he said, "Yes, I have lost my priestly vocation, but, I must admit, I lost my faith years ago. And there is no one more miserable than a priest who has no faith!" How right he was!

As Paul wrote Timothy: "But, as a man dedicated to God . . . you must aim to be . . . filled with faith. . ." (1 Timothy 6:11-12). "Keep as your pattern the sound teaching you have heard from me, in the faith and love that are in Christ Jesus! You have been trusted to look after something precious; guard it with the help of the Holy Spirit who lives in us!" (2 Timothy 1:13-14).

My brothers, this has everything to do with our formation, with our vocation, with the very reason we are here, because our people look to us as *men of faith!*

The story is told of Mahatma Gandhi: A young mother traveled eleven hours from a distant part of India to meet him and ask his help with her troubled three-year-old boy, who was unruly, hyperactive, would not sleep, always rambunctious.

"Tell me everything about him," Gandhi replied. "Tell me what he says, what he wears, what he eats, how he plays, what he dreams, with whom he plays outside." The mother did. Gandhi sat silent and said, "I know the difficulty, but I cannot tell you for a month. Come back then."

The mother made the arduous eleven-hour journey exactly a month later, and said to Gandhi, "What is wrong with my boy?" The holy man replied, "He eats too much sugar. Do not let him eat sugar and he'll be fine."

The woman, while relieved to find out the cure, was irritated and said, "If the answer was so simple, why did I have to make this terrible journey again? Why didn't you just tell me that a month ago?"

"Ah," Gandhi replied, "I could not tell you yet at that time, because I was still eating sugar."

I guess that's the eastern version of *nemo dat quod non habet* ("no one gives what he does not possess")! He knew he'd better first do what he was going to prescribe.

We spend a lot of time as priests — in the pulpit, confessional, parlor, classroom, sickbed, funeral parlor — telling people, *"Have faith!"* Well, *do we have it?* Are we men of *faith?*

Yes, our people look to us as men of faith, although theirs often is deeper than ours. How scandalous when their priests weaken their faith, by how they live, what they say, what they do or do not do. These days our people are faced with countless priests who ridicule their faith, who publicly criticize the magisterium and dismiss the truths of our Church.

I remember concelebrating midnight Mass one Christmas at the parish where my family now lives, only to hear the priest during his homily tell the people that the Gospel they just heard, one of the most moving in Scripture, one religious sociologists tell us evokes the most enduring of godly sentiments, the story of the first Christmas, was all fable, all made up, probably never happened. Can you believe it? I recall being at an RCIA session where a gentleman asked the priest-presenter to explain a bit more the doctrine of the "real presence," whereupon he answered that this doctrine was not at all stable but was being questioned and reformulated by the more enlightened theologians of the day.

As my mentor Monsignor John Tracy Ellis used to say, "No, the Church does not have all the answers, but she sure has more than any other institution on the face of the earth!" And, for God's sake, should not her priests of all people be loyal to her and in love with her?

At the zenith of the Church's year, the Easter Vigil, Holy Mother Church asks everyone to consider the same question: Are we people of *faith*? Taking the Apostles' Creed part by part, she drives home that question, *Do you believe?* I submit that it is an essential part of spiritual stewardship for us to ask ourselves these questions ceaselessly as we examine our consciences about faith.

Do we believe in God? I hope so! But, do we believe in a God who is intimately involved in our lives, who has revealed himself and truths about himself and how he wants us to live? Who took flesh in the womb of the Blessed Virgin Mary, who really was born, lived, suffered, died, rose again, ascended into heaven, and sent his Spirit?

Do we believe in a God who has created us in his own image and likeness and who has destined us for eternity, an eternity with him or without him? Who breathed into us an immortal soul, which gives us identity and personhood, and can hold the very life of God

21

imparted to us in the incomparable gift called sanctifying grace?

Do we believe God is alive and powerful in the prayers he answers and in the Church born from the opened side of his Son, that he continues to act in his seven sacraments, which really work and accomplish what they signify; that by baptism we became children of God and temples of the Holy Spirit; that in Eucharist we really and truly receive our Lord, body, blood, soul, and divinity; that in the sacrament of penance our sins are really forgiven?

That he continues to teach in the Scripture and Tradition of the Church, carefully guarded by the successors of the apostles, our bishops, especially the successor of St. Peter?

Do I believe that God has personally cherished me and called me from the moment of my conception, that he has a plan for me, that he has called me to follow his Son, who is my Lord and Savior? That he knows me better than I know myself, passionately loves me still, and is beckoning me to serve him and his Church faithfully as a priest?

Do I believe that the priesthood is an irrevocable, total, permanent commitment to Christ and his Church that actually configures me to Jesus as head, shepherd, and spouse of his Church?

Acknowledge the pivotal importance of this question: Do I really believe? Especially in an age of doubt, cynicism, skepticism, which holds that only those things verifiable under a microscope or evident in a mathematical equation are true . . . in an age that holds that *faith* is at best a curious eccentricity for weak, unstable people, at worst a superstitious sham keeping people in bondage, do I really believe?

We are men of strong faith or we are nothing! For there is nothing more pitiable than a priest without faith — and there are many. With faith we crave prayer, fraternity, spiritual growth! With faith we eagerly respond to the promptings of grace and live virtuous, moral lives! With faith we are zealous and generous with our people! With faith it all makes sense; we have peace and joy. As St. Augustine said, "There will be peace and tranquility in the Christian heart, but only as long as our faith is watchful. When our faith sleeps, we are in danger!"

Without faith — no meaning, no drive, no reason. We become cold, lazy, cynical crabs. The sacraments are empty — for we don't believe in them; preaching is boring — for we don't believe what we're saying; and we futilely seek meaning in bottles, or boys, or women, or golf clubs, or stocks, or cars, or travel, or promotion, or ambition . . .

Without faith, we're setting ourselves up for a fall. For one day, sooner or later, the crisis will come. Maybe caused by a bad assignment, fatigue over daily confrontation with evil and suffering, discouragement over our own weakness; maybe caused by failing in love, loneliness, sickness, or doubt. It will come, perhaps in the form of tortured questions: Why am I doing this? Why do I keep at it? Is the priesthood really worth it? Is there a God? Is the Church from God? Am I a fool? Unless that faith is there, we've had it!

I love the way Thomas Merton, perhaps finding himself at one such moment of trial, yet relying on his faith, expressed it:

> My Lord God, I have no idea where I am going. I do not see the road ahead of me. I cannot know where it will end. Nor do I really know myself, and the fact that I think that I am following your will does not mean that I am actually doing so. But I believe that the desire to please you does in fact please you. And I hope I have that desire in all I am doing. I hope that I will never do anything apart from that desire. And I know that if I do this you will lead me by the right road though I may know nothing about it. Therefore, I will trust you always though I may seem to be lost in the shadow of death. I will not fear, for you are ever with me, and you will never leave me to face my perils alone.

How then can we increase and protect our faith?

1. I would hope our pursuit of theological studies enhances our faith. *Fides quaerens intellectum* ("Faith seeking understanding"), as St. Anselm defined it. We dread a stale, insipid, child*ish*, defensive faith; we crave a strong, lively, confident, child*like* faith. Thus, we are not afraid to probe, wonder, question, think critically. As Pope Leo XIII said, *"La Chiesa non ha paura della verità"* ("The Church is not afraid of truth"). That's why you men are "in theology" — to bolster your faith!

And from this intense study, this critical, reflective probing, this wondering and listening, comes a faith with which we are so at home that we can express it simply, poetically, confidently, personally. My first pastor said to me as I went over to school the first day to teach, "Now we'll see if you really learned your theology when you go in to teach first grade." How right he was!

2. Our prayer increases our faith, for, at its core, faith is a gift that is ours for the asking. Those magnificent prayers of the Gospel — "Lord, I do believe! Help my lack of faith!" "Lord, increase my faith!" — have been indispensable.

I recall giving instructions once to a professor of mathematics at Washington University in St. Louis. He was marrying a Catholic girl and sincerely wanted to join the Church. Never have I seen anyone try harder for faith! He never missed an instruction, devoured every catechism I gave him, asked tough questions, even read the *Summa!* Still, no faith. "Father, what can I do?" he asked in mental agony. It then dawned on me that we were both approaching faith as if it were a discipline, a course, knowledge to be digested. But it isn't, of course — it is a gift from God. So, I said, "Have you prayed for faith, asking God to give it to you?" "Well, no," he responded. He did, and I did. He was baptized; his first son tells me he wants to be a priest. Pray for faith!

A past spiritual director once encouraged me to what he called a "prayer of articulation" where I would simply begin to tell the Lord what I believed, what I held dear, what I couldn't live without, what helped me get through — my faith. It has helped me.

3. Be careful about signs. We love to seek signs, exotic validations of our faith. Now, our Catholic tradition has always held that these things — apparitions, miracles, Shrouds of Turin, prophecies, stigmata — can *enhance* our faith but never take its place. And if all those externals caved in, really, so what? Our faith does not depend on them, but on *Him.* They're only the sauce, not the pasta.

4. Crisis, suffering — these can purify and strengthen our faith. I don't know if my faith was ever stronger than when I said the prayers after death over the still-warm body of my dad after he had dropped dead at work at fifty-one, with my mother sobbing beside me.

Faith is easy on ordination day, but tough the first time your pastor blows up at you; faith is fine when we're healthy, but elusive when sick. Faith is not needed when we're fulfilled, content, satisfied — but do we ever need it when frustrated, worried, anxious, preoccupied! Comfort, ease, security can sometimes strangle it. As we hear in the Epistle of St. James: "Count it all joy, my brethren, when you meet various trials, for you know that the testing of your faith produces steadfastness" (James 1:2-3).

5. We need the company, support, and encouragement of people who will sustain our faith. Is that not the rationale of a seminary?

Here at the North American College we pray with and for one another, we are striving for the same goal, we discuss matters of faith, and hopefully we provide one another with good example. Here we have advisers and spiritual directors who challenge us and probe us. I remember one of the first-year men telling me after about three weeks here, "Father, it is so good to be with people who share my beliefs, where I'm not scared or embarrassed to talk about Jesus, or Mary, or prayer, or temptation, or worries." Thank God we have here solidarity in prayer groups, such as Gesù Caritas, consecration to Mary, unity in apostolates, and study.

When we leave the seminary, we need friends and brother priests who will continue to bolster our faith. And believe it or not, often it is the people whose faith we try to strengthen who end up bolstering ours: Communion calls; simple people at daily Mass; normal, decent Catholic families.

What is more essential than faith?

Recently, I was at the Venerable English College for a meeting. There in the chapel is the famous portrait of the seminarians in the sixteenth century being sent to England as priests for what was almost certain martyrdom. Hundreds went from Rome back to England where the Church was persecuted. Many were arrested on the dock disembarking the ship. They were warned, threatened, sent back to Europe . . . only to catch the next ship over. Dozens, hundreds, were harassed, imprisoned, tortured, brutally martyred . . . and the stories only encouraged their brothers here preparing for the same fate. They kept going over. As one of them wrote: "Faith is readiness to die for Christ's sake, for his commandments, in the conviction that such death brings life; it is to regard poverty as riches, insignificance and nothingness as true fame and glory, and, having nothing, to be sure you possess all things. But, above all, faith is attainment of the invisible treasure of the knowledge of Christ."

On All Souls' Day at our crypt out at Campo Verano, I saw the memorial plaque for Joe Toomey, a man just a year behind me in the seminary from the archdiocese of New York. Recalling him led me to check his files because I remember to this day a letter he had sent us. I was pleased to find it:

Dear Charlie and my friends at NAC,

These past two weeks have been most trying. While I was in the hospital the doctors kept telling me that they were pushing for complete success. All of those terrible side effects returned and I fought them with renewed courage and hope. I firmly believed that the chemicals would destroy the remaining cancer.

Five days after my release from the hospital, I took a chest X-ray and was shocked by the results. The news was heartbreaking; I had made only very slight progress. The doctor very sadly told me that soon I would have to resume the nauseating weekly therapy for an indeterminable amount of time.

This news caused me to fall into a deep state of depression for a number of days. But God would not allow me to wallow in senseless despair. He kept reminding me that I must seek strength through the sacraments. Your prayers and those of my friends at home also gave me that much needed psychological and spiritual power to face a possibly long future of constant physical discomfort.

I cried tonight thinking of you all, of how much I long to return to the college. Perhaps the Lord permits me to suffer temporarily in order to add a stronger dimension of spirituality to your lives and the lives of all whom I meet. This is a joyful purpose, an actuation of true love.

Please continue to write me; I hope to see you next fall.

Cardinal Cooke ordained Joe a deacon on his deathbed, and he died seven weeks after that moving letter.

What can explain that letter but faith? What can possibly explain what we hope to spend our lives doing as priests but faith?

Let us pray the Act of Faith:

O my God, I firmly believe that thou art one God in three divine Persons, Father, Son, and Holy Spirit. I believe that thy divine

Son became man, and died for our sins and that he will come to judge the living and the dead. I believe these and all the truths which the Holy Catholic Church teaches because thou hast revealed them, who can neither deceive nor be deceived.

2

Hope

(Scripture selection — Mark 4:35-41)

Back home at Kenrick-Glennon Seminary in St. Louis, a few years ago, we had a senior in the college program named Michael Esswein. If *Sixty Minutes* had come to us wanting to do a report on "the model seminarian," we would have unanimously put forth Michael: he was holy, intelligent, handsome, outgoing, considerate, respected by his peers, a good soccer player — "man of the year" candidate!

Michael came from a very big, happy family. His older sister was a nun, and, during spring break, the first Friday of March, 1993, Michael, one of his brothers, and his mom and dad got into the family van to drive from St. Louis to Connecticut to visit that sister. Outside of Youngstown, Ohio, they ran into bad weather and hit an icy spot on the interstate; the van skidded off the roadway, tumbled down an embankment, and landed upside-down.

Michael was trapped, unconscious, upside-down, in the back seat for fifty minutes while the emergency team worked to free him. It was clear he was hurt severely, and he was taken to the nearest hospital for surgery. For eight hours the surgeons assessed and tried to repair the damage, and then came out to inform the family — who had not been injured, by the way — that, while Michael had indeed survived, his spine was irreparably damaged, and he would be paralyzed from the neck down for the rest of his life.

When he woke up, his first question was, "How is the rest of the family?" Then, seeing the apprehension on the faces of everyone around him, and sensing his powerless body telling him that something was drastically wrong, he asked, "Will I still be able to be a priest?" That's the kind of young man Michael Esswein was — and is.

Anyway, the Sunday evening following the accident, Michael's home parish planned a prayer service for his healing. St. Stephen's

Parish was standing-room-only, and the pastor led us in a moving hour of prayer for Michael, specifically entrusting Michael to the Sacred Heart of Jesus, since the Esswein family had devotion to our Lord under that title, since Michael's sister whom they were going to visit was a *Cor Jesu* nun, and since the accident occurred on a First Friday. Never have I participated in a more intense hour of intercessory prayer. At the end, with a voice full of optimism, the pastor announced, "When Michael returns, we will reassemble for a prayer service of thanksgiving."

After ten weeks in that Ohio hospital, following two subsequent surgeries and intense therapy, Michael indeed did return, and, sure enough, the same throng gathered at St. Stephen's for prayers of thanksgiving. But a pall of gloom and pessimism descended as Michael was wheeled down the main aisle, able to move only his head, and that only barely, to greet the congregation. Once he was up the newly installed ramp to the sanctuary, the service began, and, when the time came for the Scripture reading, Michael himself proclaimed the Gospel cited at the beginning of this chapter. At its conclusion, as we all sat to listen intently, Michael spoke: "You all came here for a service of thanksgiving, but, as I was wheeled up the aisle, you all thought, 'Thanksgiving for what? This young man is a quadriplegic, and will be for the rest of his life. His promising future is destroyed. This is hardly an answer to our prayers!' "

You could have heard a pin drop in that jammed church. Then Michael continued: "I must admit to you that I have felt the same way every once in a while these last ten weeks since the accident. In other words, like the apostles in the Gospel in the midst of that overwhelming storm we are tempted to think our Lord is asleep and couldn't care less. *Hope*, my friends" — Michael bellowed out — "*hope* is the gift that keeps us going when we think Jesus is asleep, and let us thank God for that great gift of *hope!*"

That was the most moving sermon on *hope* I have ever heard. I was sitting next to the chancellor of the archdiocese who whispered to me, "Let's ordain that man tomorrow."

"*Hope* is the virtue that keeps us going when we are tempted to think that Jesus is asleep. . . ."

"In God alone is my soul at rest, my help comes from him. He alone is my rock, my stronghold, my fortress, I stand firm" (Psalm 62).

I ask you to meditate with me precisely on *hope*. In the previous chapter I spoke about faith. Faith, of course, is the virtue by which we believe there is a God; *hope* is the virtue by which we trust that this God keeps his promises! "I am a man of *hope*," writes Cardinal Suenens, "not for human reasons nor from just natural optimism, but because I believe that the Lord is at work in my life, in the Church, and in the world, even when his name remains unheard."

Hope moves us to trust that the God in whom we believe will always love us and care for us, that he keeps his promises — not assuring us bliss, comfort, ease, perfection, fulfillment — but love, care, mercy, life.

I speak to you of *hope* for many reasons: Yes, every human being, certainly every Christian, needs *hope.* There are times when everything seems dark, cold, and damp, and spring is not evident— in such times we need a good chalk-talk on hope.

But, more importantly, *hope* — a deep, abiding, unflappable, calm yet noticeable *hope* — is essential for a priest! Our people want us to give them *hope,* and — here I go again — *"Nemo dat quod non habet"* ("We can't give it if we don't have it")! One of the things a priest hears most from people is: "Father, pray for me!" That means, "Father, I need hope; I don't know if I can get through this."

Our priesthood itself will hardly survive and remain vigorous and life-giving if we do not have *hope*; and we'll certainly be of no substantial service to our people if we can't give them that *hope* they crave.

"What oxygen is to the lungs," writes Emil Brunner, "such is hope for the meaning of life."

Now, let's get basic. How do we get hope? Well, we cannot obtain it on our own. We can't *get* it . . . we are *given* it! *Hope* is a virtue given us by God at baptism, intensified by the other sacraments, fostered and protected through a strong interior life flowing from a vibrant faith, and strengthened in daily perseverance through the tribulations and adversity life unfailingly brings. True, *supernatural hope* can be bolstered through *natural* habits such as a good sense of humor, an upbeat personality, a cheerful, optimistic outlook on life, and a realistic admission in the midst of trial that "this, too, shall pass."

What is of the essence, though, is the cultivation of a strong spiritual life. You have probably heard the analogy of the hurricane — in the midst of the turbulence, destruction, and overwhelming force of the storm, there is the "eye of the hurricane," an island of peace, calm, serenity. Thus is our interior life: in the midst of the storm, winds of unpredictability, setback, crisis, tragedy, or just the plain daily grind that can overwhelm us, we harbor an inner space of peace, calm, and serenity, where the Lord dwells, from which *hope* comes. Our regimen of prayer, Eucharist, devotion, spiritual direction, *lectio divina*, and the sacraments — this regimen is all directed to fostering this interior "eye of the hurricane" from which comes the *hope* to get us through what life brings.

You see it, for instance, in Pope John Paul II. Those of you who have been privileged to attend his daily private Mass know how moving it is to see him locked in intense prayer prior to, during, and after Mass. Those who seek the reason for his immense strength, determination, and *hope* need look no further than this.

I detected it in Tom Mucha, a seminarian who underwent chemotherapy for leukemia, when I talked to him on the phone several years ago. In the midst of severe pain, with chances of life fifty-fifty at best, he demonstrated an inner calm, a sense of *hope*, that must flow from a strong interior life which has been made durable by the crucible of suffering.

You see it exemplified in the life of a saint like Maximilian Kolbe, who, while stuffed in a cell with nine others slowly to die of starvation and thirst, exhibited a calm, a peace, a *hope* that inspired his co-condemned while infuriating, yet baffling the guards.

This dependable interior life, providing the "eye of the hurricane," flows from the faith we spoke of before, a childlike trust that all is in God's providential hands, that nothing is impossible for him, that, with him, all things are possible, that, although his will can be disregarded by some, his kingdom can be stopped by no one, that ultimately all will make sense because, as St. Paul writes, "all things work together for those who believe."

The Fundamentalists can teach us something about this. Flip through the offbeat channels on TV or radio at home on Sunday and odds are you'll hear some reverend yelling, "The victory has been won! The war is over! There are still some skirmishes we must fight, but these are only the last gasps of a defeated enemy! Alleluia!"

All they're saying is what St. Bernard said: "If Christ is with us, who is against us? You can fight with confidence where you are sure of victory. With Christ and for Christ victory is certain."

"In God alone be at rest, my soul, for my *hope* comes from him. He alone is my rock, my stronghold, my fortress, I stand firm" (Psalm 62).

I love the story of Pope John XXIII told by Monsignor Loris Capovilla, his private secretary. Every night, about midnight, before going to bed, Pope John would kneel before the Blessed Sacrament. There he would rehearse the problems he had encountered that day: the bishop who came in to tell of his priests massacred and his nuns raped in the Congo; the world leader who came to tell him of his country's plight in war and asking his help; the sick who came to be blessed; the refugees writing for help; the newest round of oppression behind the Iron Curtain. As Pope John would go over each problem, examining his conscience to see if he had responded to each with effective decisions and appropriate help, he would finally take a deep breath and say, "Well, I did the best I could. . . . It's your Church, Lord! I'm going to bed. Good night."

Now that's a man of *hope*! "When tempted to lose *hope*," says the Curé of Ars, "I have only one resource: to throw myself at the foot of the tabernacle like a little dog at the foot of his master."

"In God is my safety and glory, the rock of my strength. Take refuge in God, all you people. Trust him at all times. Pour out your hearts before him, for he is our *hope*!" (Psalm 62).

Let me mention a few practical observations about *hope*, which can perhaps be especially helpful for our priestly formation.

1. *Hope* can be a special struggle for priests because more often than not we do not see the tangible, immediate results of our work. A doctor can see a patient healed, even a plumber can see a leak fixed, but rarely do we see tangible, immediate results of our work as priests.

Who knows how our sermons go over?

Who knows if our words in the confessional helped?

Who knows if the marriages we have performed worked out?

Who knows if the kids we got ready for First Communion will even keep the faith?

Now, don't get me wrong — the priesthood is a life that offers immense reward, joy, and satisfaction. But there are many days we wonder if anything we're doing makes much sense or is doing any good, because our work is in cooperation with the grace of God, which works quietly, invisibly, gently, gradually, and rarely produces the fireworks of immediate, dramatic results.

So, what do you do the first time you beat your brains out preparing a talk for a parish group and nobody shows up?

What do you do when you sit for hours in the confessional and no one comes but the scrupulous person and the pious lady who was changing the altar cloths?

What do you do when you get all excited preparing your presentation for the parents of the First Communion children and all they really want to discuss is whether the girls will wear white veils and the boys sport coats?

What do you do when you're looking forward to preparing the young couple for marriage by presenting them with the Church's rich teaching and they are much more interested in the length of the center aisle?

What I'm saying is that if our happiness as priests, the meaning we find in our ministry, is based on seeing immediate, tangible, dramatic results, we're going to be terribly disappointed. That's where *hope* comes in: we trust that in some mysterious way, the Lord is working through us, even when we cannot see the effects.

This is particularly true in your first years after ordination, when you are filled with ideals and zeal, raring to go, and suddenly face the ho-humness of parish life. That's where *hope* is needed — God is working powerfully in us, through us, in spite of us, even when we can't see the results.

My first Lent as a parish priest, the president of the Men's Club said, "Father, you're supposed to give us an evening of recollection in Lent." I should have known by his lack of enthusiasm that there was hardly going to be trouble finding a parking space. But I worked hours over three talks on characters from the Stations of the Cross. The big night came — two men showed up. Needless to say, I hardly needed the microphone. Two men! I was crushed. I didn't get much help from the pastor when I went back to the rectory and he told me, "Oh, I should have told you those never work."

Twelve years later, I visited a woman from that parish in bed helpless with Lou Gehrig's disease. Her husband was so tender with her, caring for her, not leaving her side. As he showed me to the door, I told him how I admired his devotion to his wife. He said, "Oh, Father, I'm just trying to be that Simon of Cyrene you talked about." I looked at him, confused. "Yeah, remember that Lenten evening of recollection when you told us that just as Simon of Cyrene helped our Lord carry his cross, we do the same every time we help somebody else carry theirs? I'm just trying to help Ramona carry hers."

It's worth the wait . . . and *hope* helps us wait.

That's true in seminary formation too, for it takes genuine *hope* to trust that all the things that seminarians are doing will really make that much difference to them as priests. The courses they take, the training they receive, the expectations the "formators" have of them — it is understandable that at times they might ask, "Why? What good is all this to me? How is this going to help me be a better priest?" Again, it's worth the wait, and *hope* helps us wait and patiently trust that seeds planted now will indeed bear fruit later.

2. One of the great insights of priestly ministry these recent years is our need for affirmation. Priests need affirmation — from brother priests, bishops, pastors, people, families, and friends. You bet we do, and thank God for recent developments in the life of the Church that help give priests the affirmation they need. However — and I don't want to sound gloomy — *don't count on it!* When it comes, thank God, but, believe me, there will be a lot of times when the "thank yous," the "good job, Father," the "boy, is this parish ever blessed to have you" just don't come. And if we depend upon the affirmation, if we are counting on the popularity, acclaim, and external satisfaction, look out!

I hear that from young priests a lot — "My pastor never tells me I'm doing a good job." "Only time we hear from the bishop is when he sends a letter about a second collection."

In one of my parish assignments the pastor asked me to start a catechetical program for the teenagers. He warned me that others had tried and failed. I really worked to plan a program for every other Sunday evening where young couples would help me present an evening of catechetical instruction followed by athletics and pizza. Fifty-eight showed up for a smashing opening night. I returned and exuberantly reported the success to the pastor, who was watching TV and whose only remark was: "Did you turn out the lights and lock up the gym?"

Well, it's true that our pastors, our bishops, should affirm us, but often they don't. *Hope*, of course, teaches us that the real affirmation, the affirmation we crave and really can count on, comes only from the Lord. If it comes from others, alleluia! Don't count on it or let your continued zeal depend on it!

"In God alone be at rest, my soul, for my *hope* comes from him. He alone is my rock, my stronghold, my fortress, I stand firm" (Psalm 62).

3. We are tempted to put our *hope* in a lot of things, and these begin to consume us. Some are good things: we place trust in friends, in our bishops, in the Holy See, in our reputation, in the just satisfaction that comes from a job well done. But you know the day will come when even those legitimate, good objects of trust will let us down; so if we put total trust in even these legitimate things, we will one day be disappointed.

Is there anyone sadder than a priest who put all his trust in the *hope* of ecclesiastical advancement and ends his years bitter and resentful?

If you read the life of Archbishop John Ireland, one of the towering characters of American Catholic history, you see how he ended his brilliant career terribly disappointed because the "red hat" never came.

Even our friends will eventually be transferred, or drift away, or let us down . . . we cherish them and need them, but we cannot place all our *hope* in them either.

In our priestly life, we cannot *hope* in big salaries, signs of favor from our bishop, plush assignments, ecclesiastical preferment, wide acclaim. If they come, we accept them with Ignatian indifference, grateful, but able to get along just as well without them, for "we place not our trust in princes."

I tell the first-year men at the North American College on the first day they arrive, "You have left home, family, friends, security, predictability. . . . Everything has changed but one thing — your faith in and relationship with Jesus Christ: he is the same yesterday, today, and tomorrow! And perhaps the genius of study here in Rome, away from all that is familiar and reliable, is to teach us that he and he alone is the ultimate source of our *hope* — to count on anything or anyone else in this life will ultimately lead to disappointment."

"Do not put your trust in power, or vain *hope* on position. Do not set your heart on riches, even when they increase" (Psalm 62).

4. A most crucial virtue flows from *hope*, and that is *perseverance*. "Be faithful . . . always be faithful!" I remember Pope Paul VI saying to our class after diaconate ordination, "When a man says *yes* to the priesthood, that *yes* is *forever*!" To keep at it, not to flag, to continue the good fight, to remain faithful, to *persevere*, even in the midst of doubt, confusion, frustration — that flows from *hope*.

"May the God who has begun this good work in you now bring it to perfection!" the Church prays on ordination day, and we *hope* that such a prayer is being answered every day of our priestly lives. The ancient principle is that God never asks us to do something without giving us the graces necessary to accomplish it. That gives *hope*; that motivates us to *persevere* in our priestly call.

5. *Hope* is particularly needed in our prayer. The patience, persistence, and perseverance that the Master tells us must accompany fruitful prayer all spring from the virtue of *hope*. The worst mistake we can make when we are having a difficulty in prayer is to give up, to lose *hope*. There is no use denying that prayer is at times boring, unproductive, stale, full of distractions, and just plain tough. Here is where *hope* is needed:

• to trust that God is listening even when there is no response;

• to *hope* he is there when it seems he has abandoned us;

• to trust that our efforts at prayer are producing some invisible fruit when all visible signs of success are not there;

• to *hope* that "wasting time with the Lord" — as Merton defined prayer — is actually more productive than getting some practical work accomplished.

Remember St. John of the Cross. His practice was to record what happened in his prayer each day in his journal. For a long period in his life, probably his "dark night of the soul," he recorded one word: *nada. Nothing!* What went on in my prayer today? *Nada!* Not one day, but days, weeks, months, *nada!* But *hope* he kept, trusting that something would break. And we, of course, know "the rest of the story," as he is looked to now as one of those rare creatures who actually reached the heights of mystical prayer.

Along the same line, *hope* helps us in our struggle with sin. Whatever evil inclination we battle — impatience, gossip, laziness, impurity, a bad temper, a judgmental, catty tongue, whatever — we make some progress and then fall, and at times are tempted to despair and give up our journey to perfection. Never! A wise confessor once told me, "In the end, what counts is not how many times we have succeeded or failed, but how we have begun again after a failure." That takes *hope!* Fulton Sheen reminds us that there are no plains in our spiritual life, only hills and valleys, and the key to growth in holiness is not to lose hope when in the valley.

6. In the First Letter of Peter we read, "Always be prepared to make a defense to any one who calls you to account for the *hope* that is in you" (1 Peter 3:15; emphasis added).

You see, a vibrant *hope* is contagious and will attract people. Its fruits are calmness, cheerfulness, tranquility, a good sense of humor, freedom from anxiety — and these traits people find very attractive. So people can be attracted to Jesus and his Church through *hopeful* priests. But this is not some Pollyannaish, cheerleading, shallow optimism. This is a realistic, sturdy trust in God based on deep faith, born in experience, and bolstered by reason.

Such is the purpose for the Church's expectation that you are firmly grounded in theology, precisely so you can, as St. Peter says, "be able to explain the reason for this *hope* of yours."

Not that we're "know-it-alls." People don't expect an answer from us, just a reassurance that there is indeed an answer, a reason, which someday, somewhere, will be clear, even if hidden now. That gives them *hope.*

I remember once at the funeral of a one-year-old baby who had died suddenly of what appeared to be a simple cold, the child of two very active parishioners who had tried for six years to have this baby. The Church was overflowing, the parents beyond consolation. The pastor took a long time after the Gospel before beginning his homily and finally said, "If you all think I'm going to explain to you why little Matthew died, you're going to be disappointed. I don't really know why Matthew died. Even with *hope* in a loving God it makes little sense. But without that *hope* it makes absolutely no sense at all."

The parents told me those were the only words that made any sense at all in that dark time.

"The most beautiful Credo is the one we pronounce in our hour of darkness," said Padre Pio.

7. Heaven is where our hopes will ultimately be fulfilled, and we must never be afraid to speak of *heaven*.

When I lived in Washington, D.C., I used to help at the Gift of Peace House run by the Missionaries of Charity for dying AIDS victims. Sometimes I would baptize, anoint, pray with, or hear the confession of a man close to death. The sisters would always be so excited to report to me when a man had died after professing faith, contrition, asking God's mercy, for then they were confident, they told me, that he went to heaven. "That is why we do this work," one of the sisters explained, "to get souls to heaven."

Yes, they cleaned those helpless, dying men, bandaged their wounds, changed their diapers, hand-fed them, and cared for people no one else wanted. But their motive was to help a soul reach heaven.

We have grown embarrassed about speaking to people of heaven, perhaps afraid we will come across as overly pious, too otherworldly, or unconcerned about the problems of this life. But sometimes the burdens of this life can so crush people that they long to hear someone speak of that place "where every tear will be wiped away," and, if we priests won't or can't do it, who will?

As we pray in the antiphon for the *Benedictus* on the Feast of St. Agnes: "What I longed for, I now see: what I hoped for, I now possess; in heaven I am espoused to Him whom on earth I loved with all my heart."

"We did not dare to breathe a prayer or to give our anguish scope! Something was dead in each of us, and what was dead was *Hope*," writes Oscar Wilde, and this seems to characterize us today. Catholics look to their priests to be men of hope to lead them, in the words of Our Holy Father, "across the threshold of *hope*."

I remember seeing Cardinal Law being interviewed on TV outside the White House where he had just met with President Bush on averting what seemed to be sure war with Iraq. "Have you lost hope, Cardinal?" one of the reporters shouted.

"I'm in the business of hope!" responded the cardinal.

Yes, we are "in the business of hope." We are the ones who, in the boat at times about to capsize in the midst of the storm, keep on going even when it seems that Jesus is asleep.

Let us pray:

O my God, relying on your infinite promises, I hope to obtain the pardon of my sins, the help of your grace, and life everlasting, through the merits of Jesus Christ, my Lord and my redeemer. Amen.

3

Love

(Scripture selection — John 21:15-17)

The story is told of the Beloved Disciple, very advanced in years, near the end of his life in exile on the Isle of Patmos. There he lived in solitude in a cave surrounded by a few chosen disciples. Because he was the last of the Twelve, every Sunday hundreds of Christians would come to Patmos for the Eucharist and to see St. John. Sunday after Sunday the disciples would carry the frail apostle down to the crowd. When the time came for him to preach, the crowd would come closer, since his voice was barely above a whisper. Sunday after Sunday he would say the same thing: "Children, love one another! Children, love one another!"

Finally, after one such Sunday, one of his disciples, carrying him back to his cave, said, "Teacher, why do you keep repeating the same thing, over and over, 'Children, love one another'?"

"Because," replied the Beloved, "the Master kept repeating it over and over."

I want to reflect on love as the unifying principle that brings together and gives purpose to everything we do. Priestly life is full of demands and expectations; we have the requirements of daily prayer, study, and preparation for liturgies, our ministry, endless meetings to attend, and so on. The danger is that our lives can become disjointed, pulled in different directories, an engine off track. Thus, we look for a value to provide harmony, a principle to give unity, a force to give coherence, one motive to supply the direction under which everything we say and do can come — and that, I propose, is love.

St. Thérèse of Lisieux tells us in her autobiography that she had somewhat the same difficulty. The Little Flower recounts how she searched for an answer to her interior confusion, and she writes:

> I was not satisfied and could not find peace. I persevered
> . . . until I found this encouraging theme: "Set your desires on

the greater gifts. And I will show you now the way which surpasses all others" (1 Corinthians 12:31). For the Apostle insists that the greater gifts are nothing at all without love and that this same love is surely the best path leading to God. At length I had found peace! Love appeared to me to be the hinge for my vocation! I knew that the Church had a heart and that such a heart appeared to be aflame with love.... I saw and realized that love sets off the bounds of all vocations, that love is everything, that love embraces every time and place, that love is everlasting. Then, nearly ecstatic with joy, I proclaimed: O Jesus, my love, at last I have found my calling! My call is love. I have found my role in the Church.... In the heart of the Church I will be love!

— Office of Readings, Feast of St. Thérèse

Most of the time when we think of love we ponder our love for God and for his people. Natural enough — and important enough. First things first, though. The starting point of spiritual growth, the first step in true discipleship, is humble recognition of and profound gratitude for God's love for us. As the Beloved Disciple teaches, "God's love for us was revealed when God sent into the world his only Son . . . this is the love I mean: not our love for God, but God's love for us!" (1 John 4:9-10).

Those of you familiar with the Spiritual Exercises of St. Ignatius of Loyola know how he begins precisely with our recognition of God's gracious, undeserved love. You will find as priests that one of our constant frustrations is helping people accept this deep insight that God passionately loves them. That's the "Good News," isn't it? The tragedy of life is that most of us feel it is just too good to be true, and go through life avoiding it or ignoring it. Many of us can echo that gripping passage from the *Confessions* of St. Augustine:

I have learned to love you late, Beauty at once so ancient and so new. . . . You called me; You cried aloud to me; You broke my barrier of deafness; You shone upon me; Your radiance enveloped me; You put my blindness to flight; You shed your fragrance upon me. I drew breath and now I gasp at Your sweet

42

odor. I tasted You, and now I hunger and thirst for You. You touched me, and I am inflamed with love of Your peace.

— Office of Readings, Feast of St. Augustine

I remember a Jewish psychiatrist once saying to me, "Father, keep telling your people that God loves them. Most of the problems I deal with come from people who believe no one loves them, that they are unlovable, so therefore, they don't even love and respect themselves."

Every human being is loved by God and invited to love him in response; particularly are those who believe in God's revelation in his Son called to be ever aware of his love and their duty to return it. To the point, however, the priest is called to have an intense awareness of the Lord's love for him, to accept it with humble gratitude, and to return that love with such intensity that he mirrors it to his people. Not only that; we as priests are called to such an intimate love of Jesus that we are actually, at the core of our being, configured to him in his passionate love for his Spouse, the Church. Heavy words those are, and I do not pretend to comprehend their full impact. But this identification with Jesus in his spousal love of his Bride, the Church, is at the center of priestly identity and ministry.

I had better depend on the words of Pope John Paul II in *Pastores Dabo Vobis* (No. 22): "Christ's gift of himself to his Church, the fruit of his love, is described in terms of that unique gift of self made by the Bridegroom to the Bride. . . . The priest is called to be the living image of Jesus Christ, the Spouse of the Church. . . . In virtue of his configuration to Christ, the head and shepherd, the priest stands in this spousal relationship with regard to the community. . . . In his spiritual life, therefore, he is called to live out Christ's spousal love toward the Church, his Bride. Therefore, the priest's life ought to radiate this spousal character which demands that he be a witness to Christ's spousal love."

That, my brothers, is the love we are called to accept, return, and radiate. That is our lofty vocation. That is the unifying principle of everything we do here. How to accept, return, and radiate that love is precisely our lifelong program of priestly formation.

Now I ask you, how? How do we grow in our love of Christ and

43

his Church? At the risk of oversimplification, I propose we "fall in love" with Christ and his Bride, the Church, in many of the same ways we grow in relationships of love and friendship on the natural level. I ask you, then, to remember past relationships of love and genuine friendship. Or, if you have never been in love with someone before, think of people close to you who have been, or simply ask yourself what steps you would take to grow in love with someone, or to strengthen and deepen a friendship.

To grow in our love with Jesus and his Church, would we not be expected to do certain things?

1. To grow in our love with someone we first of all spend time with the other person. We converse with the other, we listen to the other, we enjoy being with the other.

The same is true in our love of Jesus, isn't it? We call being with the Lord — listening to him and then conversing with him — prayer. Thus, daily prayer is essential to our life, a *sine qua non*. Every day we find ourselves spending a chunk of time with our best friend, the Divine Lover, talking to him, listening to him. Prayer. We cannot grow in love with Jesus without it.

My mom and dad were very much in love. I heard others say they were like teenagers in their affection for each other, in the freshness and exuberance of their love. Dad left the house for work before 5:00 a.m., before any of us, even Mom, was up, but he always left a little note for Mom. At his coffee break he would call her; and when he returned home each evening at about 4:45, he and Mom would sit by themselves in the kitchen over a drink and spend an hour together. We kids just learned not to intrude. They sometimes chatted, sometimes said not much, sometimes engaged in rather animated discussion. Sometimes Mom would do the talking; sometimes Dad would. That daily time together, stealing quiet time by themselves, was the secret to their love.

The same is true in our relationship with Jesus. We must spend time alone with him daily if our love for him is to remain strong. For the priest, the liturgy of the hours is the way we "keep in touch with our beloved" during a busy day. Thus, we expect you to be faithful to daily communal morning and evening prayer. Likewise is personal prayer essential. Some of you do this early in the morning; some late at night; some depend on Scripture; some prefer the holy hour format; some call it meditation; some call it "centering." Whatever, however, whenever — if you want to fall in love with Jesus, and remain in love with him, our destiny as one of his priests, you must be with him, talk with him, and listen to him every day. That is called prayer.

2. A way to enhance a friendship or relationship of love is to share a meal with the other. In our society, you know someone enjoys your company and wants to get to know you better when that person asks you out to eat. Well — again, pardon the oversimplification — we grow in our love for Jesus by daily sharing the Eucharistic meal with him. Daily Mass is thus a staple of priestly formation. When we grow negligent, our love affair with the Master suffers. Likewise do we find ourselves savoring time before our Lord really and truly present in the Bread of Life, the Blessed Sacrament. "He who eats my flesh and drinks my blood lives in me and I in him!" (John 6:56). Pope St. Pius X wrote that the most effective way to grow in our love of Christ is to receive him daily worthily in Holy Communion.

3. When we are in love with someone, we get to know that person's family and friends, don't we? You know a young couple's relationship is getting serious when they introduce each other to their families, when they begin to get to share each other's friends.

Well, we want Jesus and his Church to be the love of our lives. Get to know his family and friends!

Particularly is this true of his Mother. So close are we to him that his Mother becomes our Mother. Thus has devotion to our Lady become a standard of priestly spirituality. We need to recognize that there are different ways of loving Mary. How we love her is an open question; that we love her is not. A filial devotion to the Mother of the First Priest is likewise a definite part of our spirituality and a practical way to grow in our love of Jesus. Such devotion has been a tradition of the North American College here in Rome since December 8, 1859, and I am grateful that it still is.

Nor do we neglect St. Joseph, John the Baptist — Jesus' family — and the apostles and disciples, his chosen friends. This city, purpled in the blood of two of his best friends, Peter and Paul, offers us a unique opportunity to come to know the apostles.

A few years back, a member of our seminary community approached me in a moment of particular trial, when he was questioning his entire relationship with Jesus and his Church. So burdened was he that he was on the brink of making what I considered a very rash decision. I urged him to at least give himself some time before he did anything final. The next day he returned much better, more confident of his love for Christ and his Church. What was the turning point? He told me he spent a few hours at the tomb of St. Peter, and concluded that if Jesus could love Peter, with all his flaws, sins, and mistakes, then Jesus could certainly love him! There's the power of getting to know the friends of Jesus so we can know and love Jesus even better.

All the saints from Peter and Paul to the most recently beatified are people we should strive to know and imitate— getting to know those friends of Christ is a practical way to grow in our love of Jesus himself.

But the people to whom we talk about Jesus don't have to all be saints! A lot of people are intimate with this man, Jesus, and they can help us develop deep bonds of unity with him.

• Thus, we confide in a spiritual director, a man wiser and more seasoned in his relationship with the Lord, who can encourage us in our love affair with Christ. At the North American College it is a requirement for every seminarian to have a spiritual director and meet with him every two weeks. This should set a pattern for the life of every priest.

• The great ascetical writers have left us a legacy of spiritual reading to help us enhance our relationship with Christ. Thus, we enjoy reading Augustine, Francis de Sales, Thomas Merton, Teresa of Jesus, just to name a few.

• Our shepherds, the bishops, are close to Jesus, especially the Bishop of Rome, who guide us in their teaching office in our search for Christ and our love of the Church.

All friends of Jesus who can help us become his friend as well.

4. When we want to grow in intimacy with someone, it is natural to try to discover everything we possibly can about that person. Same is true with our Lord. That is why the disciplined, systematic study of theology is mandated by the Church for those preparing to spend their lives passionately loving Christ and his Bride. "Theol-

ogy," wrote Aquinas, "deserves to be called the highest wisdom, for everything is viewed in the light of the first cause."

The Church classically calls seminarians in the final four years of priestly formation "theologians." The pursuit of theology, the probing of Sacred Scripture, reading, reflecting, studying, discussing, consistent class attendance — these are all part of a seminarian's growth in intimate love of Jesus, and makes no sense apart from that. Thus, daily studies are not burdens extraneous to priestly formation, but intrinsic to it. Second only to the fostering of the spiritual life is the study of theology in the preparation for holy orders.

One of the reasons the study of theology is essential is just that, when we love someone, we want to brag about the beloved, introduce others to the beloved, tell the whole world about him. That, as a matter of fact, is what we as priests want to spend our life doing — introducing the world to our beloved, Jesus the Lord. Well, we better know him, understand his teachings, and be ready to defend him with clarity, cogency, and compassion. And that's theology.

5. When we love someone, we desire to cleanse our lives of anything that could hurt our beloved. Thus, a basic characteristic of our relationship with our Lord will be a daily dying to sin and rising in virtue.

Thomas Merton describes the love of God as a brilliant ray of sunlight shining through a window. The light will always reveal streaks, or smudges, or dirt on the window. We let more light in the more we purify the window.

Thus, the way to receive more and more of the light of Christ's love is to constantly purify our life of sin. That is the exhortation found on almost every page of the Gospel — conversion, repentance, *metanoia* — call it what you want: daily wrestling with that dark side of ourselves which holds us back from the freedom and self-giving that this romance with the Lord and his Church entails will be a constant of our friendship with Jesus.

There are practical ways to help us:

• Frequent examination of conscience as we forthrightly review our day, our week, as it compares with the commandments, the beatitudes, the virtues proper to our vocation. We praise God for growth and progress and seek his mercy and help with our sins.

• Openness with a spiritual director.

• The frank counsel of friends who are confident enough of their relationship with us that they can tell us areas of our life where we need to improve. One of life's greatest blessings is a friend who is not afraid to tell us the truth even when it is painful. And one of the greatest services we can provide a genuine friend is honestly letting him know of a concern we have about him. One of the toughest things I ever had to do was share with a friend that I felt a relationship in which he was engaged was threatening to compromise his celibate chastity. He told me to go to hell.

• Healthy, wholesome friendships with brother priests are likewise a basic of effective ministry. A particular blessing of seminary life is the development of solid, lasting friendships. You know you've got a good one when you feel free to speak forthrightly to him and vice versa.

• If necessary, trust in a professional like a psychologist or specialist who is trained in helping people deal with the hurts, hangups, or tendencies that hold them back from the freedom they need to love Jesus, his Church, his people.

• The correction we receive from others.

• And, very practically and powerfully, dependence upon the sacrament of penance (or reconciliation). My first pastor always told a married couple at the wedding, "The six most important words in a good marriage are 'I love you' and 'I am sorry'. Say those frequently and your love will be enduring."

It is in the sacrament of penance that we say to Christ and his Bride, the Church, "I am sorry." Thus, frequent celebration of this sacrament will characterize our love life with the Lord. While how often you approach the confessional should be a matter of discussion between you and your spiritual director, at least once a month seems a sound policy.

6. When we love someone we will die for that person. I once saw a little child bolt from its mother on a sidewalk and run out into a busy street. Without a moment's hesitation, the mother dashed out completely oblivious to an oncoming truck. Thank God the truck stopped within inches of mother and child, but no one was sur-

prised that the mother did that. True love prompts that willingness to die for the beloved.

If we wish to grow in our intimacy with Jesus we must be willing not only to die *for* him but to die *with* him. Yes, the cross will be a part of our life. Why are we surprised when it comes? Why are priests shocked when they must suffer loneliness, frustration, failure, less-than-perfect assignments, crabby pastors, demanding people, critical congregations, aloof bishops? Why are priests tempted to think there is something wrong when sorrow and setback come? We are configured to the man on the cross, called to empty ourselves perhaps to the point of death out of love for the crucified and his Bride. He told us, "If you want to follow me you must deny yourself and take up your cross." Will not a man endure hours of dreary work daily for the woman and children he loves? So do we priests endure weariness, stress, and agony for the man and woman we love — Christ and his Church.

In my home parish there is a wonderful couple who were real pillars, happy parents of five children. She was crippled with rheumatoid arthritis at thirty-four. It became such that she could not leave her bed. He was so good to her — carrying her back and forth, bathing her, keeping her company hours at a time, feeding her. A few years ago I stopped to see them and, as we left and walked out to the car, I said, "Bill, I am so inspired at how tenderly you love Ginna."

"Father," he responded, "I love her more today than the day I married her."

So our love for Jesus and his Bride, the Church, is most proved in times of trial. In times of loneliness, rejection, suffering, tension — that's when love is pure. At times the man we love, Jesus, might seem distant; at times his Bride, and ours, the Church, might seem corrupt, mistaken, weak, scandalous — that's when we love Jesus and the Church all the more! That's when love proves itself!

The love we have for Jesus and his Church is not always a carefree, pleasing, constantly satisfying, and fulfilling intimacy. No — it will entail sacrifice, sweat, blood, tears, suffering; it will entail the cross. As the Holy Father said to seminarians in New York, "The wisdom of the cross is at the heart of the life and ministry of every priest." That is true of life here at the seminary and life in the parish. At times, "this place" will get to us, and we long to be free of it. Such is the weight of the cross that will reappear consistently throughout our priesthood. Be ready for it!

Thus, to embrace the cross now through acts of self-denial, mortification, and penance is a good way to deepen our love with the crucified. Certain exercises, such as the weekly prayer and fasting for life, are a fine example of such sacrifice.

7. Finally, if we are trying to love someone, we learn to care for the people and activities he or she prefers. When two young people fall in love, she tries to learn something about baseball, he about art, for instance, so they can share interests. When we speak of Jesus, that interest means people in need and people who are poor in soul, mind, and body. This only comes from a heart that is pastorally sensitive, and this explains the pastoral aspect of our formation program here at the North American College.

As the Holy Father said in Newark to priests: "Like Christ, the head and shepherd of the Church, you must know, tend, and offer your life for your flock. Ordination configures you to Christ the Servant, to him who humbly washed his apostles' feet because he came among us not to be served but to serve." If we want to enhance our love for Jesus, well, be interested in what he is concerned about — and that is in service to those who need it.

"The Love of Christ compels me," writes St. Paul. I don't know if I've succeeded, but what I have tried to do is demonstrate that our love of God — both the love God has for us and the love we return to him — is the steam that makes the engine of our priesthood run, the principle that brings all the facets of our demanding life together. We exist because of love; hopefully we are priests who are so convinced of the Lord's gracious love for them that we love him passionately in return, so intensely that we are configured to him and share in the nuptial love Christ has for his Bride, the Church.

Everything we are about should strengthen, develop, nurture, and intensify this love: our daily prayer and Eucharist, our devotion to our Lady and the saints, our dialog with our spiritual director, our study of theology, our struggle with sin and growth in virtue, our willingness to sacrifice and suffer, and our pastoral service of his people. We do it all for love.

Perhaps you have heard of Catherine de Hueck Doherty, founder of the Friendship House Movement, whose cause for canonization has been introduced. She was once called to one of her famous houses that served the poor which was experiencing internal strife. Her staff there were fighting and arguing, and she was called in to referee.

After listening to a couple of hours of bickering, she finally concluded the meeting and said, "I have reached a decision. I am closing this house!"

Well, shocked gasps went up all over. "But, Baroness, who will feed the poor and shelter the homeless?"

"The government can ladle soup, and make a bed as efficiently as we can! We are called to do it with love, and if we can't do it with love, we're not doing it!"

We are called to be men who love and share that love with the people we serve, and if we cannot do it with love, there's no use doing it. All the theology, all the pastoral competency, all the preaching ability, all the liturgical style, all the Roman training in the world won't amount to a plate of gnocchi if we do not have love when we're doing it. You have seen priests who are men of love, who love Jesus and his Bride, the Church, passionately, and who radiate the joy, compassion, and conviction that flow from such a furnace of love. You would not be where you are today had you not been blessed with such examples.

And you have seen a priest who has either never loved or has fallen out of love — cold, mean, crabby, petty, lazy, selfish. Oh, he loves all right — he loves himself — not in the sense of self-respect spoken of by Jesus, but in a narcissistic, selfish way. His convenience, his time, his assignment, his career, his image, his wants — they become supreme in his life. The last thing the Church needs is another such priest.

Recently in America the Holy Father urged seminarians to pray each day, "O good Jesus, make me a priest like unto your own heart."

In 1994 we placed the statue of the Sacred Heart of Jesus at the entrance to our college. The Sacred Heart, burning with love and mercy for us, is a powerful symbol of the love Christ has for us. It is the unifying principle, the driving force of priestly life; it is the only thing that gives sense, meaning, and purpose to everything we do here to get ready for that.

> Sacred Heart of Jesus,
> I place all my trust in thee!
> Sacred Heart of Jesus,
> I believe in thy love for me!
> Sacred Heart of Jesus,
> May thy kingdom come!

4

Humility

(Scripture selection — Philippians 2:5-11)

One of the most poignant retreat conferences I can remember was given by the now deceased Passionist Scripture scholar Barnabas Ahern. He began by raising the question "What was our Lord's favorite virtue?"

Faith? . . . certainly high up there . . .

Hope? . . . rank it near the top . . .

Charity? . . . think how often the Master spoke of love . . .

Justice? . . . a case could be made . . .

But all of these pale, and take second place to what Father Ahern posited to be our Lord's favorite virtue — humility.

Humility is the pivotal virtue of the interior life, the favorite of Jesus, held up by all the saints and ascetical theologians as the *sine qua non* of all progress on the road to perfection. In the simple words of the Little Flower, "The beginning of all holiness is humbly admitting that without God we can do nothing, but that, with, in, and through him, everything is possible!"

The Gospels are, of course, odes to humility, as we see on every page the divine preference for the humble:

• the sick over the healthy,

• those who lack over those who have,

• the lowly virgin rather than the exquisite socialite,

• the oafish fisherman rather than the sophisticated scribes,

• the poor over the rich,

• the nerds to the in-crowd,

• the sinner to the snug,

• children to adults . . .

"Lord, that I may see!" chants the blind beggar . . .

"If I can but touch the tassel on his cloak!" whispers the sick woman in the crowd . . .

"Lord, I am not worthy," admits the centurion . . .

"Just the scraps from the table," begs the Canaanite woman . . .

"Lord, remember me when you come into your kingdom," utters Dismas . . .

All humble prayers that move his Sacred Heart, the heart he himself describes as gentle and humble.

Why is humility so prized by Jesus?

Maybe because his mission as our redeemer was precisely to save us from the opposite of humility — pride — the original sin by which our first parents felt they could get along just fine without God. As St. Augustine observed, "It was pride that caused the Fall. . . . If you ask me what are the ways to God, I would tell you the first is humility, the second is humility, the third is humility. . . ."

Maybe because his Incarnation was the most sublime act of humility ever, as God the Son, the Eternal Word, the second Person of the Blessed Trinity, took flesh and became man. "Humility," writes St. Bernard, "is the mother of salvation."

Maybe humility is so valued by Christ because of its very definition. St. Thomas Aquinas says in the *Summa* that humility means seeing ourselves as God sees us: knowing that every good we have comes from him as pure gift, that we depend on him for everything. Is this not the "poverty of spirit" listed as first in the eight beatitudes? And, since Jesus literally saw with the eyes of God, he especially cherished those who did the same. St. Vincent de Paul expressed it well: "The reason why God is so great a lover of humility is that he is a great lover of truth. Humility is nothing but truth while pride is nothing but lying. . . . The very moment God sees us fully convinced of our nothingness, he reaches out his hand to us."

One of the welcome developments in contemporary spirituality is an appreciation of the twelve-step program of Alcoholics Anonymous. No one can recover from alcoholism, claims that extraordinarily successful program, until one admits with disarming honesty and humility that one is absolutely helpless over drink and entrusts one's recovery to a Higher Power. Apply that to all sin, darkness, addiction, struggle, vice, evil, and weakness, and begin to live, begin to grow . . . but to do that takes humility.

In our Christian understanding there is this humility before God, and then there is a humility before others — to put others first, to battle egotism, to shun honor, acclaim, and attention, to rejoice when others are preferred over us. This humility before God and others is one of the toughest virtues to cultivate but crucially necessary for the priest.

Let me enumerate what I feel are particular dangers, and then practical helps, to this cultivation of humility.

First, some of the pitfalls on the road to humility.

The Pelagianism rampant in Catholic life — that is, to think we can achieve, or merit our own redemption, to think that salvation depends on us. Of course, we know that holiness, heaven, cannot be earned but only given to one who *humbly* admits that he needs God desperately and can never win divine favor on his own merits.

Pelagianism stems, of course, from pride, the opposite of humility, an exaltation of human ability. It is a danger in seminary and priestly life because we are called to *do* so many things — daily Mass, divine office, meditation, confession, spiritual reading, acts of penance, striving for virtue, exercises of devotion — and rightly are these duties a necessary part of our spiritual regimen. We do them, though, not to earn or produce holiness — that's Pelagianism — but to open ourselves *humbly* to the power of God's love.

A subtle form of Pelagianism is found today among some in the Church: the belief that the vigor, the orthodoxy, the salvation of the Church all depend on me. At a rector's meeting I attended in England in 1995, a number of my colleagues recalled a very beneficial encounter they had the year before with the prefect of the Congregation for Catholic Education, Cardinal Pio Laghi. One of the rectors commented that he worried that some seminarians and younger priests felt they personally had a divine mandate to save the Church from rampant heresy and modernism.

Cardinal Laghi replied, "Yes, I always worry about a young man who feels he is the Church's savior. The Church happens already to have one!"

That's not limited to young priests. We had an old pastor in St. Louis who really believed the parish, the diocese, if not the entire Church, would crumble if he did not keep it going with his constant work. Because of this, he rarely took a vacation, and when he did, he would return early, frantically asking his assistants, "Is everything all right? Did anything happen?" — almost upset that the parish, diocese, and Church universal survived rather well during his absence. One year the senior assistant put up "For Sale" signs in front of the Church, rectory, and school when the pastor left to really drive the old man crazy when he got back!

Remember this when you get to a parish. There will be some things you're not happy with, some practices or ways of doing things that are not perhaps the way you would do it — humbly accept them. I'm not talking about questions of faith and morals, but style, praxis, procedures. Humbly, gradually, patiently, gently insert yourself into parish life. Admit you can learn a lot. Remind yourself that the parish was there long before you arrived, and will continue long after you're gone, and that, although the Savior will uniquely work through you as a priest, you are not the Savior.

A priest I respect very much told me that one of the problems in his diocese with younger priests was what he called their "sacristy manner." He said some fellows would come into the parish and within a few Sundays manage to have lectors, extraordinary ministers, musicians, liturgy committees, and DRE's in tears because these priests high-handedly announce that all is wrong in the parish, and that they were there to teach everybody how it really should be done. The Pelagian, proud, savior mentality! A bishop commented to me on a recent alumnus of this college. "He is very learned, personally holy, zealous, a fine preacher. I so admire his fidelity to the magisterium and the Holy Father. I need him and his energy to help me shepherd this diocese in the direction I feel it needs to go. But his style! He's already in his third assignment! He alienates everybody! He comes in and turns everyone off with an arrogant, judgmental, messianic style! He has done the cause of fidelity and orthodoxy more harm than good!"

Humility! The Church already has a savior and, Pelagianism notwithstanding, I am not he!

A second pitfall in our pilgrimage to humility is pragmatism. Especially do we Americans pride ourselves on practicality, getting things done; we are task-oriented and feel everything is possible by sweat, work, and effort. An exaggerated sense of pragmatism can stifle humility. Yes, God wants our work and effort, but, "Unless the Lord builds the house, in vain do the masons toil."

We are not defined by what we do, how much we earn or produce, or what we achieve, but by who we are, and we are usually closest to God when we are weakest, emptiest, and lowest. To admit that takes humility . . . and can drive a pragmatist nuts.

I ask seminarians to apply that to their vocation right now: four or five years of waiting and preparing, antsy, impatient, eager to move on, to produce, achieve, get at it. The Lord and the Church say: Take your time! Wait! Prepare! Get ready! Years of preparation are essential if you are to be an effective apostle. Yes, we prefer the microwave — put the food in, push the button; in a matter of minutes, the meal is ready. The Lord, the Church, prefer the crock-pot: let it brew, stew, be seasoned, mellowed, for hours, then have your meal. And the food from the crock-pot beats the stuff from a microwave any day.

Is there a better example than the Master himself? Thirty years of unrecorded preparation for three years of active ministry. No pragmatist planned that timetable! February is traditionally dedicated to the "Hidden Life of Jesus" . . . those thirty years of quiet, prayer, preparation, anticipation, listening, growing, subject to his Blessed Mother and St. Joseph — what humility! I recommend meditation on the "Hidden Life of Jesus" to seminarians who are tempted to get frustrated with the slow, crock-pot pace of seminary life.

This patient humility — countering a more aggressive pragmatism — is evident in the lives of priests who are happy and peaceful where they are. For the temptation to pragmatism that can make a man restless in the seminary will be there in the priesthood as well. So, many priests have their career all lined up; they are no sooner in one parish than they're jockeying for another. They have their plans made and their curriculum vitae all ready to be printed out and then these silly assignments get in the way. If the bishop would only listen to me and move me on . . . pragmatic? Yes! Humble? No!

Consider the humility of the promise of obedience we solemnly make at ordination to the diaconate and priesthood. On your knees — a position of weakness — with your hands bound by the bishop's, promising obedience for the rest of your life: your desires, your agenda, your preferences second to the Church's.

I was proud recently of our deacons from the archdiocese of Atlanta and the diocese of Charleston who have had their future disrupted and personal preferences pushed aside because of the pressing pastoral needs of their dioceses, as their bishops informed them they are needed at home and thus cannot return for their license. Only a heart versed in humility can accept that with resignation. "The fear of the Lord in training for wisdom and humility goes before honors. In his mind a man plans his course, but the Lord directs his steps," teaches Proverbs.

You will hear wise priests say, "Never ask for an assignment, never ask to get out of one." Not bad counsel . . . but tough for us plotting, planning, programmed pragmatists for whom humility is so elusive.

A third trap on the road to humility: an inordinate stress on personal rights. We Americans are grateful that we are citizens of a country derived from an insistence on the rights of individuals — and rightly so; we belong to a Church that champions human rights, shepherded by a pastor known as the world's most forceful defender of human rights — thank God! I am not talking of this, but about the complex that leads us to believe that we've got things coming to us, that we deserve special treatment and preference. Thus, we get down when not given the assignment we think we deserve or the recognition we feel should be coming to us. The bishop doesn't appreciate me, the pastor doesn't realize all the work I do, the people don't realize how lucky they are to have me!

We had a great priest in St. Louis who was well-known for his zeal and gentle humility. He was a pastor of a poor, struggling parish. One of the plums in the archdiocese opened up and most of the priests stayed near their phones waiting for Cardinal Carberry to call and ask them to take the plush parish.

This humble priest got the call. "I want you to be pastor of St. Clement's," the cardinal said.

"Eminence, thanks, but I'm happy here, and there are dozens more who would be much more effective."

"Now I know I want you," responded the cardinal. "I have before me twenty-three letters from men asking for the place; you don't think you're worthy — you're now the pastor."

Some of the saddest of priests are those who feel they have been overlooked. They have set their hearts on advancement in the Church and ecclesiastical honors. "Scarlet Fever" it is sometimes called, and it is a dangerous virus in the clerical life.

This exaggerated insistence on "my rights, my prerogatives" ultimately leads to a dangerous spiritual and emotional malady, that of feeling sorry for myself. This self-centered licking of wounds, rehearsing the ways we have been overlooked, taken for granted, unappreciated — look out! That's when we're setting ourselves up for a fall — in the areas of sexuality; drinking; damaging association with others who will join us in the negative, cynical carping that afflicts the clergy who feel their rights have been violated.

Humility teaches us to put all this in perspective, as we admit that we really deserve nothing at all, and that, in the long run, honors, attention, and prestige are dangerous and better off avoided. In the words of St. Paul, "If I am to boast, I boast in the cross of our Lord Jesus Christ."

This exaggerated emphasis on personal rights is an overemphasis on *me*, which is the opposite of the way it should be. Mother Teresa, in her characteristic simplicity, says the proper order of priorities in life is J-O-Y:

J — Jesus

O — Others

Y — You

A fourth obstacle to humility is machismo. Real men don't ask for help! Real men don't admit weakness! Real men can do anything they put their mind to! Real men don't cry! Real men don't have limitations!

But humble men do! Humility makes us aware of our weakness, our frailty, our faults, that we recognize we need all the help we can get — from God, from others. So we are not afraid to get down on our knees and pray, to confide in friends, to open up to a spiritual director, to seek support from others, even to seek assistance from professionals in medicine or counseling.

I have just heard of a sad case where a prominent priest has lost his parish, his diocesan status, and now the very exercise of his priesthood because he has refused to admit that he needs professional help in dealing with sexual problems and alcohol, and has rebuffed his bishop's gentle but firm insistence that he go for help or be suspended. This might be macho — but it's not humble.

And a final (Lord knows there are more) pitfall I will mention: a proud rationalism that leads us to think we have to comprehend everything, that God owes us an explanation, and that our peanut brains are capable of understanding all there is, thus eliminating the awe and mystery of life.

Compare this to the humble prayer of Psalm 131:

> Yahweh, my heart has no lofty ambitions,
> my eyes do not look too high.
> I am not concerned with great affairs
> or marvels beyond my scope.
> Enough for me to keep my soul tranquil and quiet
> like a child in its mother's arms,
> as content as a child that has been weaned.

So the greatest theologian ever, St. Thomas, surveying his life's work, said, "It's all straw when compared to the overwhelming mystery and majesty and mercy of God."

Enough of the dangers — how about some helps to humility?

No surprise that the first is prayer. As Bishop Sheen said, "Only the humble can pray, for prayer presumes we need someone and something." There's an old saying that the two most important lessons in life are, first, there is a God; second, I am not he! As the Lord spoke to St. Catherine of Siena, "You are she who is not, and I am who is!" Prayer acknowledges that.

I have found it helpful in my prayer to contemplate the eyes of Christ staring at me, piercing right through me: as he "looked hard" at the rich young man, as he gazed at the woman at the well, as he glared at Peter after the triple denial — the eyes of Christ piercing through us. No thought, word, or deed is hidden; he knows us better than we know ourselves. We are empty, open, poor, weak, broken before that gaze — and yet those eyes are loving, welcoming, accepting. That contemplation helps our humility.

In my first parish assignment, one of my Communion calls was a very prominent St. Louis woman who, the pastor told me, was terminally ill with cancer. When I called to set the time, she was very precise in saying I should not come before 11:30 a.m. on Friday. I found her looking remarkably well for a woman supposedly dying. Every Friday morning the same.

Well, one day, I was near her house, and decided to stop in

unannounced. Her nurse opened the door, and, as I entered, I saw my Communion call gasp as she quickly tried to wheel herself out of my sight. . . . She was without any makeup, without any hair, yellowish in color, drawn and old, obviously dying. . . . It dawned on me that every Friday morning she had spent hours preparing herself to look presentable, and now I had surprised her and found her as she really was — weak, ugly, bald, yellow, old, and dying. She started to cry, "Oh, Father, I never wanted anyone to see me like this. I am so ashamed!"

All I could do was embrace her and assure her that I couldn't care less what she looked like, that I loved her and cared for her soul. With that we had a moving conversation about death, about suffering, about God.

That should be our posture of humility in prayer — the Lord sees us without sham, warts and all, dying, weak, sick, helpless, and afraid. No use impressing him. His eyes stare right through us.

Julian of Norwich wrote, "It is a very great pleasure to Christ when a simple soul comes to him nakedly, plainly, and unpretentiously."

To me one of the most moving moments during the Rite of Ordination is when the candidates prostrate themselves on the floor. A position of utter humility! Before God, before the Church, they are powerless, helpless, empty, for only in such a one can God's grace take root. To use that humble posture in prayer periodically is not a bad idea.

I once heard Archbishop Emory Kabongo, formerly a private secretary to Pope John Paul II, tell about a 3:00 a.m. phone call to the apostolic apartments from the Cardinal-Secretary of State to advise the Holy Father of an international emergency.

Archbishop Kabongo called the pontiff's bedroom — no answer. Worried, he went to the bedroom, knocked, entered — no pope. He glanced in the chapel — no sign of him. He checked the kitchen, dining room, private library — still no sign. He went up to the rooftop walking garden — no one was there. He retraced all his steps, this time looking more carefully, and, in the chapel, found Pope John Paul II prostrate, on the floor, praying.

A second aid to the development of humility: regular, sincere confession. The former bishop of Springfield, Illinois, Joseph A.

McNicholas, once said at a day of recollection: "If you are faithful to an honest, humble confession, at least once a month, you'll be a good priest." At the time I thought that was simplistic, but now I see it more and more as true. Worthy, integral, regular confession is itself an act of humility as we articulate with utter candor our sins; and what a source of grace and virtue it is as well!

An openness to criticism. They say Lyndon Johnson always appointed one member of his staff to meet with him weekly to tell him bad news and to criticize him and his presidency. Johnson warned him that if he was too soft he would fire him. Bravo! Openness to criticism is a real boost to humility. From confessors, spiritual directors, our people, our collaborators in ministry, our brother priests, our superiors, we welcome criticism.

The sign of a true friend is one who is confident enough of the strength of the relationship that he can tell you things about yourself you need to hear, but perhaps would rather not.

Advice I would offer to every young priest — indeed, to any priest — is to sit down with your pastor periodically and ask for criticism. "How am I doing?" "Did I do this properly?" "Do you have any tips on my preaching, ministry, or style?" "Have you noticed any mistakes?"

None of us like to hear criticism or bad news about ourselves, because we're proud. But an openness to criticism is a great help to humility.

"Who is free from defects?" asks St. Bernard. "He lacks everything who thinks he lacks nothing."

An inner peace with the thought of being a parish priest the rest of your life cannot be overemphasized. The seminary exists to prepare men to be zealous, faithful, effective parish priests: yes, some may become teachers, some chancery officials, some even workers within the Holy See; some may go into military chaplaincy or even seminary work — but unless you have the humility to resolve to be a parish priest the rest of your life, you should rethink your vocation as a priest.

Let's be honest: Roman-trained priests are sometimes accused of having their hearts set on something beyond parish pastorates, and some bishops or vocation directors — thank God there are only a few — tell me they hesitate to send a man here because they feel the man will later be unhappy in a normal parish after five years of smelling incense in St. Peter's and shopping at Gammarelli's. "How ya gonna keep 'em down on the farm after they've seen Paree?" Totally unfair, I believe, but this criticism deserves at least a few moments of thought as we cleanse our hearts of any ambition beyond being a pastor of souls.

A willingness to admit we might *not* be called to be priests — that is an act of humility for a seminarian. We must never glide into the priesthood, simply become priests because it's the next step and, besides, Tavani has our chalice order already. True humility prompts us to admit we may not be called to the priesthood. We cannot freely, rationally, maturely accept the call to the priesthood until we have humbly admitted that we might not have such a call.

Now, this seems so obvious — but, all you have to do is listen to the gripping stories of men who have left the priesthood as they tell you, "I just coasted. I never really freely embraced the priesthood. Once I got to Rome things just happened, and I next found myself giving first blessings." How this can happen I don't know, but it does, and don't let it happen to you. Have the humility to admit that you might not be called to the priesthood.

Know yourself! Once when someone complimented St. John Vianney on being a good confessor he said, "If I'm a good confessor it's only because I am a great sinner!" We know ourselves so well; we are so cognizant of our weakness that we never place ourselves in occasions that we know can lead to sin.

A priest I know and love and respect, who had great influence on my vocation, invited me to go with him for a vacation to Las Vegas. He enjoyed golf, the shows, even a little blackjack. About two weeks before the trip I had to back out because the other assistant had emergency surgery scheduled. When I called to tell him I couldn't go, he was disappointed, and I said, "Well, you can still go by yourself, can't you?" I'll never forget his reply, "I would never trust myself alone in Vegas." This man, who was the model of priestly virtue, knew himself so well he would not put himself in an occasion of sin. Now that's humility.

You have heard of Matt Talbot, the great Irish layman, alcoholic at twelve, who through prayer, penance, and self-knowledge attained sobriety and remarkable sanctity. When he would walk home from the factory every night, he would cross the street rather than pass in front of a pub, knowing himself so well that he humbly admitted that even the smell or the sounds of the pub could tempt him severely. Now that's the kind of self-knowledge upon which humility grows.

"How can we feel our need of his help, or our dependence on him, or our debt to him, or the nature of his gift to us, unless we know ourselves?" asks Cardinal Newman.

Humility, the favorite virtue of our Lord, the cornerstone of growth in God's life, the pivotal quality for priestly fidelity and effectiveness: there are obstacles to it, there are helps to it; there are no replacements for it.

Let us pray the Litany of Humility of Cardinal Raphael Merry del Val:

> O Jesus! meek and humble of heart,
> Hear me.
> From the desire of being esteemed,
> Deliver me, Jesus.
> From the desire of being loved,
> Deliver me, Jesus.
> From the desire of being extolled,
> Deliver me, Jesus.
> From the desire of being honored,
> Deliver me, Jesus.
> From the desire of being praised,
> Deliver me, Jesus.
> From the desire of being preferred to others,
> Deliver me, Jesus.
> From the desire of being consulted,
> Deliver me, Jesus.
> From the desire of being approved,
> Deliver me, Jesus.
> From the fear of being humiliated,
> Deliver me, Jesus.
> From the fear of being despised,
> Deliver me, Jesus.
> From the fear of suffering rebukes,

Deliver me, Jesus.

From the fear of being calumniated,

Deliver me, Jesus.

From the fear of being forgotten,

Deliver me, Jesus.

From the fear of being ridiculed,

Deliver me, Jesus.

From the fear of being wronged,

Deliver me, Jesus.

From the fear of being suspected,

Deliver me, Jesus.

That others may be loved more than I,

Jesus, grant me the grace to desire it.

That others may be esteemed more than I,

Jesus, grant me the grace to desire it.

That in the opinion of the world, others may increase and that I may decrease,

Jesus, grant me the grace to desire it.

That others may be chosen and I set aside,

Jesus, grant me the grace to desire it.

That others may be praised and I unnoticed,

Jesus, grant me the grace to desire it.

That others may be preferred to me in everything,

Jesus, grant me the grace to desire it.

That others may become holier than I, provided that I become as holy as I should,

Jesus, grant me the grace to desire it.

Our Lady of Humility,

Pray for us.

5

Fidelity

(Scripture selection — 2 Timothy 1:11-13)

"Be faithful — always be faithful!" I recall those simple words spoken to my ordination class by Pope Paul VI on the eve of my ordination to the diaconate some twenty years ago. "When a man says 'yes' to the priesthood, that 'yes' is forever!" said Pope John Paul II in 1995 when he ordained forty men priests for the diocese of Rome. The decree of the Second Vatican Council on the priesthood beautifully describes how fidelity is a virtue most appropriate to a priest, since he in his pastoral ministry mirrors the faithful, fruitful love that God has for his people, and Jesus has for his Church.

"May he be faithful," the bishop prays over the men to be ordained in the "Prayer of Consecration" in the Rite of Ordination of Priests. "May he be faithful so that the words of the Gospel may reach the ends of the earth and the family of nations, made one in Christ, may become God's one, holy people."

Fidelity means, of course, that we are true to the nature and the demands of our call, that we live a life of integrity flowing from an inner conviction of who we are in the eyes of God, that we reliably fulfill the duties associated with our vocation, that we are men of our word, who can be counted on to do what we say and live as we profess.

Fidelity is what is essential in the entire life of a man who desires to be or who already is configured to Christ at the very core of his being through the sacrament of holy orders.

In a real way, formation continues outside of the seminary. As the Holy Father says in *Pastores Dabo Vobis* and our bishops in the Program of Priestly Formation, the seminary offers an atmosphere where sound values and habits of prayer, study, natural and supernatural virtue, and pastoral skill can be developed and interiorized. One of the ways a seminary does this is through its program of formation, where goals are set and expectations made to help a candidate develop such values and habits.

Now, the "proof of the pudding is in the eating," and the real test of whether or not these values and habits are interiorized comes when the external structures are removed, when, you might say, the training wheels are taken away. That comes ultimately with priestly ordination, but it also comes every vacation period, every summer, when indeed we see whether or not nine months of planting and nurturing bear fruit in the lives of seminarians. Do all the values we structure here at the North American College— daily Mass, prayer, liturgy of the hours, frequent confession, a thoughtful, reflective way of life, service to others, growth in virtue — do all of these continue when no one is watching and when the daily routine that is so much a part of seminary life is removed? Summer vacations can be the great examination of conscience, the laboratory, to see if what we do here has been interiorized, as we see if we are faithful to our vocation.

We have been blessed with examples of fidelity in our lives. Most of us were raised in homes where we saw fidelity every day in our parents, a husband and wife who lived for one another, whose whole lives were defined by their relationship, and whose every act flowed from love for each other and their children. I remember going to the emergency room of the hospital where I was summoned after my father dropped dead at fifty-one of a heart attack at work. When they gave me the bag with his effects, in his wallet were a dollar bill, his driver's license, and a picture of my mom and his five children. He literally worked himself to death out of fidelity to us.

Most of us have seen good parish priests who are reliable, dutiful, thoughtful — faithful — always there, for their people. When I returned home from that emergency room to be with my family, why was I not surprised to see our pastor already there in the living room consoling all of them? He was simply a faithful priest who could be counted upon to be with his people when they needed him.

We are blessed with examples of fidelity here, I hope. One of the values of the Institute for Continuing Theological Education for us is that twice a year we have the presence of men who have been faithful priests on the front lines. Father Terry Morgan, the director of the program, in 1995 told me that the priests of that year had a combined total of 1,141 years of service . . . fidelity. I think of seeing the *occupato* (occupied) light on at Father Donovan's door one night at 11:45 when I went to deliver a message, meaning he was with one of our students; I remember Father Vaughan kneeling on the floor with a bucket and rag wiping up the result of our strange stomach virus one winter in one of our student's rooms; I recall Dr. Greco at the photocopy machine early one morning at 5:20 getting music for Mass . . . fidelity.

Now, even though fidelity exhibits itself in reliable, consistent fulfillment of expected duties, those are only the consequences, the fruit of real fidelity. We are only faithful in what we do if we are faithful to who we are. Fidelity flows from identity.

What do I mean by that? Fidelity in our actions springs from an unshakable, confident, grateful, humble conviction of who we are as priests, that we are priests at the very core of our being. I was just reading the homily Cardinal Hickey gave at the Chrism Mass in Washington in 1995 and he touched on this point: "We are enabled to be authentic priests by the power of our ordination which changed us in the very depth of our being. Ordination makes it possible for us to act in Christ's name and power as teacher, high priest, shepherd, and spouse of the Church. We function not in our own name, but in the name and person of Jesus, the Christ. . . . By ordination our identity has been intrinsically altered; we are priests in all we do."

I remember once baby-sitting for a family in the neighborhood. I was probably fourteen or so. About 11:00 p.m. the baby woke up crying and I held her, rocking her back and forth, but she continued to cry. About a half-hour later the parents returned and the mother took the baby in her arms and rocked her. Same hold, same rocking motion, same action that I had been doing for half-an-hour unsuccessfully — yet now the baby quieted down and went to sleep. What was important to the baby was not what was being done but who was doing it.

The action was effective because of the identity of the one doing it; to use the words of the Holy Father in *Pastores Dabo Vobis*, "the being is more important than the doing." Thus, for us as priests or future priests, fidelity to our duties of prayer, study, pastoral service, and growth in virtue flows from a continual, grateful, humble, confident awareness of our identity as a priest or future priest, of one reordered, configured at the core of his being to Jesus Christ as head, shepherd, and spouse of his Church. So, fidelity cannot be imposed, can it? It flows from within, from an awareness of who we are. Thus, as priests, things like where we are assigned, what we are doing, with whom we are doing it are all secondary; that we are priests is of primary importance. Fidelity to our obligations as priests will then come naturally. People call us, not "Reverend," not "Doctor," not "Vicar," not "Canon," but "Father" — and "Father" is an identity based on being, not on function.

One of the most effective priests I know is blind, on kidney dialysis, and confined to a wheelchair — in other words, unable to do many of the things associated with ministry — yet he hears the confessions of probably a third of the presbyterate in the diocese who go to him for who he is. To quote Cardinal Hickey again: "Priestly identity is not like a judge's robe, something to be donned only when the court is in session. We retain our priestly identity wherever we go and whatever we do. . . . We need always to view our priestly identity as a way of life, a way of loving Christ and all our brothers and sisters for whom Jesus died. Our lives need to be translucent; the light of Christ must shine through us in all we think and say and do. We are called to be who we are, priests of the Church, men dedicated to God without reserve."

So, we are not faithful just to a job, a ministry, an occupation, a profession, a function. Fidelity in action — a noble goal — flows from this confident, grateful, humble consciousness of our priestly identity. We are faithful to a Person, faithful to Jesus and his beloved Spouse, the Church.

In second grade, one of my classmates asked Father Callahan, the pastor, "Father, do you have a wife?" "Yes," he answered, "I am married to the Church." Corny? Maybe. True? You bet it is! As a husband is faithful to his wife, a father to his children, so is the priest faithful to the Bride of Christ, the Church. If we are radically configured to Christ as a deacon, a priest, then we act in his person, and we develop a mystical bond with the love of his life, his Church. Is it any wonder why Pope John Paul II had so frequently and poetically spoken of this nuptial aspect of the priesthood? As a married man approached by another woman says, "I'm already taken," conscious of his fidelity to his bride, so are we priests — and future priests — already taken, spoken for, bound.

We love the Church and are as faithful to her as an excited, exuberant, buoyant young groom on his honeymoon. True, the longer we are married to our wife, the Church, the more we become aware of her flaws, her warts, her wrinkles — but we love her all the more. As Henri de Lubac wrote:

> For what could I know of Him without her? She may appear weak, her growth compromised, her means of action ridiculous, her witness too often hidden. Her children may not understand her, but at such a time I shall look at the humiliated face of my spouse and I shall love her all the more, for when some are hypnotized by those features which make her face look old, love will make me discover her hidden forces, the silent activity that gives her perpetual youth.

I remember once having the sixty-fifth anniversary celebration of a great old couple. As I sat between the couple at the dinner, the husband pointed to three of his grandchildren, observing sadly that all three were divorced from their spouses. "You know," he said, "I look back, there were a lot of times Anna and I could have split up. We've had arguments and we've each hurt each other, and there were months and maybe years that were far from happy from a worldly point of view. We were blessed 'cause we didn't even think divorce a possibility! We just knew we were married, in God's eyes, husband and wife forever, no matter what happened. So, here we are, and" — as he reached in front of me and grabbed her hand — "am I ever happy we believed that!"

Naïve? Maybe. Innocent? Probably. Impractical? Apparently . . . by today's standards. Romantic? Yes! And lovers are hopeless romantics. We as priests are in love with a woman called the Church, faithful with Jesus to her till death, for better or worse. We are faithful to a person, not an idea or a job.

Most priests discover helps to foster and guard their fidelity, and the list is long, but I want to mention three very important ones.

The first help to fidelity in our priestly life is daily Mass. I remember going to visit my first pastor a few years ago as he was in the hospital recovering from surgery. He had been bedridden for about a week and when I went into the room, he was smiling. I asked how he was and he almost beamed as he said, "Fine . . . they said I could say Mass tomorrow." That's how important daily Mass was to him. I would probably have beamed at the thought of my first meal of solid food — for him, it was saying Mass.

The great Jesuit confessor of the faith Walter Ciszek relates how in his years of imprisonment in a Siberian work camp he would save a crust of bread from breakfast and, with a bit of wine snuck to him by a sympathetic guard, he would go off to a corner of the barracks each night before lights went out and offer Mass from memory. When Rob Jaskot and I met Cardinal Keeler after he arrived from Baltimore one day, the first thing he said once he was settled in, was, "Well, I'll shower and shave, say Mass, and then take a nap." You will find that faithful priests are faithful to daily Mass.

The legendary Father Theodore Hesburgh, who could legitimately brag about many things, is proudest of one accomplishment in his autobiography: that in his half-century of priesthood he missed offering Mass only one day. If you want to remain faithful to your vocation, be faithful to daily Mass.

A second aid to fidelity is the daily prayer of the liturgy of the hours. Dr. Greco was telling me of a priest close to him who had gone through a lot of troubles and even vocational searching. When he asked this priest if he had any advice for future priests, he said, "Yes, tell them to be faithful to the office." The breviary I use I inherited from the pastor of my home parish, who was a very faithful and beloved priest. When the executor of the estate sent me the four volumes, I looked at the one he would have been using at the time of his death and — sure enough — the ribbons were up to night prayer for the evening he died — faithful to the end.

You will hear married couples relate how they check in with each other during the day — they chat in the morning before work, call at lunch, visit when the workday is done and they're both home, converse before retiring. Is that not what we do in the divine office with the Lord: keep in touch throughout the day with Jesus and our common Spouse, the Church, as we pray the liturgy of the hours?

The first priest I ever knew who left the active priesthood told me how he went to tell the archbishop he was leaving. The archbishop was very kind and, among other things, advised the departing priest that he was no longer bound to the divine office. The man snickered when he relayed the incident, observing, "Hell, I haven't said that thing in years." Case closed. No doubt about it, fidelity to the office fosters fidelity to our vocation.

A third help to fidelity is a regular, consistent way of life. You hear more and more from spiritual directors, therapists, and self-help experts that a careful, planned, regular daily regimen, balancing prayer, study, work, recreation, exercise, time for friends, eating, sleep — is good insurance for a healthy, happy life. No matter where we are or what we're doing, no matter if here or on vacation, certain things are constant — I just mentioned two, Mass and office. But there are others, from proper sleep and exercise, time for friends and reading — you all know what I mean.

I have heard more than one pastor complain that his assistant does not know how to organize his life, to plan his day, to be proactive, not reactive to crises and difficulties.

We live a very hectic and demanding life, with spiritual, academic, apostolic, community, and hospitality demands. To learn to balance them with a sense of prudence and proportion will be perhaps one of the most valuable lessons you can imbibe.

A consistent, orderly way of life helps us through the tough times. It is precisely when we are most pushed, most confronted, most challenged, that we fall back on those stables, those basics. Remember Cardinal Newman's advice to those who wanted his secret of success? "If you ask me what you are to do to be perfect, I say, first, do not lie in bed beyond the due time of rising; give your first thoughts to God; attend Mass; say the Angelus devoutly; eat and drink to God's glory; say the rosary well; be recollected; keep out bad thoughts; make your evening meditation well; examine yourself daily; go to bed in good time . . . and you're already perfect."

Any farmer could tell you the same! Any successful person could tell you a regular, consistent, balanced way of life is the secret; any faithful priest will tell you the same.

Fidelity to the Lord, fidelity to his Church, fidelity to our vocation. The proof comes in times of great joy and fulfillment or in times of great trial and difficulty. As the Scriptures tell us of our Lord, "Avoid ignoring him in prosperity and cursing him in adversity." The crunch comes in remaining close to him in the highs and lows, loyal to him in the successes and failures.

We have the perfect example of fidelity in our Blessed Mother, Mary. We call her both "the cause of our joy" and "Our Lady of Sorrows." She is ever close to him, the faithful disciple and Mother, at the happiest moment of salvation history — Bethlehem; and the saddest — Calvary.

- from the wood of the manger to the splinters of the cross;
- from the swaddling clothes to the bloody shroud;
- from the bouncing new life to the lifeless body . . .
- faithful woman, whose only message to us would be her last recorded words, "Do whatever he tells you!"

I once heard a psychologist say that the first moment a child is conscious of his or her own unique identity is when that baby stares into the eyes of its mother. You and I find ourselves in prayer staring into the eyes of our spiritual Mother — it might be the haunting eyes of Our Lady of Czestochowa, the soothing eyes of Our Mother of Perpetual Help, the confident eyes of the *Salus Populi Romani*. As we gaze into the eyes of our Blessed Mother, we become conscious of our identity: a child of God, beloved of the Father, redeemed by Jesus, called by the Eternal High Priest to be configured to him at the very depths of our heart. It is from the consciousness of that supernatural identity, learned from her, that fidelity to God, his Church, his call comes.

As Pope John Paul II said in his Holy Thursday Letter to Priests in 1995: "If the priesthood is by its nature ministerial, we must live it in union with the Mother who is the Handmaid of the Lord. Then our priesthood will be kept safe in her hands, indeed in her heart."

6

Obedience

(Scripture selection — Hebrews 5:7-10)

"If today you hear his voice, harden not your hearts," could be the most frequent verse in the divine office, since we repeat it seven times each day during the Invitatory. Wise mother she is, the Church knows we need that daily exhortation to live the virtue of obedience.

Obedience could be the easiest virtue to describe, but the toughest to live. Obedience is simply conforming our lives to the will of God, submitting ourselves to his dominion as expressed in the Bible, in the Tradition and magisterium of the Church, in natural law, in the directives of our legitimate superiors, in the dictates of a well-formed conscience, and in the prompting of the Holy Spirit interpreted prudently in discernment.

So basic is it that it was the only virtue expected of our first parents, and the Creator's gracious design was tragically distorted by that "original sin" which was an act of willful, proud disobedience. As the French philosopher Montaigne observed:

> The first law that ever God gave to man was a law of obedience. It was a commandment pure and simple, wherein man had nothing to inquire after or to dispute, for as much as to obey is the proper office of a rational soul acknowledging a heavenly superior and benefactor. From obedience and submission spring all the other virtues, as all sin does from self-opinion and self-will.

Thus is the generous act of obedience by Our Lady at the Annunciation seen as the "right" wherein the primordial "wrong" of the first Eve is corrected by the second. As Irenaeus remarked, "The seduction of a fallen angel drew Eve, while the glad tidings of the holy angel drew Mary, to begin the plan which would dissolve the bonds of the first snare. . . . So the Virgin Mary has become the advocate for the Virgin Eve. . . . Life has triumphed by the Virgin Mary's obedience, which has finally balanced the debt of disobedience."

Thus is Jesus extolled as the perfectly obedient Son. "Thirty years of our Lord's life are hidden in these words of the Gospel: 'He was subject unto them,' " preached Bossuet. However this is even more evident in his embrace of the cross — as tragic, illogical, desperate, useless, and spiteful as pride might interpret it — that Jesus was most obedient. "For Christ became obedient, even unto death, death on a cross." Irenaeus again: "In the first Adam we offended God by not performing his command. In the second Adam we have been reconciled, becoming 'obedient unto death.' "

However, as much as we recognize its pivotal importance, obedience is one of the most difficult virtues to practice, because it goes against a power that makes the neutron bomb look like a Bic lighter: the stubborn, proud human will.

". . . Obedience! / Bane of all genius, virtue, freedom, and truth / makes slaves of men, and of the human frame / a mechanized automaton. . . ," muses the poet Shelley in what has to be the common understanding of obedience.

My own spiritual director believes that it is precisely in obedience — not in celibacy, strangely enough — that the priest of today is most countercultural. For we live in a world that divinizes the will, holding that true happiness only comes when you have the license to do what you want, when you want, with whom and to whom you want, how you want, where you want; and that any restraint based on obedience to any higher authority is unjust, oppressive, and to be defied — since, as a matter of fact, there is no "higher authority" than my own wants, needs, and will.

This culture of denigrating obedience is particularly obvious in our beloved United States of America, which was founded on disobedience. We legitimately celebrate the courageous patriotism of the revolutionaries who risked all to gain independence from an oppressive king, yes, but we also admit that at times we tend to equate liberty with license, freedom with rights unbridled by duty; that we exalt dissent over docility, and view with suspicion authority, tradition, and accepting things purely on faith. Those familiar with the history of the Church in America know that a major reason for the ingrained anti-Catholicism of American society is the stereotype that Catholics are mindless, shackled peons who are required to give blind obedience to a corrupt, medieval, foreign system. We grudgingly admire the shrewd public relations coup of the pro-abortion lobby that has so effectively used the "pro-choice" label, pandering to this American resistance to the thought of anyone forcing me to do anything. Astute foreign observers of the American scene, from Tocqueville to Solzhenitsyn, and from Bedini to Mother Teresa, have keenly perceived this flaw in American society, namely to resist obedience to God, to tradition, and to moral principles, for the sake of choice, convenience, or personal preference. Recent emphasis on self-fulfillment, self-actualization, taking care of oneself — all legitimate goods, by the way, when properly understood — has only deepened this American suspicion of obedience.

So, my spiritual director's hunch is probably correct. It is precisely in obedience that we are most countercultural: in a society that urges us to keep all options open, not to be tied down, always ready to move on to something more attractive, to place conditions on all pledges, to protect our own interests above all else, to move up and make more, to demand rights and resist restrictions — we pledge complete obedience to one man and one confined area of God's vineyard. That's obedience. That's countercultural!

And, of course, the paradox comes because we are signs of the deeper truth: that it is precisely in obedience to God that the fullest freedom comes, that lasting peace is attained only when we are led not by our will but by his.

When I was newly ordained there was a fine woman religious as principal of our grade school. She was one of the youngest and most talented in her order, and I worried about her because her congregation was collapsing, regrouping, closing apostolates, and in seeming disarray. I once asked her, "What will your future hold?" I never forgot her answer.

"I don't know and I don't really care. How freeing it is not to have to worry about my future. That's the gift of obedience."

Thus the paradox: the most liberated people are those most under obedience. The martyrs of the city of Rome by their example converted thousands who came to watch them die, expecting to see frightened, shackled, and depressed slaves forced to their deaths, but instead saw courageous, confident, free, joyful men and women more liberated than their persecutors, people whose obedience to God freed them from all earthly trepidation, compromise, or doubt. Is this not what St. Thérèse of Lisieux had in mind when she wrote her Carmelite superior: "Isn't it extraordinary what a lot of nervous strain you can avoid by taking the vow of obedience? How enviable it is, the simple creed of the religious, who has only one compass to steer by, the will of her superior? She knows for certain that she is on the right path."

Or, as St. Philip Neri observed, "Entire conformity to the divine will is truly a road on which we cannot go wrong, and it is the only road that leads us to taste and enjoy the peace which sensual and earthly men know nothing of."

Can we take a look in more detail at obedience, and begin by considering it in the broadest sense: obedience as listening to God? How many times have you heard in a homily that "to obey" and "to hear" come from the same Latin root? So, let's examine this obedience to God for a few moments.

I recall once meeting with a seminarian when I was spiritual director back at Kenrick Seminary in St. Louis. In response to his forthright expression of quandary over his priestly vocation, I launched into a glib exposé on the necessity of obeying God's will.

"Father," he pleaded, "my problem is not obeying God's will; my problem is finding out what it is!" How very true! When God's will is clear, it might take sacrifice to obey it, but at least we know what we should do. The problem comes when his will is not clear. Then what?

As Archbishop Giuseppe Pittau said so touchingly when he presided over the installation of lectors in 1999 at the North American College, seminarians want to be priests not just because they desire to do the things priests do, not only because they have the talents and qualities necessary, not only because people they love and trust have told them that they'd make good priests; no, seminarians want to be priests first and foremost because priests sincerely and humbly believe God is calling them. If that is his will, then obedience is the only appropriate response.

The process of discovering God's will is called discernment, and it is a noble and sacred enterprise. One phenomenon essential to discerning God's will and then obeying it is prayer. If obedience is predicated upon listening to God, then we had better listen hard, and that comes in prayer.

We cannot be obedient disciples unless we ensure that there is a period of prayer every day, and one of our major duties in life is to develop the habit of prayer. We cannot know God's will unless we pray.

The legendary president of Notre Dame, Father Theodore Hesburgh, remarks in his autobiography that the achievements of his life could never have happened "without inner peace, born of prayer, especially to the Holy Spirit, in search of light, inspiration, and courage. I have a simple three-word prayer that has served me well for many, many years: 'Come, Holy Spirit.' It has never failed me."

But I have a particular form of prayer in mind that is essential to this listening to the Lord that is at the core of obedience. Most of us would get a "B" or above when it comes to a more active type of prayer: daily Mass, the divine office, our rosary, spiritual reading, devotions, quick visits to the Blessed Sacrament, and favorite prayers. Not to take away from the importance of this more "active" prayer, but I'm afraid most of us hover around a "D" when it comes to that more passive kind of prayer where we do nothing but open ourselves to our Lord's movements. That's meditation; that's contemplation; that's hard. To listen to the voice of the Lord, to sense his presence, to absorb his love, grace, and mercy . . . that's when we listen so we can obey.

We'd rather talk, wouldn't we?

I am reminded of the story of the father who died, leaving behind a grieving wife and two sons. The one son was not home when his dad died and rushed back, went right to his brother, who had been at the bedside when his dad had expired, and asked, "Tell me how dad died. Did he have any last words?"

To which the other son said, "No, dad had no last words. Mom was there with him till the end."

That's us: so busy talking, telling God what we want, telling him how to be God, that we miss his subtle whispers. "The value of persistent prayer is not that God will hear us, but that we will finally hear God," writes William McGill. This quiet, patient, calm, passive, listening prayer is hard, slow, and painful work. But keep at it we must. We cannot discern his will, much less obey it, unless we keep at it.

"If today you hear his voice, harden not your hearts!" Obedience to God.

Now, that to God is obedience in the broadest sense. We'd best particularize it, and begin to consider the more specific types of obedience appropriate to priests.

The first and most obvious is obedience to our bishop. Key to the understanding of diocesan priesthood is the obedience we owe our bishop. "Do you promise respect and obedience to me and my successors?" the bishop asks the ordinand at diaconate and priesthood ordinations. For God's sake, know what you're promising by that!

"Do you intend to spend the rest of your life in service to God's people in your diocese in obedience to your bishop?" as I ask every third- and fourth-year man at evaluation for approval for holy orders.

The respect and obedience to your bishop shows itself in your loyalty in word and deed. You support his programs, you speak well of him, you never scandalize people by mocking him or criticizing him. If we ridicule him, they may giggle and you may think they admire you for your independence and bravado, but they are scandalized. They admire you far more when they see you loyal and supportive, especially if they know that's tough for you to do.

Once at a retreat the priest-director shocked us by saying, "You know, I don't like my bishop. I don't enjoy his company, I disagree with the direction he is taking the diocese. I am at odds with his ideology, and I am hurt by the way he has treated me. I don't like my bishop . . . but, I do love him, and I have given him my solemn word that I will obey and respect him, and I will, and I will do it well. I will live for him and I would die for him." Please God, we will both like and love our bishop, but that priest's point was well taken.

We see obedience to our bishop as liberating, as a gift, not as a chain. Unlike our contemporaries, we do not have to fret about job security, about where we will next be assigned, about applications and curriculum vitae. We have freely placed our future in another man's hands, and how liberating that is. So, on the one hand, we can obviously disobey our bishop by refusing to accept the direction and assignment he gives us; but on the other hand, we can also disobey our bishop if we maneuver for appointments, plan for our career, and harbor ambitions for certain positions and assignments.

As you know, bishops today try their best to consult and collaborate in assigning their priests. They have personnel boards and often will even ask you if you want a certain assignment. So, we are obedient when we cooperate with that process. If a bishop asks us whether we would like to take a certain assignment, we are obedient by being honest with him. If our diocese has the system where men can apply for a parish or assignment, we are obedient by cooperating. But, the bottom line is always, "Bishop, since you asked, I'm happy to give my own preferences, but I will still do whatever or go wherever you want."

When I left the Apostolic Nunciature in Washington, my archbishop, John L. May, asked me what I wanted to do. "Do you want to be a pastor, or do you want to go to the seminary?" I said, "Archbishop, I want to do whatever you want."

He said, "Fine. Thank you. I will indeed tell you what I want you to do. But you will help me decide that by telling me what you would like to do."

So, I said, "I would like to be a pastor."

He sent me to the seminary. He did his job. I did mine.

Some priests claim externally they want to be obedient in accepting an assignment from their bishop, but internally are angry, thinking they have been passed over or mistreated; so, they go, but they never really accept the assignment and never work at it. They childishly say, "I'll show him. I'll go, but I'm not going to do anything." The people of course are the ones who then suffer. Obedience is not only accepting an assignment, but doing it well. As St. Bernard preached, "If you begin to grieve at your assignment, to judge your superior, to murmur in your heart, even though you outwardly fulfill what is commanded, this is not obedience, but a cloak over your malice."

The old-timers say, "Never ask for an assignment and never ask to get out of one, or you'll regret it." Some truth there. Another old-timer, Monsignor McRae, tells the deacons each year before they depart, "For God's sake, don't be a pain in the . . ." Some guys are never happy. They're always complaining about their assignment. After a few years as a priest, I was elected to our priests' personnel board — a real headache — then went off it after my three-year term, only to be reelected six years later. I'll be darned: at the first meeting of my second term there I saw the same names of priests who were complaining six years before. Don't be one of those.

Now, what if the bishop asks you to consider a special assignment, yet tells you he will not order you there but will only assign you if you sincerely agree to go? Well, take him at his word. Be honest with him. Consult people whom you trust. There would be some acceptable reasons not to take the offered assignment, I suppose. These are three that are not acceptable:

"Sorry, Bishop, I'm so happy where I'm at that I do not want to move." He didn't ask you that, did he? In the long run, pardon the bluntness, but your contentment has nothing to do with it. We all get settled, comfortable, and happy at a place — and maybe that's when it's best to move on. Just because you're happy at one place does not mean you should say no to another.

A second untenable answer: "Oh, Bishop, I'm so needed here; it would not be fair for me to move now. The place couldn't survive." Remember the old saying: "Cemeteries are filled with indispensable people."

A third excuse that does not hold water: "Oh, I could not do that. I'm not qualified." Well, apparently your bishop thinks you are, since he's asking. Remember what Archbishop Pittau said: "The Lord is not calling you because you're the strongest, most talented, or most qualified. The Lord is calling you because he loves you, and can work in you."

The scales are always tipped in favor of the bishop and the Church, not you, your wants, or preferences. That's obedience.

Another part of obedience to your bishop, very relevant today: your obedience is to the bishop of the diocese. Two corollaries here:

It is a wonderful blessing when you personally have a strong relationship, an affection, a reverence, and a deep personal loyalty to your bishop. Many of you can thank God for that. Some of you trace your vocation to the direct personal influence of your bishop. Thank God! But . . . your obedience is not to the man but to the office, and "there will come a pharaoh who knows not Joseph." And you will be called to respect and obey the new one as much as you did the old. Your priestly vocation, certainly your promise of obedience, is not dependent upon the name of the man who sits in the cathedra, but to the office.

As diocesan priests our obedience is to the diocese. That's why the ideal is that a man is a priest in the diocese he calls home, in the diocese in which he was raised. I know there are legitimate reasons why a man may be a priest in a diocese other than his home, as some of you are. But make sure you are not attracted to it for some ephemeral reason, such as the personality of the bishop or the present regnant ideology. When Anthony O'Connell was ordained first bishop of Knoxville, he took his new ring, put it on his finger, and said, "People of the diocese of Knoxville, with this ring I do thee wed." That's the bond we diocesan priests have with our diocese. We love her; we know her inside and out; we want to spend our life in her service; we want to die there.

Not only are we obedient to our bishop, but to our priesthood. By this I mean that we are faithful to our priestly call, we generously obey the expectations the Church has of us, we daily foster and strengthen our priestly identity, and we avoid anything or anybody that can threaten it.

Ever heard the term "the long obedience" to describe those priests who are quietly faithful, day in and day out, who accept assignments willingly, who look for no advancement, who love their people, and who keep at it year after year? The "long obedience" . . . the long obedience to our priesthood . . . it's not just a function, a career, a job, or a ministry that we can leave when tedium, frustration, or failure comes — as they will. It is a call, a life, a vocation that calls for the long obedience. It is fragile and must be protected; it is a flame that can flicker and must be fanned; it is a gift that can be taken for granted or even forgotten, unless we are daily obedient to its demands.

Funny enough, we are often tempted to a disobedience toward our priesthood, not just when frustration, tedium, or failure comes, but when popularity, acclaim, and success come.

In his opening talk to the new graduate priests at the Casa each year, Monsignor Elmer sobers them by urging them to "protect your priesthood," because very often, it is the priest who achieves his advanced degree who gets a big head, becomes haughty, proud, too independent — and ends up leaving. Dominic Maruca observes the same phenomenon when, in his analysis of priests who leave, he discovered that those who were most popular, sought after, highest paid, and very acclaimed, ended up forgetting obedience to the essentials of their priesthood and leaving.

Obedience to our priesthood means a vigilant attention to the duties of our vocation: our daily Mass and divine office, meditation, growth in the virtues of chastity, humility, simplicity of life, wholesome friendships with brother priests, a daily regimen, a reliance on the sacrament of penance, our annual retreat, and spiritual direction — all those things that keep us faithful to our priesthood.

That obedience to vocation starts in the seminary. One of the first-year men recalled his first weeks here at the college: "I was terribly homesick, lost, confused, wondering why I was here, convinced I should go home. But, I thought, no, I must be obedient. Those wiser than me sent me here; the faculty and my brother seminarians tell me to give it time. God wants me here. I will trust him." And now he is grateful for that obedience. So we immerse ourselves fully in the demands of our vocation: no second-guessing, no getting around things, no "I know better." If a man is one of those always looking for the exception, always figuring he is above the demands others might be held to, he is not obedient to his vocation.

Then comes obedience to our people. Yes, they are our bosses. We serve them. The salvation and care of their souls are our daily task. A priest I respect so very much wonders aloud if we have lost what he calls "our sense of duty." He explains, "It used to be that, if a parishioner was in the hospital, I could not rest until I had visited him; if one had died, I could not finish the day without going to the funeral parlor; if one called to speak to me, I would return the call as soon as possible; if one asked to see me, I'd make time right away. It was my duty; I owed that to my people, to be there always for them. But now I find it so easy to excuse myself, to skip it, to crave to be left alone and not bothered." A sense of duty; an obedience to my people. I owe it to them as their priest. The Lord did not give me the priesthood as a cozy, comfortable benefice, but to serve his people.

Some years ago a missionary priest from the United States, Father Jim Tully, stopped to see me. He had been working in the African country of Sierra Leone and had just barely escaped with his life. As he was hiding in the bush, he watched as the marauders burned down his little church, school, clinic, and began rounding up his people. With the other refugees he had made it out of the country, and finally to Rome for consultation with his general there. His only desire? To go back to his mission.

"I have to see my people again. I must see if they are all right. I did not even have time to say 'good-bye.'" That's what I mean by obedience to our people.

Finally, obedience to suffering. "Son though he was, he learned obedience through suffering," as the Epistle to the Hebrews reminds us. And so will we. It may be the suffering that comes from accepting an assignment we do not want, and plunging into it; it may be the trial of living with a man who is not our "cup of tea"; it may be the weariness of tough and demanding work that hardly seems to matter and which only seems to multiply; it may be failure, sin, or struggle that wears us down and tempts us to cry "*basta*" ("enough")! In all of this, we are obedient in our suffering, often finding on our lips the words of the Eternal High Priest, "Father, let this cup pass; but, not my will, but thine be done."

In fact, St. Ignatius tells us that difficulty can be part of the very act of obedience, in that, if we are given the choice between two assignments, it is better to take the hardest one, the one least appealing. Far cry from today where we check the bank account and see how nice the rooms are before we give our assent. Sometimes it is the disappointment of an assignment that burdens us, as we feel useless, wasted, or not being utilized properly. Obedience to suffering reminds us that, ultimately, it is not what we do as a priest that counts, not where we're doing it, but who we are as a priest doing it.

A monk at the Abbey of Gethsemani told me how he was happy with his work in the bakery when one day the abbot told him he wanted him to be ordained a priest. After his years of preparation, he was ordained and, the day after his first Mass, waited for the abbot after morning prayer to ask what his new assignment would be. The abbot was surprised and said, "Why, return to the bakery, of course." "But," the young monk replied, "that's what I did before

I was ordained." "Yes, but now you'll do it as a priest," replied the abbot.

It was precisely at the lowest point of his earthly life, at the time he felt most abandoned, most forgotten, the most useless, the time he hurt the most — it was precisely at the time of greatest suffering — on the cross, obedient even unto death, that Jesus accomplished the most.

If the goal of our lives is conformity to Christ, then obedience is the path to get there. St Ignatius Loyola taught: "Obedience is a whole burnt offering in which the entire man, without the slightest reserve, is offered in the fire of charity to his Creator and Lord. . . . Few souls understand what God would accomplish in them if they were to abandon themselves unreservedly to him, and if they were to allow his grace to mold them accordingly."

St. John Vianney, who himself was tempted often to leave Ars for other easier assignments, but who each time accepted the bishop's will, preached, "Obedience makes the will supple. It gives the power to conquer self, to overcome laziness, and to resist temptations. It inspires the courage with which to fulfill the most difficult tasks."

Obedience then is that mediating virtue through which all the others come; we pursue holiness, humility, chastity, simplicity, and charity because we are attentive to God's will, obedient to his designs, and we know this is what he wants. He has a plan for us, and we cooperate. It is rarely clear as we anticipate it in the future; it usually is as we reflect upon it looking back, if we have been obedient.

As we find in Cardinal Newman's meditations:

> God has created me to do him some definite service; he has committed some work to me which he has not committed to another. I have my mission — I may never know it in this life, but I shall be told it in the next.
>
> He has not created me for nothing. I shall do good, I shall do his work, I shall be an angel of peace, a preacher of the truth in my own place — if I do but keep his commandments and serve him in my calling.
>
> Therefore, I will trust him. Whatever, wherever I am, I can

never be thrown away. If I am in sickness, my sickness may serve him; if I am in sorrow, my sorrow may serve him.

He does nothing in vain. He knows what he is about. He may take away my friends. He may throw me among strangers. He may make me feel desolate, make my spirits sink, hide my future from me — still he knows what he is about — and I trust him.

So, in our obedience as priests we are most in conformity to Jesus, placing our plans, our desires, and our wills at the disposal of the Father. We close with the *Suscipe* of Charles de Foucauld:

> Father,
> I abandon myself into your hands;
> do with me what you will.
> Whatever you may do, I thank you:
> I am ready for all, I accept all.
> Let only your will be done in me,
> and in all your creatures —
> I wish no more than this, O Lord.
> Into your hands I commend my soul;
> I offer it to you
> with all the love of my heart,
> for I love you, Lord,
> and so need to give myself,
> to surrender myself
> into your hands,
> without reserve,
> and with boundless confidence,
> for you are my Father.

7

Courtesy

(Scripture selection — Philippians 2:1-4)

One of the most prominent historians of the Catholic Church in the United States, Monsignor John Tracy Ellis, whose magnum opus is his magisterial two-volume life of Cardinal James Gibbons, was fond of telling a story about a prominent citizen of Baltimore whom he interviewed while doing research for the biography. The man told how as a young boy his parents took him for a walk every Sunday afternoon following dinner. Sure enough, every Sunday they would pass a small but distinguished-looking cleric also on a stroll who would unfailingly tip his hat, smile, and say "good afternoon" to the family. Each Sunday, the man recalled, he would want to return the greeting to the kind gentleman, and even chat with him, so courteous did he seem, but his parents, who never returned the greeting, pulled him quickly along. Seems they were prominent Presbyterians who would explain to their little boy that the man in black was a Catholic priest with whom they did not associate.

Well, so engaging was the priest's smile, so sincere his greeting, Sunday after Sunday, even when constantly ignored by the parents, that, so the man related to Monsignor Ellis, he became more and more curious about Catholics, to such an extent that, at twenty-two, to the horror of his blueblood parents, he took instructions and joined the Roman Catholic Church. How moved he was when, at the Cathedral of the Assumption to be confirmed, he saw process up the aisle the gracious gentleman who had been unfailingly courteous to him on the Sunday strolls, now in regal vestments, blessing the crowd who whispered in awe to one another, "It's Cardinal Gibbons."

I begin with that simple story, because it shows the supreme importance of courtesy. The constant kindness, even when not returned, of a priest on a Sunday stroll won a soul for the Church. As Belloc wrote:

Of courtesy, it is much less
Than courage of heart or holiness,
Yet in my walks it seems to me
That the grace of God is in courtesy.

Now, courtesy is a virtue I hope needs no definition. We know it when we see it; we sure know it when we do not. It has to do with kindness, consideration, with manners, propriety, and decency. I presume it comes under charity, the supreme Christian characteristic. St. Francis observed: "Realize, dear brother, that courtesy is actually one of the properties of God, who gives his sun and rain to the just and the unjust out of courtesy; and courtesy is the sister of charity, by which hatred is vanquished and love is cherished."

"God is in the details," as the old dictum goes, and, so is the devil, I might add, and I propose that courtesy governs the details, the nuts and bolts of charity. Courtesy is based on three principles:

• One, self-respect: we honor and reverence ourselves as a child of God, made in his image and likeness, his priceless work of art, redeemed at the cost of his only Son's precious blood, destined for eternity. This gives us such a healthy self-respect that we treat ourselves with dignity, and only allow words and actions to flow from us that are worthy of our birthright.

• Two, a respect for others: what I believe about myself I firmly believe of others, and thus will only treat them as the reflection of the divine that they truly are — that means, courteously.

• Three, courtesy: this virtue is built on the commonsense conclusion that society —whether as small as my corridor or as large as the Church — can only survive, prosper, and fulfill its purpose if it is well ordered by self-evident rules of civility, consideration, and care.

Let's bring it a little closer to home. I could give a conference on courtesy to the Rotary Club, the Masons, or the pickpockets of Rome for that matter, because it is a basic human duty, usually taught in one's earliest years in the family. Courtesy is incumbent upon everyone. But it is absolutely essential for a priest! Our people expect us to be gentlemen. I do not mean foppish, snobbish, goody-goody, "Mr. Manners," experts on protocol and etiquette, but thoughtful, considerate, polite men. Why? Because Jesus was, and we dare to represent him! And we are thus hypocrites if we are thoughtless, inconsiderate, sloppy, crude bores!

I was just reading a fascinating interview with Dr. Laura Schlessinger, this amazingly popular author and TV and radio personality. Listen to what she says:

> If I have an ice-cream company and you drive one of my trucks which says "Schlessinger Ice Cream" on the side, looking like a bum — your hair is filthy, you've got a cigarette hanging out of your mouth, you're dressed sloppily, and you're mean to the kids — who is held in disrespect? Schlessinger Ice Cream Company, that's who! So, a person who sets himself up as a religious person *de facto* represents God, and is responsible for God's good name in the community.

Thanks, Dr. Laura! You said it better than I could! By our courtesy we attract people to Jesus, his truth, his Church — as Cardinal Gibbons did that young man. And by our rudeness or lack of courtesy? We drive them away!

Let me mention another reason why courtesy is so crucial for a priest. When I begin to get specific in a minute, you might comment about an example or a point, "That's a bit trivial. With all the violence, crises, and troubles in the world, Dolan is talking about how to use a knife and fork?" All right, maybe writing thank-you notes is way down the list after such things as faith, chastity, integrity, and holiness . . . but I still maintain courtesy is not an option for one serious about the road to perfection . . . and, if you're not on that road to perfection, you should not be on the road to priesthood.

"Thoughtfulness," claims Mother Teresa, "is the beginning of great sanctity. If you learn the art of being thoughtful, you will become more and more Christlike. . . . Our vocation . . . must be full of courtesy for others." All right, so maybe acts of courtesy by themselves are rather small and insignificant. "If they are," claims Emerson, "so are the dewdrops which give such a depth to the morning meadow."

Okay . . . to the details. God is in the details, remember! Here's how I will tackle this: I have enumerated eight characteristics of courtesy — could be more, I admit; could be expressed differently, granted — but eight attributes, under which I'll give specific instances, many of which have been thoughtfully submitted by many priests and seminarians I have known.

The list: a courteous man is — deferential, friendly, hospitable, reliable, civil, magnanimous, grateful, and dignified.

A gentleman is deferential. "Do nothing from selfishness or conceit," St. Paul writes the Philippians (2:3), "but in humility count others better than yourselves. Let each of you look not only to his own interests, but also to the interests of others." There — that explains well what I mean by deferential. We always place the needs of others before our own. Henri Nouwen taught that genuine Christian love is not just an awareness of the needs of others, but the anticipation of them. Even now do I recall my father, obviously the hungriest one at the supper table, after a hard day's work, always taking his food last, deferring to his wife and children.

The courteous man will be deferential to everyone, but there are some who especially deserve our deference:

• Our parents and family, in obedience to the fourth commandment, merit special piety and respect from us.

• Those in authority merit our deference. It is the mark of a well-mannered man that he would stand up when anyone enters the room. That's deference. When in a parish, always defer to the pastor, not only in leadership decisions, but also in simple things, like seating, leading a prayer, and referring to him with respect. Authority deserves deference.

• Women have a right to our deference. I do not mean we patronize them, but I believe that certain elements of chivalry are still valid, such as standing when they enter a room, opening doors for them, watching our mouth around them, and holding the chair for them at the table.

• The weak, the sick, the elderly, and the handicapped merit deference, again, not in a patronizing way, but in a subtle sensitivity to them. I once heard of a parish priest, the celebrant at a standing-room-only Sunday Mass, who watched a visibly pregnant woman walk up and down the aisle looking for a place to sit. This priest began to fume as none of the parishioners made a move to help her. He finally said from the chair, "Ma'am, come up and take my seat." Not too wise liturgically, was it? Not too wise even as far as manners go, since he probably embarrassed the woman; but he sure made that an unforgettable "teaching moment" on the duty of courteous deference!

"Defer to one another out of love for Christ."

A courteous man is friendly. Let me tell you a paradox of my nearly six years as rector. One of the frequent compliments I hear about my seminarians is, "Your men are so friendly! They are quick to welcome, to introduce themselves, to greet people, and cheerfully offer help." The paradox? One of the frequent condemnations I hear is, "Your men are not friendly. They walk by me without a word of greeting, they do not return a salutation, they will not initiate an introduction, and they are snobbish and rude." Which description is the accurate one? Obviously, both! I firmly believe the first dominates, and I hear my men commended for friendliness much more than condemned for lack of it. But, enough people have noticed a rude lack of friendliness in some of you to merit drawing attention to it.

A few examples:

• "Not saying 'hello' when someone greets him." That is elementary courtesy, something we would expect from a bus driver. When I first arrived at the North American College, I said "good morning" to a man on the stairwell as we were both heading for the chapel; no reply. Figuring he did not hear me, I repeated the greeting; no reply. I stopped him: "It is rude not to return my greeting." To which he replied, "Oh, I'm just not a 'morning person.' " To which I responded, "Then don't be a parish priest, because you will meet most of your people almost every morning before 8:00 a.m."

• "Not giving the sign of peace at Mass." Forgive me — that, in my mind, is matter for the confessional.

• "Going to the other side of the corridor and keeping your head down to avoid greeting someone."

Not the courteous man, who is unfailingly friendly.

Closely allied: a courteous man is hospitable.

Not long ago, Father Williams and I visited Mount St. Mary's, Emmitsburg. We arrived late in the evening, about 9:30, parked the car, and went to the trunk to get our luggage. Three of the seminarians who had been chatting on the steps walked over, and, in a very genuine way, introduced themselves, welcomed us, and helped us with our luggage to find our rooms. I commented to Father Williams, "To be on the receiving end of hospitality reminds me how important it is. I only hope our men at the North American College are as hospitable to guests as these three have been to us!"

Always introduce a guest! Always introduce yourself to a guest! If you wonder if you have already done so, say, "I can't remember if I have met you or not. I am Monsignor Dolan, the rector. And you are?" Always give your name when someone introduces himself to you! I can't believe how many I see who, once someone says, "Hi, I'm Bill Smith from Kansas," responds, "Oh, hi!" Introduce yourself!

A courteous gentleman is hospitable. The Master — who in his Blessed Mother's womb was turned away from innkeepers at Bethlehem, who was welcomed warmly into the homes of Martha and Mary, Zacchaeus, and Matthew, and who was snubbed as a guest in the home of the leading Pharisee — has a special place in his Sacred Heart for those who are hospitable.

And what a priestly virtue! To see the newcomer, the stranger, the visitor in our parish, and to make that person feel at home. *Venit hospis, venit Christus* ("When a guest comes, Christ comes").

The courteous man is reliable. When we have commitments to fulfill toward others, we do so, since our self-respect and our respect for them demand it. Some particulars:

• We are reliable in assignments. It is a poor reflection on a man's courtesy when he misses his appointments, whether liturgical or pastoral.

• Priests are notorious in not responding to invitations. When you receive an invitation, reply with acceptance or regret; if you are due somewhere, be there! People count on you to be reliable.

Clericalism is a curse of the Church. It means priests believe they deserve special treatment. It is evident when priests think they are exempt from normal rules of courtesy, like responding to invitations and showing up when they are expected.

• Never leaving for an overnight without informing those we should notify of where we can be reached and when we will return.

• Promptness: to come late constantly is a rude violation of reliability. Why would you selfishly presume your time is more valuable than another's?

A courteous man is reliable!

The courteous gentleman is civil. By that I mean that a tone of respect for the other, a lack of acrimony, and a climate of trust should characterize our public dealings, especially in more tense or unpleasant situations.

Wise voices in society — and our Church — lament the loss of civility. Like it or not, everyone agreed with at least the one aspect of the late Cardinal Joseph Bernardin's "Common Ground Initiative" that urged a return to civility in all public discourse. The name-calling, suspicion, and vitriol that characterize the written and spoken word among Catholics is nothing less than sinful. Augustine claimed that the greatest of all heresies was lack of charity.

A few observations:

• Never should we get *ad hominem.* "Don't listen to him — he's a heretic!" "She's not orthodox." "He's a right-wing fanatic." The presumption for the civil man is that each person is good, honest, and respectable. We may disagree with what he or she says or does, but we are always civil to the person. "I wouldn't let Sister talk to the RCIA — she's a heretical feminist!" No, she's not . . . she's a child of God and consecrated daughter of the Church, whose particular views on a given issue may be wrong — and need to be corrected — but she deserves our respect, and our words about her are always civil.

• Civility means no name-calling, no angry outbursts, no accusatory charges. We express our criticisms calmly, charitably, and respectfully.

• Civility also means that, when we have made our point and brought it to the proper authority, we let up, and trust the goodwill of those who have proper responsibility to take care of it. We do not then wage guerrilla warfare to accomplish our goal.

The bishop of Pittsburgh, Most Reverend Donald Wuerl, issued a pastoral letter on this very topic not too long ago. "We cannot highlight evangelization and then destroy its fondest hopes by the way we talk with or about one another," the bishop wrote. Listen to the principles he enunciated:

> "To enter a dialogue convinced that the others engaged in the effort are dishonest, deceitful, or intent on harming us negates the possibility of a wholesome outcome."

"Successful dialogue begins with trust."

"Basic to Christian discourse is the belief that the truth itself is strong enough to win the day."

The shock-talk, trash-mouth name-calling so popular on TV and radio shows cannot become the style of discourse in the Church.

Courtesy demands civility.

A gentleman is magnanimous. By that I mean there is a wideness of spirit, a largeness of heart about him. The best way to understand magnanimity is to name its opposite: pettiness. So, to judge a man's liturgical propriety by whether or not he wears an amice is not magnanimous; to do an autopsy on the priest and deacon after every Mass and homily is petty.

The magnanimous person has a wideness of spirit that shows itself in notes of sympathy to those who have lost someone dear in death, or in a word of support to the sick. The magnanimous quickly forgive and do not nurse grudges; they overlook slights and give others the benefit of the doubt.

Likewise is magnanimity shown when I can remain courteous to someone who is always rude to me. There's the real test. We often learn courtesy from feeling the lack of it ourselves.

The courteous man is magnanimous.

Grateful: everything we have comes from a good God through generous people, and that leaves us grateful. "Thank you" is the phrase most often found in the conversation of the courteous man, his conversation with God in prayer, his conversation with others.

Gratitude exemplifies itself in thank-you notes to benefactors and those who host us, help us, present us with gifts. Priests are notorious for not writing notes of appreciation.

Gratitude is apparent in the care we give property and our surroundings. As priests, we live in homes and enjoy comforts given us by God's people. To exercise careful stewardship over them is a mark of courtesy. To care for our rooms and furnishings, to close outside doors and turn off lights, to pick up trash and clean up after ourselves, to return items we have borrowed — these are all areas of stewardship, which would flow from a gratitude for what we have been given.

It is not coincidental that among the first words we are taught is "thank you"; it is not accidental that gratitude and grace come from the same root word.

A final characteristic of courtesy: dignity. Our self-respect as well as our respect for others gives us a dignity, a poise, a sense of propriety. All of us have a base side that threatens our human dignity, and courtesy and manners keep this animal side under control.

Again a few examples:

• It should not surprise you that our animal side needs to be tempered by our dignified side at table! We have, I am afraid, capitulated to the habit of eating as quickly as possible, immune to those around us, getting it over with fast. Meals are meant to be enjoyed, savored, with human company the best course of all.

• I should also observe that courtesy demands that we do take our meals with the community or, when a priest, in the rectory with the pastor. Since I have never missed a meal in my life, I am startled when I hear pastors today comment that their associates rarely eat at the rectory. This is not good; it can be rude if overdone.

• We show our dignity, for ourselves and for others, in our dress and appearance. I think we do well when we are in clerics; I sometimes cringe when we get informal. We expect a collared shirt; we expect dress slacks. We are public people. Never leave your residence without clean, presentable clothes. The only hat a gentleman would ever wear inside in a public area is a zucchetto or biretta — which would then raise other questions, not about your manners but about your mental health. Unless you are growing a beard — which should always then be clean and trimmed; so remember to shave every day.

• And, as much as I am reluctant to admit it, I must: it does violate our dignity and that of others to smoke (or use chewing tobacco) when others are present. Go outside, use the privacy of your room, or make sure you are in a place — more and more difficult to find — where smoking is allowed and others are not bothered.

We show dignity at the table, in our dress, and in our personal appearance and hygiene.

May I conclude by holding up our Lord as the perfect example of courtesy, grace, manners, and consideration? To close, consider this from Belloc:

On monks I did in Storrington fall,
They took me straight into their hall.
I saw three pictures on a wall,
And courtesy was in them all.
The first the Annunciation,
The second the Visitation,
The third the Consolation
Of God that was our Lady's Son.

Jesus, divine courtesy incarnate:
deferential in coming to serve, not to be served,
so friendly that people would not leave him alone,
hospitable to even the cheat and prostitute,
reliable even to his appointment on Calvary,
civil to the arrogant and self-important,
magnanimous in the expanse of his burning heart,
grateful in attributing all to his Father and wanting nothing
    more than for all to return to him;
dignified even in the stable, when tired, when insulted, when
    crucified.

The courtesy of Jesus, the courtesy of his priests . . . is it too much to suggest that, in our consideration of others through manners and thoughtfulness, we enter the paschal mystery? As one of the seminarians at the North American College observed, "Courtesy is another way of dying unto self," best expressed in the golden rule from the Gospel, "Do unto others as you would have them do unto you."

In this age of "entitlement," where we are told to watch out for number one, where we are led to believe that we have everything coming to us, where we are tempted to ask what others can do for us instead of what we can do for them, that God, country, society, Church, and this college owe us something but can ask nothing from us in return, where privacy, pleasure, and convenience seem the only inalienable rights, for us baby boomers thought to be spoiled and you "generation X-ers" said to be selfish, we are asked "to think humbly of others as superior to ourselves."

As John Andrew Holmes wrote, "Genuine courtesy is a splinter from the true cross."

8

Integrity

(Scripture selection — 1 Timothy 6)

On April 28, 1997, armed Hutu militiamen attacked the major seminary in Burundi, forcing all thirty-four resident seminarians to the courtyard in front of their chapel, where the leader of the invaders demanded that the seminarians divide themselves into Hutu and Tutsi groups. The seminarians refused, huddling together instead of declaring themselves members of any one tribe. The commandant insisted again, ordering his cutthroats to aim their rifles at the united group of students, threatening to open fire if the men did not obey his command to divide into the two ethnic groups. The seminarians remained united, defiant of the threat. The commandant ordered his men to open fire, mercilessly cutting down in cold blood those thirty-four young Africans who wanted nothing more in life than to be conformed to the Prince of Peace as his priests.

I begin with this contemporary episode of martyrdom to exemplify the virtue I want to address. Admittedly, many come to mind after hearing that account:

• How easy it would be to speak of fortitude, as these brave young men fearlessly stood up to the threats of thugs to witness Christian principle.

• How vividly their courage illustrates Christian and priestly identity, as they were aware that their identity as children of God, disciples of Jesus, and men sharing a mutual vocation to priesthood, superceded any racial division.

• How movingly their martyrdom teaches the power of love, as they knew that to divide into groups would seal the fate of their Tutsi brothers, and hoped that their common unity in the threat of violence would protect the defenseless. . . .

But may I propose that their martyrdom dramatically instructs us about integrity, as they wanted their exterior stance of fortitude, their claim of fraternity flowing from Christian and priestly identity, and their common desire to love one another even to laying down their lives, to mirror what they believed inside. For these courageous seminarians, there was no division between what they claimed to believe and how they acted, no danger of hypocrisy in preaching devotion to one principle but compromising it in reality, and no dishonesty in their conviction that they were men of God whose allegiance was totally to the King of Kings, not to the armies of this world. These were men of integrity who proved faithful, reliable, trustworthy, and honest even under the ultimate threat, joining such people as John the Baptist, the apostles, Thomas à Becket, John Fischer, Thomas More, and Maximilian Kolbe. To the brutal taunts as to whether they really believed what they claimed, they answered "yes" with their innocent, young lives. And that is integrity.

Often have I asked what the Church, what the world, expects of priests, and I have answered my own question by responding, "Holiness." True enough! A very close second, and certainly related, is integrity. The Church, our people, and, yes, even the world, long for priests who are men of integrity.

And what does that mean? Integrity is one of those traits rather tough to define but very easy to recognize. A man of integrity is a man of honesty, without guile, a genuine, authentic man, whose interior convictions are externally evident, who outwardly shows in word and deed that he is what he claims to be: a man of sincerity, truth, principle, character, and reliability, whose word can be trusted, and who inspires respect in others. As the father of our country wrote, "I hope I shall possess firmness and virtue enough to maintain what I consider the most enviable of all titles, the character of a man of integrity." John Cassian used the term "transparency" as he described the man of integrity as "one found the same, day and night, the same in bed as in prayer, the same alone as surrounded by others, with absolutely nothing to hide."

As with so many virtues, we find it easier to recognize when it is lacking. For integrity, the greatest example of what it is not comes from the Pharisees, who earned the charge of hypocrite from the Master, hypocrisy being the opposite of integrity.

The problem with the Pharisees was not, of course, in what they professed — their attention to the law, ritual, worship, doctrine, and morality was commended by Jesus — but with their lives: their words and deeds were so far from what they professed that they were seen as hollow and cynical.

• They eloquently preached the message of compassion, charity, and justice found in the teachings of the prophets, but then treated others with arrogance, harshness, and spite.

• They refined the intricacies of the law with scrupulous precision and urged obedience, but then discovered loopholes that let them get by without observance

• They set themselves up as models of virtue but then became arrogant and judgmental with others.

Simply put, they lacked integrity.

We as priests and future priests hang our heads in shame every time we hear of the scribes and Pharisees in the Gospel, for what they were to the Old Israel we are to the New Israel. We claim to be men of faith, prayer, love, simplicity, chastity, fidelity, honor, and generosity — and often we are not. Our promises, our preaching, and our worship can all become "lip service" unless we are men of genuine integrity. Not for nothing does the Church require us every year for a week to ponder in the Office of Readings St. Augustine's burning castigation of those in holy orders, his commentary on the bad shepherds of Ezekiel. Priests without integrity are the Pharisees, scribes, and hypocrites of today, and he who thinks that such does not apply to him is the worst one!

There seem some specific areas where our people especially expect their priests to display integrity. Let me mention six of them:

The first is in the area of chastity. It is very interesting that the *Catechism of the Catholic Church* speaks of chastity precisely in terms of integrity. I was only a priest for a few weeks when a woman in the parish came to the door asking to see a priest, and since I was on duty that day, I went to the parlor to see her. For nearly an hour she confided in me about the sexual troubles she was having, revealing to me intimate details that made me wish I had taken, not my moral theology classes, but my college biology classes, more seriously. This suffering woman did not even know my name but she could call me "Father," and, because I was a priest, she could speak to me in absolute trust. In a world filled by men who had sexually used her, I was for her one who saw beyond her body into her soul. Knowing only men who viewed her as a sexual toy, she saw me, a priest, as one who respected her person, her interior beauty. Existing in a world where her every move had been interpreted as seductive, she could relax around one she trusted as pure and chaste.

Our people believe us when we say we are chaste celibates, that we can love and accept them purely, that we respect them not for how they can gratify our sexual appetites but for who they are. Now, how they can still believe us when we say we are chaste celibates is beyond me, when so many of us have seduced women, broken up marriages, and pursued their sons. But they continue to believe we are men of integrity in matters of chastity, and, thank God, most priests are. In a world gone mad with hormones and promiscuity, we are looked upon as "safe," that means, men who are pure, self-controlled, confident about their sexual identity, and who have incorporated the charism of chaste celibacy.

As I have said before, one indication to seminarians of whether or not you will be chaste as a priest is whether or not you are so now. An ongoing genital relationship with another person, man or woman, or a tendency to look for such in our relationships; an inability to speak of sexual matters in a calm, mature manner; an inclination to view others with lust, as objects to gratify one's sexual desires; constant fantasizing leading to frequent masturbation; use of pornography (magazines, books, videos, movies, even the Internet!), or so-called "cruising" for sexual partners or even prostitutes, or an attraction to young boys or girls — all would be a cause for much concern and should lead the man of true integrity to stop and settle issues about his own sexuality before pledging himself to a life of chaste celibacy. For God's sake, the Church does not need another priest who hurts himself, others, the Church, and the Lord with a violation of integrity in the area of celibate chastity.

A second area where people expect integrity in their priests is in reliability. They look to us to be men of our word, whose promises can be trusted. "People must think of us as Christ's servants," as Paul wrote to the Corinthians, "stewards entrusted with mysteries of God. What is expected of stewards is that each one should be found worthy of trust" (1 Corinthians 4:1-2). Generically, yes, they expect us to be reliable in living the kind of life we profess as an *alter Christus*. In very practical ways, though, they want to be able to count on us. When they make an appointment with us, they count on us being there; when they leave a phone message for us, they count on us to return it; when we are due at a meeting, we are there; when they expect us to bring them Holy Communion when they are sick, we show up; when we are scheduled for 6:30 Mass, we are there, and we start on time; when we are due to teach the second graders, we are there. We are reliable; we keep commitments and we are men of duty and responsibility . . . integrity. . . . We can be counted upon, and, as our Lord tells us, he who can be trusted in small matters can be trusted with greater.

We all wish to be reliable, so I ask: Can you be counted upon now?

One area of trustworthy reliability in which priests should excel is confidentiality. People believe they can trust us with secrets. They can bring to us matters they could speak about to no one else and we will bring that knowledge with us to the grave. The gossipy, chatterbox, flannel-mouth priest violates integrity. At the North American College I so admire our spiritual directors and staff counselor, Father O'Brien, who are models of confidentiality, or a man like Monsignor Daniel Thomas, who has a delicate position at the Holy See but is impeccably discreet about matters in the office.

In my first assignment lived my mother's doctor, and I knew she had gone in the day before for a physical, and I asked him after Mass how the exam went. He replied, "Oh, Father, I'd rather you ask your mom." He was so sensitive about his professional confidentiality that he did not want to speak of his patient to me, even though she was my mom and I was his parish priest. So do we need always to be discreet, always a man of prudent reserve.

It is best to say nothing rather than risk violating confidence. This especially, of course, applies to the confessional, where we are bound by the most rigid confidentiality. Priests of integrity never refer to the confessional, and would never even identify someone as one of their penitents. In my first parish assignment I saw one of our auxiliary bishops come to the rectory every Saturday morning. I would comment to the pastor that I saw Bishop McNicholas at the rectory that morning and he would simply respond, "Oh, yes, when he's in the neighborhood he stops by to say hello." It was only years later that Bishop McNicholas told me he came to confession every

Saturday to Monsignor Flavin. That would have been so natural for Monsignor Flavin to have told me that the bishop came weekly for confession, but he had too much integrity for that.

It is so easy to compromise confidentiality if we are not careful. Once a young couple came to me to begin preparations for their marriage. That Sunday I saw the girl's parents at Mass and congratulated them on the good news of their daughter's marriage, only to be met with stares of disbelief. It turns out that the young couple was going to surprise them that day with the good news, but Father Big Mouth ruined it. I vowed then that never would I say anything to anyone about things I learned as a priest, whether they be good, bad, or indifferent.

I am afraid that sometimes priests are rather known as gossips. Some say the "pontifical secret" means you can only tell one person at a time, or that everyone in Rome knows it except the pontiff! It is said that the reason we do not have a fire alarm here at the North American College is that news of the fire would get around the house faster than an alarm. If you are a gadabout gossip now, eager for the latest news and always good for the most recent dirt, how can you be worthy of the confidence your people will place in you as a priest?

A third specific area where our people expect integrity from their priests is in always telling the truth. "All you need say is 'yes' when you mean yes, 'no' when you mean no; anything else comes from the evil one," warns Jesus (Matthew 5:37), whom St. Paul describes as "never yes and no, but always yes" (2 Corinthians 1:19). Or, as Cardinal Newman wrote, "Let us aim at meaning what we say, and saying what we mean; let us aim at knowing when we understand a truth, and when we do not."

Our people want to hear the truth, even when they protest. Doctrinally, they look to us to present Church teaching faithfully, even if, regrettably, many of them will disagree with it; morally, they expect to be challenged with the truth, even if it makes them uncomfortable. King Louis XIV had a succession of court preachers, all of whom entertained and pleased him, but finally selected the famous Père Jean Baptiste Massillon, explaining to the preachers he rejected, "Up until now I have been very pleased with the preacher, but now I am displeased with myself." Yes, we strive to present the truth gently, humbly, positively, nonjudgmentally, but we never compromise the truth. How, when, where we say it is negotiable — that we speak it is not.

A fourth type of integrity people look for in their priests is fairness. They expect us to be consistent, clear, evenhanded, and judicious. Especially will they sniff favoritism. And what a temptation that is! To favor the wealthy, attractive, happy, healthy, affirming, nice-looking, who make us feel so wonderful! That is a great temptation for a priest.

President Lyndon Johnson became very fond of the priest at the parish in which the LBJ Ranch was located, where he periodically worshiped on Sunday. When asked why, he related the story that, as he left Mass one Sunday, this priest greeted him, and the president invited him for Sunday dinner that day. The priest replied, "Thanks, Mr. President! What an honor! But, I can't come, because I have a baptism, and I promised that family I would come for dinner afterwards!" The president was astonished to find a man who would pass up the chance to have dinner with the president, a man of such duty, such integrity, to whom a family in his parish was as important as the president of the United States, and that priest became a close confidant.

And a final area of priestly integrity is in charity. We publicly claim to be men configured to Love Incarnate, to the One who flawlessly exemplified mercy, patience, gentleness, generosity, and care. Integrity would demand that we act as we claim. Perhaps this is the area of greatest scandal in the lives of priests — not so much drinking, sexual indiscretion, laziness, or poor preaching, as tragic as those are — but that we do not practice what we profess in the area of plain, simple charity, and can be known as cold, heartless, and uncaring crabs! We all have our stories; we all have perhaps personally felt the sting of a priest's petty meanness.

I remember reading the best-seller *Angela's Ashes*, written by Frank McCourt, and how I could only hang my head in shame as the author depicted the arrogant, callous priests who ignored and failed to help that suffering family growing up in Limerick. Yes, there were dozens of caring priests, but it was the heartless ones who made the impression on young Frank McCourt. Integrity demands that our words and actions reflect the promise we made at diaconate when we said "I am" to the bishop's inquiry, "Are you resolved to shape your life always according to the example of Christ . . . and serve the people of Christ?"

Enough on specific challenges to our integrity; how about helps to sustaining that integrity of life we all crave? Again, thank God, there are many.

May I mention as primary a humble self-knowledge? Funny enough — one of those paradoxes that abound in Christian discipleship — a great help to gaining and maintaining integrity is admitting that we are far from it. Beware of the one who likes to tell you what a man of honesty and integrity he is! Emerson said about a guest at dinner, "The louder he talked of his honor the faster we counted the silverware!"

You see, all of us certainly long to be people of integrity, but we are far from the ideal!

• We want to be honest, yet we are daily tempted to lie, deceive, distort, or avoid the truth.

• We crave to be men of reliability, trustworthiness, principle, and character, and yet find ourselves fickle, wavering, compromising, and letting ourselves and others down . . .

• . . . and a big help to integrity is to admit that and work on it. So, we have integrity not only with others but with ourselves, because we are honest and forthright with ourselves. As St. Thérèse of Lisieux, recently proclaimed a doctor of the Church, wrote, "humble self-knowledge is the beginning of sanctity."

So, you can bet that the one who laughs off concern expressed by those who care for him that he drinks too much and boasts he has no alcohol problem indeed does have such a problem, while he who asks for help is on the road to the integrity of sobriety.

Watch for the one who is defiant when confronted about dangerous sexual inclinations to appear one day as the latest headline about sexual abuse by priests, while the one humbly aware of his weakness becomes a compassionate, holy priest.

Wager that the one constantly griping about the unfairness of his superiors, the unfriendliness of his brother priests, and the misunderstanding of his people is the one very hard to live with, while the guy who apologizes for his moodiness is a great companion in the rectory.

Because, as Edward Benson observed, "How desperately difficult it is to be honest with oneself! It is so much easier to be honest about the foibles of others!"

Now, a second help to obtaining and sustaining integrity is the ability to hear the truth about yourself. For, if it is true that "it's desperately difficult to be honest with yourself," we will need to cherish people of integrity who will tell us the truth about ourselves, even when it stings. I mentioned that people expect their priests to preach the truth; well, a priest of integrity should likewise be willing to hear the truth!

When researching the man whose biography I wrote for my doctoral dissertation, Edwin O'Hara, I discovered that, in his seventeen years as bishop of Kansas City-St. Joseph, he always had one priest among his close pastoral collaborators whom he would always appoint "court critic." This man saw him every Monday morning at nine o'clock, and his duty was to criticize the archbishop, to tell him bad news, to let him know what the priests and people were saying about him. Now, it takes a man of real integrity to set up such a system.

As Samuel Goldwyn said, "I don't want yes-men around me. I want men who will tell me the truth, even if it costs them their job."

So, to cultivate the habit of being able to hear the truth about yourself is a great boost to achieving integrity. If a friend talks to you about a concern he has about you, do you listen, accept it, and work on it? Or do you drop him as a friend? Such would be sad because he was a true friend. If someone brings some flaw or shortcoming to your attention, do you say, "Thanks — that's what I'm here for, to be a better priest, and I need to be aware of whatever is in my personality that needs refinement"? Or do you say, "You don't know me! You have never liked me because I'm conservative — or liberal — and, besides, look at how you let so-and-so get away with worse things!"

Ninety-nine percent of priests who experience trouble in their ministry — in sexuality, loneliness, lack of clarity and confidence in their identity, drinking, whatever — will admit that the problem started long ago, and they denied it or ignored it. Those generous souls who work with troubled priests will tell you their constant refrain is, "Oh, if I had only owned up to this a long time ago!" Well, this is the time to do it!

A man of integrity wants to hear the truth about himself, and appreciates it when people whom he respects tell him.

A third help to integrity follows: namely, the cultivation of vehicles to hear about oneself. Here I mention two:

First is an honest, consistent relationship with a spiritual director. Suffice it to say that the honesty, humility, and character — the integrity you seek — can hardly be found without consistent, candid spiritual direction. A man of integrity knows he needs a spiritual director and freely, joyfully, and dutifully sees him regularly in a relationship characterized by utter honesty.

We have no problem seeing a doctor the minute we cough — and well we should. How much more do we need doctors of the soul to take the temperature of our fervor, listen to the breathing of the Spirit within, and to see where the congestion and infection blocking God's grace is located.

Closely related is frequent confession. St. Francis de Sales said it well when he remarked that a good confession was the soul looking in a mirror. If integrity depends upon humble self-knowledge, it would be hard to think of a spiritual tool more helpful in fostering it than the sacrament of penance. "Hide nothing from your confessor, for a sick man can be cured only by healing his wounds," writes St. Margaret of Cortona. One could make the point, as paradoxical as it seems, that we are most a person of integrity when in the midst of this sacrament of penance.

A fourth help to developing integrity is to accept responsibility for your own life. The man of integrity is aware of his gifts and his flaws, knows clearly his principles and convictions and his obligation to live them with honor and duty, and takes responsibility for it when he does and when he does not. He knows it is soothing but inaccurate to blame others for his own faults.

There was an excellent article in *Human Development* (a journal edited by, among others, our own Father O'Brien), by Father Thomas Morgan, entitled "The Anatomy of Priestly Morale." He concludes with the startling observation that a priest's low or high morale depends first and foremost on himself! "Responsibility for morale means the individual priest is accountable to God, self, and others for the quality of his spiritual, emotional, and physical life. We cannot justify blaming others for the quality of our lives. The individual priest has the capacity to increase or decrease his own morale, which is a reflection of the quality of his total wellness and holiness. No bishop, major superior, spiritual director, counselor, or anyone else outside of us can give or take away a priest's morale. . . . We must take responsibility for our feelings and our behavior. . . . Assuming responsibility for our own morale is the first step toward improving our lives."

The Directory for the Life and Ministry of Priests issued by the Congregation for the Clergy notes, "It is the priest himself who is the person primarily responsible for ongoing formation. In reality this duty of being faithful to the gift of God and to the dynamism of daily conversion falls upon each priest."

Strive to be a man of integrity who can hear the truth about yourself, even bad news. I had two terms on the priests' personnel board at home, and was surprised to learn how some priests could not take responsibility for their actions, and would always blame someone else for faults. "This pastor is lousy — get me out of here!" in one parish; "These people are so unappreciative — get me out of here!" in parish number two; "Boy, the other assistant here is impossible to live with — get me out of here!" in number three; "He won't let me do anything!" in number four; "He expects me to do everything!" in parish number five. And finally, someone — the archbishop, the personnel director, the vicar for priests — has to say, "Brother, the problem is you," whereupon the bearer of the bad news becomes the latest entry in the litany of those who are out to get the poor misunderstood victim.

I mention this ability to accept responsibility for one's own actions and effectiveness as an aid to integrity precisely because a failure to do so severely hinders it. When we are unable to accept responsibility for our own lives with calmness, humility, and trust in Providence, we become catty, petty, and vindictive, all verboten to a man of integrity. We begin to fudge on principle and lose the noble principles and convictions that firm up our honor and character. We get huffy and easily bruised, quick to find fault in others, easily aggrieved, and childishly feeling everyone is picking on us.

In his wonderful work *The Return of the Prodigal Son*, Henri Nouwen meditates on how we are called not only to admit we are the Prodigal Son, but also the pouting brother, and, ultimately, the embracing, welcoming Father:

> Isn't there a subtle pressure in both the Church and society to remain a dependent child? Hasn't the Church in the past stressed obedience in a fashion that made it hard to claim spiritual fatherhood, and hasn't our consumer society encouraged us to indulge in childish self-gratification? Who has truly challenged us to liberate ourselves from immature dependencies and to accept the burden of responsible adults? Aren't we ourselves constantly trying to escape the fearful task of fatherhood?

Michael Medved, the social commentator, recently observed that society is suffering an "epidemic of whining," where everything wrong with me is someone else's fault, and where society breaks down into rights' advocacy groups to see who has been most aggrieved.

My point is that it is tough to be men of calm, magnanimous integrity if we lack the honor of accepting responsibility for our own lives.

And, a final help to integrity of life is the cultivation of a genuine inner serenity and purity of heart. "The Lord alone is my comfort and my refuge. In him I put my trust!" chants the psalmist (144:2).

It is interesting that the word "integrated" comes from "integrity." We strive for the inner serenity and purity of heart that come only from an integrated life, where there is an evident harmony between what we profess and how we live, a concert between our external actions and our internal convictions. Our life is in order, with clear goals and basic principles directing our words and actions. Thus, a "well-integrated person," who knows what he's about and is at peace with his God, himself, and with others, is a man of integrity.

A person who lacks integrity, who lies, deceives, is unreliable, hypocritical, and prompts fear and suspicion instead of trust, evidently lacks an inner serenity and purity of heart. Living a lie eventually takes its toll:

- a man who preaches a principle but then compromises it,

- a man who vows love but is selfish,
- a man who speaks of faith but is filled with doubt and cynicism,
- a man who claims simplicity but spends, consumes, and hoards,
- a man who promises obedience but craves independence and calling his own shots,
- a man who pledges chastity but is leading a double life . . .

. . . such a man cannot be a man of integrity, and living that lie will take its toll on moral, spiritual, emotional, and physical health. . . .

While, on the other hand, a man who has achieved, with God's grace, a life where there is integration, symmetry, and harmony between the internal and external, such a man has a genuine inner serenity and purity of heart that sustains integrity.

When that happens we need not curry favor with superiors, or seek advancement, prestige, and acclaim, because our worth comes not from outside but from within.

When that happens we do not get resentful, petty, or snide when overlooked or misunderstood, for our value comes from inside.

When that happens we need not waffle on principle, be two-faced or duplicitous, because our goal is not to please others but to please God by remaining true to the principles that we hold deep within.

When that happens we are people of integrity.

So, our life is rather simple and uncluttered. Our convictions are clear and our attempts to live them out consistent and sincere. There are certain things we must do and certain things we just can't. We have a clean, clear conscience that serves us well and is regularly examined; we trust people of honor who tell us when we are wavering, and find that others approach us because they trust us. When asked by a biographer to state his driving goal in life, Don Bosco replied, "To remain in the state of grace." What he meant was this integrated life, at peace within, which flows without in a life of integrity.

Three former seminarians whom I have known over the years come to mind as examples here. One left the seminary and was struggling to find a job, and finally was hired at a prestigious real estate office where he began to do very well. After six months he was promoted and prospered even more until he discovered that part of his job was exacting bloated rent payments from elderly black people in a shabby ghetto tenement. He quit. "I couldn't live with myself if I did that," he told me.

Another man left the seminary to land a promising job with a pharmaceutical company, until he discovered it would mean selling abortifacients and contraceptives. He quit. "I couldn't live with myself if I did that," he told me.

Another man decided against priesthood only two months before ordination. "I have a divided heart," he said, "and there are troubling questions I have to settle before I can truthfully go ahead. I know I couldn't live with myself if I went ahead."

God bless those men of integrity. They could not have lived with themselves because they would have been bad company, at odds with what they claim to believe and stand for.

I remember an excellent homily Father Walsh preached once on purity of heart. Taking Jesus as our model, we long for a heart undivided, not torn by interior dissension and a confusion of agenda. Our heart is pure, totally given in love to Jesus and his people. Christ reigns in our heart, not Satan or this world, and the result of that reign is purity of intention and action — integrity.

Remember the famous newsclip of Pope John Paul II's visit to Poland where he is standing next to General Wojciech Jaruzelski, the communist leader of Poland? The Holy Father is calm, completely steady, and perfectly at peace, while the general is reading an address of welcome, the paper shaking in trembling hands, his knees literally knocking, he was so nervous. No wonder: the one had inner serenity because his message was based on truth and he had earned the trust of people, while the other was a nervous wreck because his message was based on a lie and he had caused only fear and distrust.

Oh, for that inner serenity, that purity of heart which flows from a good conscience and fosters integrity!

Bringing it all together, I'd like to mention something that is both a specific area where people look for integrity in their priests, and also a help to integrity, namely prayer.

Prayer is an area of priestly life where our people expect integrity precisely because we profess to be men of prayer. Rarely a homily goes by without our exhorting our people to pray, so integrity demands that we do it. Not a day goes by without one of our people asking us for prayers for a certain intention and we glibly say, "We'll keep you in our prayers," and integrity demands we do it.

And, of course, prayer is a help to achieving and maintaining integrity. In prayer we rehearse our deepest beliefs, principles, and convictions, and we seek divine assistance to live without betraying them.

In prayer as well we foster the honesty that is a synonym for integrity, for in prayer as nowhere else can we be completely honest with ourselves and with God. With the psalmist we pray:

> O Lord, you search me and you know me. . . .
> You discern my purpose from afar.
> All my ways lie open to you.
> Before even a word is on my lips,
> You know it, O Lord.
> Oh, where can I go from your spirit?
> Where can I flee from your face?
> For it was you who created my being,
> Knit me together in my mother's womb.
> Already you knew my soul,
> I held no secret from you.
> Your eyes see all my actions. . . .
> — Psalm 139

No secrets from God! No hidden agenda! No duplicity! No lying! No compromise! No divided heart! How absurd to try to deceive him. He knows us better than we know ourselves, every wart and ounce of fat, every thought and deed, every sin and embarrassment — and he still loves us and accepts us passionately! If that recognition in prayer does not engender integrity, what can?

Mother Teresa recommends a style of prayer that has us imagine Jesus staring right at us, through us. "I worry," she wrote shortly before she died, "that some of you still have not really met Jesus — one to one — you and Jesus alone. Have you seen with the eyes of your soul how he looks at you?"

That's a beautiful style of prayer, imagining Jesus staring at us. Do you recall how he "looked at" the rich young man? Remember how, after Peter had denied him, the evangelist tells us that Jesus walked by and "looked at him," and Peter went out and wept bitterly. When we allow Jesus to look at us, the only sentiment is utter honesty, upon which integrity is built.

"All he really wants is to tell you he loves you, even when you don't feel worthy. Not only does he love you, but he longs for you!" as Mother Teresa concluded about our Lord. Prayer like that fosters the honesty that results in integrity.

A number of years ago, I had the privilege of giving instructions in the faith to a fine young man, happily married with three children to a woman in the parish. He was so impressed with the parish, the priests, the Church, his wife, the teachings of the Church, he became a great Catholic. About five years later, his wife left him . . . for a priest. He came to see me. "You know what hurts most?" he asked me.

"Sure, losing Kathy," I replied.

"No," he answered. "How stupid I was to think all that stuff in the Church was really true!" Now, what do you say to that?

Some of you have already heard — the rest of you will, please God, one day — these words addressed to you by the bishop:

> My son, you are now to be advanced to the order of presbyterate. . . . Meditate on the law of God. Believe what you read, teach what you believe, and put into practice what you teach. . . . Let the example of your life attract followers of Christ, so that by word and action you may build up the house that is God's Church. . . . Know what you are doing and imitate the mysteries you celebrate. . . . Do your part in the work of Christ the Priest with genuine love and joy, and lead the people effectively through Christ to the Father.

In other words, be a man of integrity.

9

Prudence

(Scripture selection — Proverbs 9:1-18)

Scripture shies away from telling us what prudence is but prefers ever so beautifully to describe for us the prudent man, how he acts, what he does, what he avoids. Think even of the different words we can use for prudence, its sister virtues such as wisdom and counsel, or allied traits such as discretion, circumspection, perspicacity, insight, sageness, and sound judgment. See how evasive it is, how it defies tidy categorization, this prudence?

Yet none of us doubt its pivotal role in discipleship. I wonder if there is any virtue, save faith and justice, more extolled in the Old Testament than wisdom and prudence, to such an extent that the judicious, discreet, insightful man becomes the hero, the prototype of the perfect man of God. In the Christian dispensation, prudence is so essential that it has classically been listed as the first of the so-called cardinal virtues. So critical is it that Basil the Great remarked, "Prudence must precede every action that we undertake; for, if prudence be wanting, there is nothing, however good it may seem, which is not turned into evil." Strong words!

Perhaps St. Thomas Aquinas can help us define prudence. The Angelic Doctor describes it as involving correct judgment, acquired by the infusion of grace, and by one's own trial and error in making choices through life. It is the intellectual virtue that allows us to recognize the good and evil possibilities in any situation and to act correctly, in accord with God's will, on the basis of this foresight.

We really don't use the word "prudent" too much anymore, do we? I sometimes wonder if the term "common sense" has taken over some of its meanings. Monsignor John Tracy Ellis used to begin each academic year by telling us at The Catholic University of America, "If you lack wisdom, God can give it to you; if you lack knowledge, I can give it to you; but if you lack common sense — nobody can help you!"

Now, prudence, or wisdom, is certainly a much-needed virtue for any believer, but it is essential for the priest. Our people look to their priests to be wise, holy, prudent men. Often, to our consternation, they will seek our assistance in settling disputes or in making tough choices in life. I remember in my first assignment being startled when a young man asked me to help him choose between two women with whom he was in love, and here I was, celibate; or when a well-known physician twice my age sought my guidance in a tough moral question. I was twenty-six, newly ordained, with little practical experience in either of the areas, yet, because I was a priest, my parishioners presumed I had good judgment, clear thinking, wisdom. Likewise do they look to us to act with prudence, not to be silly, indiscreet, irresponsible fools. They expect us to act with probity, sobriety, and care. Prudence in our choices, prudence in our behavior.

But you already know this: there is not one of you who cannot point to the wise counsel received from a priest whose prudence you respected in helping you discern at some point in your life. As St. Augustine writes, "The greatest good is wisdom." Thus we owe it to the Church to cultivate this most crucial virtue.

As I survey the assessments that seminarians receive from summer pastoral assignments, or the observations often made in the annual faculty evaluations, or, most profitably, as I hear comments from pastors and bishops of our men recently ordained, I rarely hear a criticism about their doctrinal orthodoxy, their devotion to prayer, their homiletic ability, their obedience, or their chastity — thank God for all of that! — but I do hear some observations about a lack of prudence, and, this hardly shocks me, since, as St. Thomas reminds us, prudence does come with experience and age.

The rub is, of course, that prudence most often involves not the what we do, or even the why, but the how, the when, and the where! Let me give some actual examples where prudence was lacking!

• Thus, for instance, to correct the lector at Mass who, in attempting to give instructions for reception of Holy Communion to the congregation, keeps using the word "bread" for the body of Christ, and "wine" for the precious blood, is a good thing; to do so from the altar, in an angry voice, railing against lack of belief in the Real Presence right before holding up the Host and saying "This is the Lamb of God" — as a pastor told me his assistant did — is imprudent. That was not the how, when, and where to do it. His intention was good, and his message was sound, but his good judgment stunk! So, to disagree with the DRE when she tells the RCIA catechumens that the reservation of priestly ordination to men is unjust, obsolete, and will soon change, and then to present the Church's clear teaching, is good; to call the DRE a heretic and warn the catechumens that anything she says is suspect, is imprudent.

• Thus, to try to find shelter in the parish for a teenage boy who has been thrown out of the house by an abusive, drunken father, is good; to invite him to spend the night on the couch in your room is imprudent.

• So, to participate in sports is a very good thing; to engage in contact sports when you know your knee is still healing from surgery is imprudent;

• Thus, to welcome visitors to the college graciously is a beautiful virtue; to bring women guests in our living quarters is imprudent.

• To make those divorced and remarried outside the Church feel welcome in the parish is laudable; to invite them to be Eucharistic ministers is imprudent.

You get my point: motives might be excellent, what needs to be done clear — it's the how, when, and where that can wreck us — unless we have prudence. And that prudence, as Coleridge remarked about common sense, is, I'm afraid, most uncommon!

Let me now go through some practical observations about prudence, especially as they apply to a priest.

For one, prudence very often has to do with decisions, but a particular kind of decision. The virtue to choose the good when faced with the choice between the moral and immoral is not prudence — that's obedience! No, prudence is the ability to choose well between two goods, or, at least two possibilities both morally neutral.

When a man comes to tell me he is leaving priestly formation, I ask him to assure me that his choice has been characterized by the three "p's": (1) Has it been prayerful, seeking enlightenment from the Lord? (2) Has it been patient, meaning slow, careful, thoughtful, not sudden or impetuous? (3) Has it been prudent, that is, sober, calm, reflective, and considerate of the input of those wiser than him — spiritual director, advisers, bishops, vocation directors, close friends, family, yes, even rectors? If such a decision has indeed been prayerful, patient, and prudent, I can add a fourth "p," for I can *praise* God that this seminary has done its job in helping a man reach such a mature decision. The decision to leave the seminary is one between two goods — priesthood or another mode of discipleship such as marriage — and thus requires prudence.

Here let me speak of the need for prudence in the more common decisions we face.

A *sine qua non* of prudence is that we never, ever, make a decision in anger, in lust, in discouragement, or in haste.

We never, ever, act in anger. "How much more grievous are the consequences of anger than the causes of it," observes Marcus Aurelius. Yes, it takes heroic control, but the prudent man will never make a decision while angry; he will "sleep on it," or put it aside, or postpone it until he can weigh things calmly and coolly. A wise man is not afraid to admit, "I am too angry right now to make a decision." As Dag Hammarskjöld remarked, "How fewer widows and orphans the world would know if leaders learned to wait till their tempers had subsided before making a decision for war."

We never, ever, make a choice in lust! It's no mistake that our brains are above the belt, but as the old saying goes, our reason declines as the parts below the belt incline. How many priests have rashly left their vocation because they acted in lust! The prudent man will again step back, and give himself space and distance, before allowing himself to be ruled by lust. A priest I know told me he was thinking of leaving because he had fallen in love with a woman. I encouraged him to prudence, to do all possible to protect his vocation. He told me not to worry, that he and his lover were going to go away for two weeks by themselves to decide just what he should do. Fat chance his vocation had! As Shakespeare wrote, "The strongest oaths are but straw to the fire in the blood."

We never, ever, act while discouraged. Having suffered a failure, having fallen to sin, or having made a stupid move — all these things discourage us. That's not the time to make a decision. We don't ask for a transfer just because the pastor yelled at us and we're down in the dumps; we don't abandon the priesthood because we've become lonely or depressed. The prudent man never compounds one bad mistake by making another.

We never, ever, act in haste. While a priest must be able to make decisions confidently, he will never do so rashly. He will weigh options, consult, pray, reflect, take a reasonable amount of time, and then act.

A second help in prudence is the maintenance of a balanced approach to life. Our day is firmly grounded in the Lord through our prayer and a confidence in our priestly identity and mission. Come what may, no matter what happens, there are certain things a prudent man will never miss on a given day. This is protected by a rhythm of life, a daily regimen. Yes, the priest, especially the parish priest, must be very flexible, for he never knows what a given day may bring, but the wise priest always has a basic outline to his day. He is not a "gadabout" but a man of purpose and direction, calmly and deliberately approaching his day.

In his *Journal of a Soul*, Pope John XXIII records this entry for August 14, 1961:

> Considering the purpose of my life I must:
>
> • Desire only to be virtuous and holy, and so be pleasing to God.
>
> • Direct all things to the service and glory of the Church.
>
> • Recognize that I have been sent here by God, and therefore remain perfectly serene about all that happens.
>
> • Entrust myself at all times to Divine Providence.
>
> • Always arrange my day in an intelligent and orderly manner.

Now, that is a wise man!

Often have I quoted from Cardinal Newman who, when asked the road to perfection, responded: "He is perfect who does the work of the day perfectly . . . first, do not lie in bed beyond the due time of rising; give your first thoughts to God; make a good visit to the Blessed Sacrament; say the Angelus devoutly; eat and drink to God's glory; say the rosary well; be recollected; keep out bad thoughts;

make your evening meditation; examine yourself daily; go to bed in good time . . . and you are already perfect."

That simple, prudent daily plan from the man many consider the most towering Christian intellect since Aquinas!

Each of us learns what he needs for a purposeful, productive life. I know, in my own life, that no matter how hectic things get, I must every day ensure prayer — Mass, divine office, some period of meditation — at least six hours of sleep, some exercise, and three meals, or I get fatigued, irritable, and ineffective.

Monsignor Cornelius Flavin, my first pastor as a priest, was very close to his sister. I got a call one afternoon that she had died. It was about 3:30 p.m., and I knew he would any moment be coming in from his hospital visits, because he went every afternoon. Sure enough, I heard the garage door open, and went to give the sad news. He was visibly shaken; I extended condolences and offered what help I could; he went to his room, had, I suppose, a good cry, called his two brothers and the funeral home. The next thing I know is that he's coming out of his room, and going over to Church for his daily holy hour, which he made every day from 4:00 to 5:00 p.m. At a time of crisis and personal loss, his regimen of prayer, his daily duty, has not been neglected.

The prudent man has such a rhythm, a planned regimen of the day that makes sure the basics are covered. This is not running from responsibilities but wisely assuring we meet them more effectively.

This balanced approach to life avoids excess. Exercise is important, but can be overdone; sleep is essential, but can be disproportionate; food and drink necessary, but can be abused; recreation and time off needed, but can be exaggerated. Even, believe it or not, can prayer be misused.

A bishop told me of a recent alumnus from here who told him, "You know, Bishop, I'm a contemplative."

"I suppose by that you mean," responded the bishop, "that you need some time of contemplation every day to give energy and meaning to your ministry?"

"No," the young priest replied, "I mean that I'm a contemplative!"

"Well," answered the bishop, "I ordained you to be a zealous, active parish priest, not a contemplative!" The bishop was right! The young priest was imprudent in his approach to his prayer.

Especially is this balanced, proportionate, even approach to life essential in times of crisis, and we will have many. When tragedy comes, either to ourselves personally or to our people; when temptations and discouragement arrive; when demands pile up and seem to overwhelm us — then more than ever does prudence come through to insist on a calm, reflective, dependable approach to life, grounded in the essentials, avoiding extremes.

A third way prudence helps us is in keeping a focus about us, keeping our priorities straight. "Why did God make you? To know him, love him, and serve him in this world, and to be happy with him in the next," as many of us learned in our catechism. Or, in the hauntingly simple words of St. Ignatius of Loyola's "First Principle and Foundation":

> Man is created to praise, reverence, and serve God our Lord, and by this means to save his soul.
>
> The other things on the face of the earth are created for man to help him in attaining the end for which he is created.
>
> Hence, man is to make use of them in as far as they help him in the attainment of his end, and he must rid himself of them in as far as they prove a hindrance to him.
>
> Therefore, we must make ourselves indifferent to all created things, as far as we are allowed free choice and are not under any prohibition. Consequently, as far as we are concerned, we should not prefer health to sickness, riches to poverty, honor to dishonor, a long life to a short life. The same holds for all other things.
>
> Our one desire and choice should be what is more conducive to the end for which we are created.
>
> — Louis Puhl, S.J., *The Spiritual Exercises*

Prudence helps us keep our goals clear and in focus, thus keeping our lives well-ordered and purposeful. The wise man will often remark, "That's really none of my business," as he realizes he has his own duties and need not get excited over other people's.

So must parish priests concentrate on their assignment. When in a parish, that becomes your priority. You will be avalanched with invitations to say Mass elsewhere, to give days of recollection and retreats outside, to become chaplain of this group and that group — but prudence keeps us focused! Yes, I can accept other duties, but only if they do not interfere with my first responsibility, this assignment.

And, of course, prudence protects our fundamental goal, eternal life through fidelity to our priestly vocation, and is this sure important. Because our life with Christ in grace is fragile, our priestly vocations frail, and wise is the man who protects these pearls of great price at all costs!

A very respected vocation director was here visiting the North American College once and expressed concern in this very area. Lamenting the departure of two of his young priests, he commented, "How could they think their priesthood could survive when they went out six nights a week and did not roll in until after midnight? How could they think their celibacy would survive when they kept exclusive company with attractive women? I worry," he concluded, "that some of our young priests are overly confident, almost cocky, and do not realize the delicacy of their own vocation. Why are they not more vigilant?" Vigilance — yet another synonym for prudence.

So the wise man knows his limitations. We used to call them "occasions of sin," defined as any person, place, or thing that makes sin easier. Certain people lead us to gossip, griping, cynicism — we best avoid them; when we go to a certain place where we tend to drink too much — we avoid it; when we feel ourselves attracted sexually to another person — we avoid her — or him. Because the prudent priest knows that his uncompromised priority is eternal life through fidelity to his vocation, and that pearl of great price must be protected at all costs!

I read an excellent article by Father Dominic Maruca, S.J., on just this point. "It is considered a mark of wisdom," Father Dominic says, "not to overestimate one's own strength or underestimate the vehemence of passion." He then goes on to elaborate four danger signs that, from his experience, usually result in a priest leaving the active ministry. They are: an absorption in secular activities instead of the classically priestly ones of preaching, teaching, and celebrating the sacraments, with a consequent desire to live alone and shun external signs of the clerical state such as dress and title; plenty of money; a declining interest in prayer and the sacraments, especially Mass and confession; or an exclusive affective relationship. What this sage spiritual director exhorts is that we be prudent in protecting our frail priestly vocation, because we cannot do it alone.

St. Francis de Sales expressed it well: "Be ye prudent as the serpent who, in danger, exposes his whole body to preserve his head. In the same way, we must risk everything, if necessary, to preserve the love and presence of our Lord whole and entire within ourselves, for he is our head and we are his body."

I am moved every year when Monsignor Charles Elmer speaks to the new priests at the Casa. "I am not worried about your academic life," he tells them, "for rare is the man who leaves here without fulfilling his scholastic duties. What I do worry about is your priestly vocation, your spiritual life. I know from experience," Monsignor Elmer continues, "that when the breviary goes unopened, when daily Mass is left uncelebrated, when one is in restaurants and shops more than in the chapel, when one ignores Jesus and his Mother, when months go by without confession, one's priesthood is in big trouble."

Prudence helps us keep our focus on what is really essential.

A fourth asset of prudence: we are realistic in what we have left behind. We know what we are getting into as a priest. As the apostles left their nets, their boats, their father, their livelihood, to follow the call, so do we realize what we have left behind.

A pastor told me that his newly ordained associate approached him a couple of weeks before Christmas and asked, "Well, what do I have off, Christmas Eve or Christmas morning?"

The pastor, perplexed, inquired, "What do you mean?"

"Well," continued the associate, "I certainly have the right to be with my family on Christmas, so I would expect to be free either Christmas Eve or Day."

Can you imagine — that a parish priest would not have realized that, as a matter of fact, the parish was his family, that leaving behind such a legitimate joy of holidays with one's family was a realistic expectation of diocesan priesthood, and that he should be relishing his first Christmas of total immersion in his parish?

It is sometimes as if we think Jesus was only kidding when he told us the cost of discipleship, things such as loneliness, frustration, opposition, discouragement, sacrifice, and suffering. The wise man knows what he is getting into, and, just as importantly, what he is leaving behind, namely genital sexuality, a career, fame, popularity, the warmth and support of a wife and a family, and a lot of money.

Prudence helps us realize what we have left behind.

A final area of prudence I wish to mention is best described by the word "discretion," yet another synonym for the virtue.

Discretion is very helpful in speech. Earlier when I spoke about integrity I dwelt on the necessity of a priest keeping confidence. Rarely do we get into trouble for saying nothing. As Ben Franklin noted, "Far better to keep your mouth shut and be thought the fool than to open it and prove it." Not to feel we have to comment on everything, with ceaseless chatter and idle talk — people respect a priest who listens well, who reserves comment until appropriate, and whose words are tactful, appropriate, and spare. Likewise are we discreet about vulgarity and cursing in our language.

Discretion is valuable in picking our battles. You already know from your own parish experiences that when you are assigned to a parish, you will find a lot that bothers you, much you want to change. Prudence, discretion, directs you to be patient and respectful, to bide your time and earn trust, before waging war. So the deacon self-communicates at Mass! I know he shouldn't; the time will come when I can help him understand that. But is it worth an immediate battle? The pastor does not like Eucharistic exposition. Should I yell, demand, threaten, or harangue? Or should I earn his trust, patiently and gradually coax, and then state my case? A bullish, arrogant, haughty, know-it-all approach usually hurts the cause, for a man of discretion prudently picks his battles. There are some things you must go to the mat over; there are other things that you can put up with while not compromising your integrity. Wise is the priest who knows the difference.

Discretion is helpful in humor. A sense of humor is a real blessing in a priest, but it must always be guided by discreet prudence. Be careful of any humor about sex or ethnic identity, for our people can be easily shocked or hurt.

Especially avoid what I hear referred to as "campy" humor, which someone explained to me as implicit homosexual innuendo, such as referring to men by female names, or speaking to one another as women do. That is insulting to women and to our own chastity. Good Lord, in some places our reputation is so bad that parents lock their sons in their rooms when the priest visits, and then you hear some priests or seminarians calling each other "Mary." Really funny!

Discretion is valuable in developing the art of criticizing. It is a virtue, a sign of loyalty even, to point out to our superiors imperfections and ways things can be improved. It is laudable to express worries, fears, and criticisms of the Church which we love so much that we long to see her perfect. Again, it is the when, where, and how we do it that demands prudence and discretion.

So, for a consecrated woman religious to criticize a cardinal of the Church and call for disobedience to him on national TV, or for a priest to castigate the Holy Father week after week in terms that can only be defined as nasty in a syndicated newspaper column, or for a priest to call a theologian, even one dissenting from the magisterium, a "cancerous tumor on the Mystical Body" on TV, is imprudent, to say the least!

For a priest to question Church teaching from the pulpit or in a classroom, a discussion group, or RCIA session, is hardly discreet.

Let me point out four characteristics of prudent criticism: it is never *ad hominem*, as the good name, character, and motives of the other person are never impugned; it always follows proper channels; its tone is always charitable and respectful; and, once the point is made, the case is dropped, as one does not become a boorish zealot for a single cause.

And, finally, discretion prompts us to avoid, not only evil, but even the appearance of evil. We owe it to our priesthood, the Church, and our people — who have suffered so much from priestly scandal — not to risk giving mixed signals. I'm sorry, but there are just certain things we cannot do, as much as we know they are innocent. It may be as pure as snow to travel with a handsome young man, with the thought of any impropriety a million miles from our mind, but I'm afraid we can't do it. You may mean nothing partisan at all by showing up at a political fund-raiser, but people are going to interpret it in the wrong way. You may have the most innocent of motives in dressing in coat and tie and taking a beautiful young woman in the parish to dinner and theater, but scandal will be given. Discretion helps us avoid, not just evil, but even the appearance of doing evil.

Prudence can itself be abused. We have all seen priests stored frozen away from any type of creativity, zeal, dare, risk, or love because they are afraid of being called "imprudent." "But we've never done that before" seems to be the mantra of many listless priests who are scared of trying anything fresh. Listen to John McKenzie: "Prudence has long been, not the virtue by which one discerns the Christian thing to do, but the virtue by which one finds sound reason for evading the Christian thing to do! I have never read of any martyr who, if he or she had the course in prudence I had in the seminary, could not have evaded martyrdom with a clean conscience!"

• From a purely natural point of view, it could be said that our Lord himself acted imprudently in the company he kept and some of the doctrines he taught.

• From a solely worldly perspective, Mother Teresa was terribly indiscreet to speak so strongly against abortion in front of the president and first lady.

• From an exclusively rational viewpoint, Cardinal O'Connor was quite unwise to question the value of capital punishment at the funeral of a murdered policeman.

But, ours is not a purely natural, solely worldly, or exclusively rational perspective, is it? "Human, carnal, or worldly prudence only has worldly prosperity in view," writes St. Vincent de Paul. "Christian prudence takes Eternal Incarnate Wisdom for its guide. . . . It is regulated by the maxims of our faith."

Prudence never holds us back from pastoral charity — it only protects it and refines it. Listen to Padre Pio:

> You must always have both prudence and love. Prudence has the eyes, love has the legs! Love which has the legs wants to run to God and others, but its impulse to rush is blind and at times can stumble! So it must be guided by prudence, which

has the eyes. When prudence sees that love could become un-bridled, it loans its eyes to love. In this way love restrains itself and, guided by prudence, acts as it should and not as it would like.

So, to be prudent does not mean a lack of creativity, dare, risk, and gamble. To be prudent does mean knowing how, when, and where to be so! For, as St. Paul writes, "The wisdom of this world is foolishness with God."

Are you wondering if, indeed, you will ever have the wisdom you so admire in others, the prudence the Church expects of you? Good! Then you're on your way to get it. The fool, of course, thinks himself wise, while, as the *Imitation of Christ* teaches, "To have a low opinion of our own merits and to think highly of others is itself evidence of wisdom."

While age, learning, experience, and practice can help us become wise, it is ultimately a gift from the Lord. Even Walt Whitman admitted such in his "Song of the Open Road":

> Wisdom is not finally tested in the schools,
> Wisdom cannot be passed from one having it to another
>   not,
> Wisdom is of the soul, is not susceptible of proof.

So we daily ask for it, and never fully gain it; and the one who realizes that wisdom comes not from us but from the Lord is the most prudent man of all. As the Little Flower concluded, "I know Christ dwells within me, guiding me whenever I do or say anything. A light, of which I caught no glimmer before, comes to me at the very moment when it is needed."

10

Penance

(Scripture selection — Joel 2:12-13)

The name of Gene Hamilton may be new to you if you are not from the archdiocese of New York or have not read *A Priest Forever* by Father Benedict Groeschel (published by Our Sunday Visitor in 1998). Gene was a seminarian for that archdiocese at St. Joseph's Seminary, Dunwoodie. From all accounts he was a fine student, a friendly, sincere young man, eager to be a priest. He was diagnosed with cancer, and the final years of his life were a real cross for him — pain, decline, hopes way up after surgery and treatment only to have them dashed with another outbreak. In his brave struggle a saint emerged, and I use that word purposefully.

In his pain, agony, and dwindling strength, a man of deep faith, indomitable hope, and genuine love arose; a seminarian of prayer, who never complained, thought more of the needs and difficulties of others than his own. A man driven by one desire: to be united with Jesus in his passion and death, hopefully, yearning to do so as a priest. There was a lot of longing for a miracle by his family, brother seminarians, friends and admirers; many, including doctors and other medical personnel, told the young man, "You're going to beat this, Gene." Dozens who just knew he was too good, too innocent, too pure and holy to die so young and painfully, prayed for his recovery.

In January of 1997, Gene Hamilton was too ill to come on the pilgrimage here to Rome with the men from Dunwoodie. Bishop Edwin O'Brien, realistic and thoughtful man that he is, with the late Cardinal John O'Connor, approached the prefect of the Congregation for Catholic Education, the dicastery of the Holy See under which seminaries come, for permission to ordain Gene Hamilton should he worsen, and received the proper dispensation. Upon his return to New York, Bishop O'Brien visited him in the hospital, and, having been briefed on his condition, with Cardinal O'Connor's approval, ordained him a deacon and a priest on his hospital bed. Two hours later, Father Gene Hamilton died, at twenty-four years of age.

His long struggle and his dying have moved many people. Dozens have told stories of his patience in suffering, his closeness to the cross of Christ, his enduring conviction that all that really mattered was "Christ, and him crucified." Apparently, during his stays in the hospital, he would pray a lot. One of his favorite devotions was the Stations of the Cross. At the end, without the strength to reach the chapel, he would shuffle down the corridor of the hospital, dragging his IV and oxygen, and stop at fourteen different hospital rooms, designating each of them one of the stations, recognizing in each cancer patient the suffering, bleeding Savior on the *via crucis*. To Gene Hamilton, his life had meaning, purpose — his suffering was salvific — if united with the passion and death of Jesus. And the sentiment of the Church of New York is that this priest of two hours, so configured to Christ on the cross in life, is now indeed a sharer in his resurrection.

To be in union with Jesus in his dying so we can join him in his rising. . . . Jesus and his Church expect every priest to be like Father Gene Hamilton, configured to Jesus in his passion and death. The virtue of penance is essential in the life of every genuine disciple, one particularly necessary in the life of a priest.

The virtue of penance . . . call it self-denial, mortification, self-abnegation . . . it means curbing, taming, controlling, dying to the cravings, comforts, lusts, longings, and appetites of the flesh, of this world, to live more freely and intimately with Jesus. It is not a popular virtue today, this one of penance. But, then, it never has been. As Thomas à Kempis wrote in his *Imitation of Christ* centuries ago:

> Jesus has always had many who love his heavenly kingdom, but few who bear his cross. He has many who desire consolation, but few who care for trial. He finds many to share his table, but few to take part in his fasting. All desire to be happy with him, few wish to suffer anything for him. Many follow him to the breaking of the bread, but few to drinking the chalice of his passion. Many revere his miracles, few the cross.

Penance has never been popular, but especially not today. The historian in me wants to figure out why this age thinks itself exempt from the call to self-denial and mortification. Is it the loss of the sense of sin, which would, of course, render self-abnegation superfluous, since one of the reasons we practice penance is in reparation for our sins? Is it the New Age thinking that sees every human desire and urge as basically good and deserving to be satisfied? Is it due to the bogeymen of secularism and materialism? Is it just raw hedonism? It could be a loss of the sense of the supernatural, since people today are frantically practicing self-denial through fasting and painful exercise for the earthly benefit of good health. I don't know the reason why this age belittles the spiritual value of penance, and, I don't really care, since none of them amount to a hill of polenta, because haunting us always are the words of the only person who really makes a difference:

"Unless you do penance you shall perish!"

"Unless you take up your cross and follow me you cannot be my disciple!"

As the Holy Father preached a few years ago on Ash Wednesday at Santa Sabina: "When we forget the need for penance, self-denial, and sacrifice, we forget the fact of our sinfulness. When we forget we are sinners, we forget our need for Christ. And when we forget we need Christ, we have lost everything!"

Or, as he says to those of us involved in preparation for the priesthood in *Pastores Dabo Vobis*: "Jesus Christ, who brought his pastoral charity to perfection on the cross with a complete emptying of self is the model and the source of the virtues . . . which the priest is called to live out . . . in pastoral charity. In accordance with St. Paul's words . . . the priest should have 'the mind of Christ Jesus,' emptying himself of his own self so as to discover, in a charity which is obedient, chaste, and poor, the royal road of union with God and unity with his people" (No. 30).

It seems to me that penance can come in three ways:

• One, as we voluntarily take upon ourselves practices of mortification.

• Two, as we accept the rejection that necessarily comes from the world when we are loyal to the Gospel.

131

• Three, when we gracefully embrace the adversities and sorrows that just plain come with life.

I want to elaborate on each of these three avenues of penance, especially in the life of a priest.

We conform ourselves to the passion and death of Jesus by freely taking upon ourselves acts of self-denial. This is the mode of penance most associated with Lent, as we voluntarily give up certain food, drink, smoking, entertainment, or legitimate pleasure, or take upon ourselves a practice we find difficult, such as rising earlier or walking when we could ride.

It is especially this first kind of penance that has today declined in popularity. Those of you older can remember when this kind of penance was legislated by Church discipline, resulting, for instance, in mandatory Friday abstinence all year and required fasting every day of Lent. The canonical requirement is gone, a move which was meant to purify our motives but not eliminate voluntary penance. Unfortunately, the baby went out with the bath water.

Be that as it may, it is safe to say that voluntary acts of self-denial are a singularly effective way of growth in holiness. It would be difficult to find any saint who did not have specific practices of mortification as part of his or her spiritual regimen. I remember being very moved when I read in a biography of Paul VI that he wore a hair shirt as an act of penance. (Those are tough to find at Gammarelli's, by the way.) Anyway, since the priest by definition is a man serious about holiness, we can conclude that acts of voluntary self-denial must be part of every priest's life.

Why are acts of self-denial effective in our spiritual growth? The ascetical theologians give us some answers. For one, acts of mortification allow us to feel closer to the passion of Christ. The temporary, passing discomfort caused by denying ourselves a legitimate comfort or pleasure reminds us of the love of Jesus exemplified most dramatically in the supreme act of voluntary self-immolation, the cross. Two, giving something up usually creates a vacuum in our lives, an emptiness which then, so the ancient wisdom goes, can be filled by the Lord. Three, denying ourselves a legitimate pleasure trains us to deny the illegitimate ones. If I can curb my appetite for ice cream, for instance, well, then, maybe I can curb my tongue when I am tempted to say something unkind. In other words, we train ourselves to say no to acceptable comfort and pleasure so we can then, with the grace of God, say no to the temptations to sin that come along.

It is a rather practical, effective, simple wisdom here, one backed up by Scripture, Tradition, and the example of Jesus, who himself fasted. May I mention three special areas where voluntary acts of self-denial are particularly appropriate for priests?

1. The sacrifice of time. It would be difficult to find a commodity more precious to us than time, and a penance the good priest must always embrace is to sacrifice time.

Time with the Lord in prayer! Henri Nouwen once defined prayer as "wasting time with the Lord." How sacrificial for us, pragmatic that we are, to mortify ourselves by giving the Lord the time he deserves in prayer. I remember the first time I made an eight-day Ignatian retreat. The first day I had a real problem persevering through my four assigned hours of meditation. I reported that fact to my director the next day, reasoning that I needed to be practical and thus should trim the hour to forty-five minutes. Whereupon he prescribed four one-hour-and-fifteen-minute periods of prayer for that day, informing me that St. Ignatius insisted that we add to the hour the time we are tempted to cut. Needless to say, I did not complain again!

Fidelity to that set time of daily prayer, in our divine office and meditation, even when nothing seems to be happening, can be a real sacrifice of time, but one most appropriate for the priest. We all occasionally find ourselves wondering if the batteries in our watch have gone out as we periodically struggle through our set time for prayer. That is an act of penance most fitting for us, sacrificing time, "wasting time with the Lord" in prayer.

We also sacrifice time for God's people. The demands made on our time! How the priest longs for an evening alone, an afternoon without the phone or doorbell interrupting him, a day without appointments. Again, we are asked to sacrifice our time, freely to give up something we find precious for the service of God's people. This is especially true of a parish priest whose people expect his presence. Woody Allen said "half of life is just showing up," and that's very true of the parish priest. To be there, after Mass, at the meetings, in the classroom, in the home, at the hospital, funeral parlor, nursing home, playground, basketball game, reception, party . . . you name it. "Father, can you come? Father, will you be there? Father, we'll be looking for you!" Priestly presence! It calls for a real sacrifice of time, which can be a penance.

2. A second style of voluntary penance that is most called for in priestly ministry is simplicity of life. Monsignor John Tracy Ellis once said in a conference to priests, "Luxurious living and display of affluence in priests have probably been the source of greater scandal to the faithful than would be true of his succumbing to the weakness of the flesh or excessive drink." I'm afraid it's true. You all have been turned off by priests who drive the flashiest cars, eat at the most exclusive restaurants, join the most prestigious clubs, go on the most exotic vacations, wear the most expensive clothes. Our people do not expect us to be poor, but they do look for us to be simple. I propose to you that a genuine simplicity of life entails voluntary self-denial, because it is very natural for a priest to become sated, comfortable, cozy, and just plain spoiled. Thus, to learn to deny ourselves some comforts, possessions, and perks to protect our evangelical simplicity is a lesson essential for the priest.

3. A third area of freely undertaken penance most appropriate for a priest comes in our ongoing struggle with our dark, unredeemed side. As Fulton Sheen said, "A saint is only a recovering sinner." The wise priest is acutely aware of his weaknesses, his inclination to sin, his dark side. All of us, redeemed though we are, have evil spirits lurking within, and the first step in victory over them is identifying them, owning up to them. Our life then becomes a constant struggle to keep them in check, to make sure that only Jesus, and no one or nothing else, has dominion over us. The sacrifice comes because that is hard work! We can never let up in our vigilance and self-control! The minute we think we're strong and have mastered our sinful nature, we're setting ourselves up for a fall.

What will lurk deep within you for the rest of your life? Laziness, a temper, lust, a desire for recognition and prestige, a longing to control, anger, a sharp tongue, drink, gluttony? We all have one, or two, or three of these unsettling, dangerous spirits. To control them, moderate them, keep them in check, is a lifelong struggle that demands sacrifice.

I remember once in college seminary when Cardinal John

Carberry, the archbishop of St. Louis, came to talk with us about the priesthood. Now, Cardinal Carberry is one of the most pious, saintly gentlemen you would ever want to meet. After his talk, he invited questions, and one of the guys said, "Yeah, Your Eminence, when does the priest stop having bad thoughts and temptations against purity?" Well, there was a gasp from all of us! This was just not the kind of questions one should address to the cardinalitial presence! But, without missing a beat the cardinal responded, "Oh, about five minutes after you're pronounced dead." This pious man knew well the struggle with sin never lets up! And it cannot be won without self-denial.

Now, before I conclude this consideration of voluntary penance, let me mention a few caveats:

1. While some freely embraced mortification is essential for all of us, it is always wise to discuss it with a spiritual director. We can at times get excessive in our penance. If our voluntary acts of mortification harm our health, sap our energy, or make us crabs, they are counterproductive.

2. Be careful of pride! Sometimes voluntary penance can be counterproductive when we start congratulating ourselves for being so heroic for God. If our freely embraced acts of mortification attract attention to ourselves, they are counterproductive. As Padre Pio said, "Self-denial is not our gift to God, but allowing God to do more for us!"

3. In our Catholic tradition, voluntary penance is particularly beneficial when it leads to charity for the poor, acts of mercy to those in need. As St. Peter Chrysologus said: "When you fast, if your mercy is thin your harvest will be thin; when you fast, what you pour out in mercy overflows into your barn. . . . Give to the poor, and you give to yourself. You will not be allowed to keep what you have refused to give to others."

We are called to penance by gracefully accepting the difficulties and opposition that come from our loyalty to the Gospel.

The Eternal City is filled with examples of men and women who excelled in this kind of self-sacrifice. We call them martyrs. They gave their lives simply because their convictions clashed with the prevailing values.

In 1997 when I was at home in the United States, I spent time with Cardinal O'Connor. One of the priests closely associated with him told me that, in spite of the cardinal's protests, the New York Police Department regularly has two plainclothes officers near him at each public appearance because of the multiple threats on his life. Think of the burden the late cardinal had to be under because of that hostility. Why? Because of his ardent defense of the unborn and his perceptive questioning of the militant homosexual lobby.

Or consider the late Cardinal Joseph Bernardin, who bore the heavy cross of vicious, scurrilous accusations, fed, it now turns out, by a priest who detested him because of what he called his "liberal policies." That's what I'm talking about: two brave priests who faced harassment and persecution because of their loyalty to the Gospel of Christ. Now, this was not voluntary penance, because neither had asked for it. This type of mortification had come to them simply as a result of their principles.

And so will this kind of penance come to any priest worth his salt. You will not be ordained very long before you are backed into a corner at a cocktail party by someone irate over the Church's strong stand against abortion, or by someone incensed by the Holy Father's pleas for clemency on behalf of prisoners about to be executed. You can even expect harassment from within the flock, from those who berate you for refusing to support the ordination of women, to those who think you're a modernist because you accept and promote the genuine liturgical renewal of the council. Get ready for it! The days when priests were considered too noble or sacred for barbs, criticism, and ridicule are over. One priest told me they should start painting targets on rabats because the priest gets shot at from all sides.

If we do not unite this with the supreme persecution and rejection that Jesus experienced during his passion, it will wear us down. Remember the eloquent quote of Paul VI: "When it is hard to be a Christian, it is easy to be a Christian. And when it is easy to be a Christian, it is hard to be a Christian." We are often tempted to interpret rejection and opposition as signs of failure, whereas in the dispensation of Christian paradox they are proofs of the authenticity of our discipleship. When we face slings and arrows because of our fidelity to Christ, we share in his cross. Remember what St.

Thomas said, that the greatest lesson of the cross is that Jesus could have avoided it, but instead freely embraced it to demonstrate dramatically the intensity of God's love and the horror of sin.

We, too, can escape the cross, and sink into a bland, comfortable, feel-good preaching and style of ministry. As Thomas Reeves, a biographer of John F. Kennedy, wrote in the October, 1996, edition of *First Things*: "Christianity in modern America is, in large part, innocuous. It tends to be easy, upbeat, convenient, and compatible. It does not require self-sacrifice, discipline, humility, an otherworldly outlook, a zeal for souls, a fear as well as love of God. There is little guilt and no punishment, and the payoff in heaven is virtually certain. The faith has been overwhelmed by the culture, producing what is rightly called cultural Christianity."

Well, sorry, but, as much of a cliché as it has become, we are called to be countercultural, and as most of us learned on the playgrounds in first grade, when you oppose the in-crowd, you better be prepared to be ignored, ridiculed, and knocked down. Chesterton said that "Christianity not only comforts the afflicted but afflicts the comfortable." I am afraid that the world still apes those who taunted Jesus to "come down off the cross," for they much prefer a religion of ease, affirmation, agreement, and soothing. So is the priest called upon to be countercultural because:

• to a society of violence and revenge he stands for peace and forgiveness;

• to a world sated with sex he himself is celibate and preaches chastity;

• to a society frantic to spend, own, and horde, he models simplicity and sharing;

• to a country that blames and scorns the poor he urges care and justice.

And that will cost you in terms of popularity, prestige, and power; and this, I contend, makes sense only if we interpret it as penance, as a chance to conform ourselves to the rejected, scorned, persecuted Savior.

Fidelity to the specifics of our priestly commitment will also require sacrifice. Yes, it is good to view obedience, celibacy, and evangelical simplicity as positive, liberating promises, and that they are. But we must not ignore that each has a sacrificial side, and that they cannot be successfully integrated without some self-denial.

A life of loving service to the Church in obedience to our bishop is a freeing, creative promise. But you are really naïve if you do not think obedience will at times require dying to self. To accept an assignment we dread, to hear of our transfer without any consultation, to be told "no" to a request we think most logical, to watch others move ahead or be preferred over us, to wonder if we have been forgotten and overlooked — all of these come with the promise of obedience, and I have yet to meet the person who can be consistently obedient without some dying to self.

Perpetual celibate chastity is first and foremost seen by the Church as allowing a more expansive and important love, but by now you know it also entails giving something up, saying "no" to one of life's most beautiful and natural urges. To cut short a relationship you know is going to get physical and exclusive can hardly be done without a real act of dying to very potent desires.

All I am saying is that penance will come necessarily if we are true to a life of fidelity to our Lord, his teaching, his Church, and our vocation. Be ready for some pain, rejection, and mortification. Maybe not a "red" martyrdom, but certainly a "white" one. It only makes sense if we unite it all to the passion of our Lord.

Finally, penance enters our lives as we gracefully embrace the adversities that just plain come with life. As C. S. Lewis wrote, "Christianity does not take hardship from life; it simply gives one a reason to endure it." Father Gene Hamilton did not voluntarily ask for his fatal cancer, did he? Nor did it come to him as a result of his fidelity to the Gospel, did it? His cross came like most do — because tears, sorrow, sickness, and adversity come with life. And the virtue of penance is an invitation to give them meaning, make them redemptive, by interpreting them as opportunities to conform ourselves to our suffering Savior.

Aleksandr Solzhenitsyn observed that the great heresy of modernity is to believe that progress, prosperity, health, and happiness are the ordinary, expected conditions of life, and that, thus, frustration, boredom, sickness, pain, setbacks, and struggles are flaws, failures, and glitches that must be avoided and from which we must escape at all costs. And yet, we have a Master who says, "He who loves his life will lose it; he who loses it for my sake preserves it to eternity."

Life is jammed with frustrations and heartaches. One of the greatest blessings of the Gospel is that it provides a reason to bear them joyfully and achieve life and happiness through them.

Every one of you carries a dozen crosses a day, some heavy, some trivial. All those crosses come naturally just because you get out of bed each morning — which, by the way, is usually the first cross of the day.

The cross is there! We cannot get away from it! And in every one of those we hear the whisper of Christ, "Take up your cross and follow me!" This is penance in its purest form! Every single one of us is invited daily to embrace the cross. Listen to St. Francis de Sales:

> The everlasting God has in his wisdom foreseen from eternity the cross that he now presents to you as a gift from his inmost heart. This cross he now sends you he has considered with his all-knowing eyes, understood with his divine mind, tested with his wise justice, warmed with loving arms, and weighed with his own hands to see that it be not one inch too large and not one ounce too heavy for you. He has blessed it with his holy Name, anointed it with his grace, perfumed it with his consolation, taken one last glance at you and your courage, and then sent it to you from heaven, a special greeting from God to you, an alms of the all-merciful love of God.

Let me mention a few of the more predictable crosses that come to the priest, not because he asks for them, not because he is prophetic in witnessing to the Gospel, but just because he gets out of bed each morning and wants to be a decent priest.

One is the penance of listening. A wise priest I know back home says that listening is the full-time job of a priest, listening to the Lord, listening to his people. "Ministry of ears," it is sometimes called.

I remember being in the parish only a couple of days when a woman called up and asked to see me. When I entered the parlor and introduced myself, that was the last word I said. For a solid hour she talked, cried, talked some more, and then got up and said, "Thank you, Father, I am much better!" I had not said a word!

We listen in the confessional, outside of Church, in the parlor, and, especially at meetings. We listen to the bishop, and the chancery tells us what we should be doing; we listen as our people tell us what we're not doing. To listen with attention, sensitivity, and interest is a skill — and can be a penance. Learn it now. Do you listen attentively, looking at people, interested in what they say? Or are you a chatterbox, self-absorbed, bored with the conversation of others, preparing your next response. Listening is a wonderful pastoral skill, one expected of a priest — and takes mortification.

Another common penance that is a part of every priest's life is that of waiting and trusting that our work will bear fruit. I remember my brother telling me about the excitement of his first baby, there in the delivery room with his wife, and the thrill of holding their newborn daughter. Here was a living, breathing, physical result of their love.

We don't have such a thrill. We love, too, and we hope our love bears fruit, but more often than not the priest does not see it, and that, my brothers, is a penance. Are our people moved by our sermons? Sometimes we'll hear a reaction; most of the time we just have to trust. Do our converts persevere? We might never see them again. Did the seed of faith planted through the baptism we administered to a baby blossom to full, vibrant, adult faith? We'll mostly never know. Oh, don't get me wrong — we will be privy to wonderful workings of God's grace through our unworthy ministry, but not all that often. Most of the time we do our best, and wait and trust that it will one day blossom. We do not have the joy of holding the fruit of our love in our arms. And that can be a cross.

Then there is "goodness fatigue." Ever hear of that? We just plain get tired of doing good! Dorothy Day claims that one of the most important lines of Scripture is: "My brothers and sisters, never get tired of doing good" (2 Thessalonians 3:13). Daily do we battle sin, vice, evil, Satan, selfishness, sickness, and it takes its toll. At times we just get weary of doing good. St. Mark says, "Jesus went about doing good," and so do his priests. But doing good constantly is hard work, a daily cross. We want to run and hide, turn off the phone, lock the door, have a couple of drinks, spend the day in bed, become a cable TV junkie, retreat to the clubhouse for the week, tell people we're sick of their whining . . . but daily are we called to do good, and that can be a cross.

The "blahs" can be another daily mortification for the priest. Yes, it can be one of the most exciting, interesting, challenging ways of life around, but there can be tedium and boredom. There's a lot of things like turning out lights, filling out Mass cards, sweeping up rice, and mopping up overflowing toilets that can get to us, making us ask after a while what we got into, and if this is why we were ordained. Unless we daily accept these doses of the "blahs," again, as an invitation to persevere with Christ on the road to Calvary, the "blahs" can ruin us.

Finally, a fifth penance you will find in every priest's life: the daily cross of just doing well the ordinary, routine duties of our priesthood for the glory of God and love of his people.

At the celebration in honor of Cardinal John Newman in 1997 at San Giorgio in Velabro, Archbishop John Foley preached well on this very point, using as his theme the quote from Newman, "If we wish to be perfect, we have nothing more to do than to perform the ordinary duties of the day well." So, we do our work, fulfill our responsibilities, generously and graciously, without notice and complaint. Such is the lot of most priests . . . day in day out, the "Cal Ripkins" of the Church, exercising their ministry reliably with reverence, joy, and zeal. But yet, my brothers, such daily, unswerving attention to our priestly duty has a penitential dimension.

Has anyone said it better than the Little Flower? She longed for some heroic, dazzling, exotic ministry: would it be as a missionary in China? Would she be a martyr, perhaps? And then to arrive at that insight so plain and simple that it evades most of us: that the secret of sanctity is to do the ordinary things of life extraordinarily well for the glory of God and love of his people. And that entails what we might call a "passive penance" as daily we pick up our cross and advance a bit with Jesus in his passion and cross.

Is this not the reason we look back with love and admiration upon people who have had a real impact upon our lives, our mothers and fathers, some priests in our lives — nothing dramatic, nothing big sticks out, just day in and day out, reliably being there?

141

Yes, penance enters our lives as we gracefully embrace the hardships and difficulties that just plain come with life.

St. John of the Cross says: "I saw the river over which every soul must pass to reach the kingdom of heaven, and the name of the river was *suffering* . . . and I saw the boat which carries souls across that river, and the name of that boat was *love*" (emphasis added).

Love and suffering . . . the key words to describe penance, as we are configured to Jesus in his passion and cross so that we may be so in his resurrection. "We carry in our bodies the dying of Jesus," as St. Paul described it.

The old-timers used to describe the priest being a victim for his people. What did they mean? That the priest joins Christ in taking upon himself the sins, troubles, and sufferings of his people.

Our Lord already did that. He is the Lamb of God who takes upon himself the sins of the world. Sometimes he would absorb so much sickness, sadness, and brokenness that he would sigh; he would groan. St. Bridget of Sweden in her mystical revelations wrote that our Lord's deepest wound was not his hands, feet, or side, but his shoulder, gashed deeply from carrying the cross, so heavy it was.

He beckons those who claim to act in his person to join him as such a victim for his people, to take upon their shoulders the sins, sufferings, and trials of their people.

It will dawn on you during Mass one morning in the parish as you look out at your people. There is the man in the back pew, the faithful husband and father of four who has been out of work for five months and is close to despair; there's the wealthy executive two pews over who, while the picture of success, is twisting within because of the downsizing going on at the company; there's Sister Elizabeth, the DRE, who tomorrow will go in for her six-month checkup after her mastectomy and who fears the cancer has returned; there is the wife whom you have twice gotten into a shelter because her alcoholic husband beats her; there's the couple who come to you for marriage counseling; and there's the kid whom you visited in the drug rehabilitation center . . . all with their crosses . . . you know them all because you are part of their lives and they have shared their crosses with you. And at Mass you take them all, and put them on that paten and pour them in that chalice and make them literally the body and blood of Christ and sacrifice them again to the Father! You do that at Mass; you live that out as a priest.

Dated it is, maudlin and overly romantic probably, but true and valid all the same are the well-known words of Lacordaire:

> To live in the midst of the world without desiring its pleasures;
> To be a member of each family, yet belonging to none;
> To share all sufferings;
> To penetrate all secrets;
> To heal all wounds;
> To go from men to God and offer him their prayers;
> To return from God to men to bring pardon, peace, and hope;
> To have a heart of fire for charity and a heart of bronze for chastity;
> To teach and to pardon, to console and to bless always;
> My God, what a life;
> And it is yours, O Priest of Jesus Christ!

Let us pray:

We adore thee, O Christ, and we bless thee! Because by thy holy cross thou hast redeemed the world!

11

Human Formation

(Scripture selection — Philippians 4:7-9)

The whole work of priestly formation would be deprived of its necessary foundation if it lacked a suitable human formation. The priest, who is called to be a living image of Jesus Christ, head and shepherd of the Church, should seek to reflect in himself, as far as possible, the human perfection which shines forth in the Incarnate Son of God and which is reflected with particular liveliness in his attitudes towards others as we see narrated in the Gospels. . . . In order that his ministry may be humanly as credible and acceptable as possible, it is important that the priest should mold his human personality in such a way that it becomes a bridge and not an obstacle for others in their meeting with Jesus Christ. . . .

— No. 43

The foregoing comes from the apostolic exhortation of Pope John Paul II, *Pastores Dabo Vobis*, and is perhaps the most quoted passage of that entire providential document. Commentators speculate that this statement was considered almost revolutionary by many because, although the Church had presumed it for centuries, no pope had ever stated it so officially or bluntly. The Holy Father is simply declaring the primary importance of human formation in the whole enterprise of priestly preparation, that a candidate for holy orders must develop human, natural virtues in addition to supernatural ones; that our personality, our humanity, our temperament, our character, constitutes the matter, the "stuff" of our priesthood, what the Lord "reorders" and uses in the sacrament of holy orders; and that our personality, our temperament, our character, as a priest, either attracts people to Jesus and his Church, or drives them away.

All the Holy Father is saying is that "grace builds on nature," to use the legendary expression of St. Thomas. God's grace enhances, works through, and transforms our nature. We supply the raw material for God's amazing grace. As I mentioned once at a Mass, "You can't make good gnocchi without good dough." I want to speak to you about the dough we supply for the Lord to work on. What is it in our personality, our character, our temperament, that is supple to God's grace, that is clay in the hands of the Divine Sculptor, that he can use to bring people closer to him? And what is it in our person, our nature, that is resistant to his grace, that could drive people away from Jesus and his Church? In other words, human formation.

"As the seminarian, so the priest," as the adage goes. Most often we apply that to the supernatural life — if you pray and practice virtue as a seminarian, so you will as a priest; but if you don't, you won't as a priest either, because holy orders, while radically transforming your spiritual identity, will not alter your habits of life. Apply that to the human as well: if a seminarian is lazy he will be a lazy priest!

• A crab as a seminarian? Another crabby priest!

• A slob as a seminarian? A slob as a priest!

• Always late before ordination? You'll irritate people by not being on time as a priest.

• A shy seminarian who avoids people? Someone unlikely to do the aggressive evangelization the Church expects of her priests.

• Someone with b.o. or bad breath? A priest people will avoid.

• Someone who bores people silly with incessant chatter? People won't answer their doors when you come visit.

• A gossip as a seminarian? So we will have another flannel-mouth priest!

• Someone who flies off the handle at the slightest thing? Another mean priest!

Because grace builds on nature, the Lord can only work with what we give him.

Now this is nothing new, but, as the reaction to the Holy Father's statement shows, the Church seems to be waking up to the value of human formation today. I hear it from bishops, vocation directors, pastors, and laity all the time: rarely do I hear them criticize any recent alumni of the North American College for lack of prayer, for dissent on Church teaching, for failures in piety — what they criticize are human flaws.

Recently I asked a bishop about one of our alumni and he sadly replied that the pastor had already asked to have him transferred. Why? I asked. A failure in preaching, in pastoral commitment, in theological preparation, in habits of prayer? None of the above! Why did the pastor ask to have the man transferred? Because his room was a pigsty! The housekeeper refused to go in. The man did not even flush his toilet. Now, that's not a supernatural problem, is it? That's about as human as you can get! Yet it debilitated this man's ability to function well as a priest. Human formation. . . .

I asked a pastor about another of our alumni. He rolled his eyes and shook his head. Again the litany of questions: Is it his preaching? No. His liturgical style? No. His lack of a prayer life? No. His inadequate theological foundation? Not at all. What's the problem, then? Answers the pastor, "The guy's just obnoxious." He elaborated that the guy was haughty, dismissive with the people, selfish with his time, arrogant with the staff, a know-it-all with the people. Again, human formation: nothing all that supernatural here, but a man whose manner, style, and personality drive people away instead of bringing them closer to Christ.

We are called to be bridge-builders, from *pontifex*, to use the local word. Our manner, our style, our personality is to attract people, not shock, scare, hurt, and alienate them. Thus must we be aware of those traits in our character that do indeed serve as a magnet to draw people to Jesus and his Church, and constantly enhance, refine, and improve them; and thus must we candidly confront those characteristics that wound, scatter, and scandalize people, and work to purge them from our temperament.

When you talk to priests in a rectory, what do they usually find trying? The human tension, right? A guy that won't talk, won't socialize; a guy that leaves lights on and comes in late; a guy that leaves the sacristy a mess and won't carry his share of the work. All human failings.

I'm not telling you anything new. Most of us have been profoundly affected by the positive influence of a priest in our life, maybe in the parish, at school, in the confessional, there at a tough period in our lives. His humanity — his sincerity, his genuine love, his care, his compassion, his sensitivity, his patience, his friendship — his humanity was the vehicle, the bridge for us encountering the divine, the sacred, the supernatural. We all want to be a priest like that! And yet you all have met priests who have shocked you, not with a defect of their interior life, since that is unknown to us, but by their personality, their character — their harshness, their lavish lifestyle, their sexual exploits, their drinking, their temper, their vocabulary, their callousness, their laziness. To quote the Holy Father again, "It is important that the priest should mold his human personality in such a way that it becomes a bridge and not an obstacle for others in their meeting with Jesus Christ."

When Carl Mengeling was ordained bishop of Lansing, during his sermon he looked at Cardinal Maida, who was to consecrate him, and said, "Eminence, when it comes time for you to place the book of the gospels on my head, will you please press down real hard, because I've got to let that gospel penetrate through a thick, stubborn skull that very often resists the promptings of that gospel?" Don't we all? Sometimes we call this "evangelical effectiveness": in other words, what in my personality makes my preaching and living the Gospel smooth and effective, and what does not?

At the North American College we stress the spiritual and intellectual life. Our seminary exists to provide an atmosphere where a seminarian can grow intimately in love with Jesus and learn his Revelation with rigor and precision. I am proud that we get high marks in these two areas. Our men in general leave here with a solid, disciplined, firmly rooted spiritual life and a fine theological education. But this will not help much if the human qualities are not as refined and attractive. What good will the prayer and learning be for the priest whose personality repels people? A man might know all about the theology of marriage, but, if he's so shy that he can't introduce himself to people, he won't have any young couples coming for marriage at all. A man's homiletic skills might be dazzling, but they won't do a bit of good if he yells at a crying baby from the pulpit.

Archbishop Fulton Sheen told the story about one of his first sermons as a priest in the parish. He had prepared it so well and polished it so much that he was sure it would go over. After the Mass he greeted the people and waited for some comment, but no one said a thing about his sermon. Finally, when all were gone, he asked the usher what he thought. "Frankly, Father, nobody could hear you." Now, knowing Fulton Sheen, I am confident that the content was marvelous . . . however, because of a simple human flaw — he spoke too softly — his sermon helped no one.

A man was golfing with his pastor and admired how the pastor sank every putt, while he himself was three- and four-putting every hole. He finally asked the pastor his secret. "Well, before every putt I say a 'Hail Mary.' " Next green, the pastor sank a long putt; the parishioner confidently said a "Hail Mary" and proceeded to miss the hole by three feet. The pastor looked at him and said, "Won't help you a damn bit if you don't know how to putt."

We have to know "how to putt" so that people are attracted to Jesus and his Church through us. Like it or not, the personality of a priest can decide whether or not a person stays in the Church or not. When I was a parish priest I would visit fallen-away Catholics and I was surprised to find that, second only to irregular marriages, the major reason people left the Church was because a priest or nun had hurt them. "Oh, I was in the hospital and called and asked Father Smith to come see me and he never did." "My mother was dying and I asked Father Jones to bring her Holy Communion and he never did." "When my kids were going to school we fell behind in tuition and the pastor sent the kids home."

Those people left the Church because of a priest. Now, that's not logical, is it? To leave the Church because you do not like a priest is silly, and we know it. I remember as a child at my grandparents on a Sunday morning getting ready to go to Mass. My grandma said to my grandpa, "Come on, Tim, time to go to Mass."

He was comfortable in the easy chair reading the Sunday paper and replied, "I'm not going . . . I can't stand that new pastor."

To which my grandma responded, "Yeah, well, you can't stand the bartender up at the corner, either, but you sure as hell haven't quit going up there." He got up and went to Mass. Sure, it's silly to leave the Church because of the foibles of a priest, but many certainly do, and we must be scrupulous in seeing that we never give anyone such an excuse. God forbid anyone should ever grow apart from Jesus and his Spouse, the Church, because of something we said or did, or something we did not say or do when we should have.

In 1996 I was at a reception at John Cabot University to celebrate the anniversary of the *New York Times,* when a well-known journalist came up to me. I had chatted with her in the past. This time she was very intense. She said to me, "Tell your men to be careful!" I asked what she meant. "Rome can teach them a lot about what's good in the Church, but it can also teach them to be nasty, mean, ambitious, backstabbing clerics." She went on to tell me that she had attended the big Mass in honor of newly beatified Edmund Rice at St. Peter's on Monday, and when she left, it was pouring down rain. She had a deadline to meet and struggled to get a cab and had just found one, was actually opening the door to get in, when a priest pushed her aside and jumped in. She was furious. No telling how the nasty rudeness of that priest will affect her coverage of the Church in the future.

We are ever conscious of the fact that we are a public persona in the Church. For better or worse, rightly or wrongly, we represent the Church to people. How people think of Jesus and his Church often depends on how we come across, how our human qualities are perceived. What a heavy responsibility! People can be driven away by us, and thus we must avoid not only any wrongdoing but even the appearance of wrongdoing. On the other hand, people can be attracted to our Lord and his Mystical Body through us — and what a joy that is!

Once on an airplane I sat next to a man who told me that he had converted to Catholicism because of the example of Cardinal Cooke. I said, "Oh, yes, his patience and resignation during his agonizing death were so inspirational."

"Yes, they were," he replied, "but I had converted long before that. One day at an airport, there was a terribly long line to get the shuttle, and Cardinal Cooke was waiting in line in front of me. An attendant came up and whispered to him, 'Your Eminence, follow me. I will take you to the front of the line.' 'That's very thoughtful of you and I appreciate it, but I can wait my turn,' replied the cardinal. That act of simple humility moved me so much that it sparked my interest in becoming a Catholic."

We can bring 'em in; we can drive 'em away. Yes, the supernatural is essential, but we usually attract them or distract them by the human, natural side of our personality.

Now, let me mention three specific human qualities — and there could be dozens more — that people find particularly attractive in priests.

The first is nebulous, I admit, but the only word I can use is "kindness." People love kind priests. Cardinal John O'Connor tells the story that, shortly after he was ordained, he asked an older priest if he had any advice. The veteran said, "Why, yes, three pieces of advice: Be kind! Be kind! Be kind!"

A few years ago I had the privilege of attending the first Masses of three newly ordained priests. At each of those joyful events, looking at the people who filled those churches, I had the same thought: these people are the reason I'm at the North American College — to form kind, good priests who will mirror to them the love of God. I looked at those people; many of them had on the only decent set of clothes they owned; they were beaming with joy at having had a part to play in the life of a new priest; they loved their spouse, their kids, their parish, their faith, their God; they loved their priests, and all they asked in return is that their priests be kind to them, care for them, show them God's love. And they've all had more of their share of priests who had let them down, ignored their needs, hurt them, or shocked them. But they kept hoping. Those are the people who deserve our kindness.

Charles de Foucauld wrote, "To be an apostle, but how? With goodness and kindness, brotherly affection, a virtuous example. . . . Being patient as God is patient, being good as God is good, being a kind brother."

In one of Jon Hassler's novels, *North of Hope*, there is an episode where the struggling priest, Frank, was talking to the old pastor, Adrian, who had spent most of his life as chancellor of the diocese.

"I thought it was all so important then," says Monsignor Adrian, reflecting on his life in the chancery. "I thought the Church needed my talents as an administrator, and, maybe it did, but now that I'm a pastor again, I see what being a priest is all about. A man's talents are best put to use in parish work, Frank. And do you know what parish work consists of? What it comes down to? What our job really is?"

"What?" Frank asked.

"Being nice to people."

"That's all?"

"Loving kindness. Nothing more or less."

"Isn't that oversimplifying it, Adrian?"

"Nothing simple about it."

That's for sure. Being nice to the people. There's nothing simple about it. Because I'm not talking about being some smiling childish airhead; I'm talking about a loving kindness that reflects the burning compassion of the Sacred Heart of Jesus. St. Francis de Sales in his *Introduction to the Devout Life* says we attract more souls with honey than with vinegar.

There's nothing simple about it, being kind. We are tempted to dismiss people, to yell, to get fed up, to say we're too busy, to ask them how stupid they can be. To keep the smile, to let people think we've got all the time in the world for them, to exhibit a genuine interest, to ask about their families and remember their worries so we can inquire about them, to follow up on cases and get back to people . . . to be kind. The Holy Father calls this "Affective Maturity" in *Pastores Dabo Vobis*: the ability to relate to people confidently, effectively, and maturely.

You want to know a few of the things that will appear unkind to people and that you should be aware of in your human formation?

Anger: never, ever, lose your temper and lash out at someone. One time while I was hearing confessions I lost my temper and yelled at the penitent. She left the confessional — I'm sure in tears — in the middle of my tantrum. To this day I repent of that sin. To this day I pray for her. To this day I know that when I stand before the judgment seat of God that point will be brought before me.

I am not saying we are not to be firm, clear, and challenging with people. As a priest there are times we must be decisive, say no, state that certain behavior is unacceptable. A priest I know claims the great heresy today is "nice-ism," with priests and bishops so afraid of losing popularity or unsettling people that they turn into fluffy, least-common-denominator Christian ministers. That's not what I mean.

I'm saying watch how you do it . . . and never act in anger and risk hurting someone.

Hurriedness: a second attitude that can appear unkind is always seeming to be on the run, busy, with no genuine time for people. They are then afraid to approach us because we give them the impression we have more important things to do.

Brusqueness: "I said 'good morning' to Father and he didn't even look at me." The appearance of being aloof, unfriendly. Not that we all have to be backslapping, hail-fellow-well-met, campaigning-for-mayor type people. No . . . but, believe it or not, after all that has happened, people are still in awe of their priests. So we have to take the initiative.

Some of you are shy and always will be, but make sure people never interpret your shyness as a brusque unfriendliness. We must take the initiative. After Mass we learn to initiate a greeting with such expressions as, "You know, I see you all the time but can't remember your name." A cool, detached brusqueness detracts from the kindness people long for in their priests.

Be kind! Be kind! Be kind!

A second human trait that will enhance our evangelical effectiveness: reliability. People want to depend upon their priests.

• So, if we make an appointment, we keep it.

• If we promise to call someone, we do.

• If we are in charge of a particular parish organization, we make the meetings.

• If we have 6:30 a.m. Mass, we start at 6:30 a.m.

• If we teach eighth grade on every Tuesday afternoon from 1:00 to 1:30, we're there.

Reliability. People have a right to expect us to do what we're supposed to, to put in a good day's work.

One pastor told me he got a new assistant who said to him at their first meeting, "I'll be gone every day from about 1:00 to 4:00 because I have to visit my old aunt in a nursing home."

The pastor said, "I don't think that will work. There are duties you will have in the afternoons."

The assistant answered, "Well, surely you don't expect me to place my aunt second to these parish duties, do you?"

"As a matter of fact, I do," replied the pastor. We have a duty to our family — our parish — and the people have a right to our reliable, effective presence.

I recently read a "letter to the editor" in *America* magazine from a parish priest in the Bronx, speaking about his ministry: "Once you're known, if you're available and approachable, if you believe the Gospel yourself, they'll be knocking at your door, dialing your number, and stopping you on the street. There's enough pain out there, enough anxiety, enough hunger for God to keep you busy all day, every day. How do you get known? You greet the people after Mass, you go into the school on a regular basis, you attend all the parish affairs, you visit shut-ins. Once you're known, if you're available and approachable, if you believe the Gospel yourself, you'll be busy."

A reliable availability to the people. You are there for them. Recently I called a rectory at home and got a tape message: "Please call only during normal working hours, 9:00 to 1:00." Normal working hours? Normal for where? What's going on here? That's availability? No emergency number to call. Does it not dawn on them that most people cannot approach a priest during "normal business hours," since most of them happen to be working?

A common complaint you hear from our people is that they never see their priest. Traditionally a good parish priest is immersed in the lives of his people, there in times of need. He is a "father." They can rely on him. Cultivate that human trait of reliability.

Start now! That's why a rhythm of life is so essential. If we are dependable, we get up at a certain time and go to bed at a certain time; we avoid late nights and late mornings; we have a faithful time for prayer, exercise, study, and fostering of friendships. And we get our work done. One of the highest goals of human formation in the seminary is the development of a rhythm of life from which a pastoral reliability comes. We are men whose word can be trusted, who fulfill our duties, who are immersed in our communities, and are present to those with whom we live — we are reliable.

And a third human trait people look for in their priests: an upbeat, hopeful attitude. While such a posture must certainly flow from the supernatural virtue of hope, people are attracted to Christ and his Church through a priest who exhibits a sense of cheer and confidence, even in the midst of suffering, setback, and difficulty.

They often approach a priest in times of emergency and trouble, and can reach the God who is a Rock in times of distress through the ministrations of a priest who exudes a serene, sunny confidence, even in the midst of woes.

There are tendencies in all of us that militate against this upbeat, hopeful attitude people expect from their priest. One is a thin-skinned hypersensitivity that causes us to take offense at the least provocation. Some priests become easily aggrieved. They always think they're being cheated, overlooked, put upon. Their pastors don't trust them, their bishops don't use them properly, their people don't appreciate them. So they're always mad, upset, feeling sorry for themselves, and thus hardly exhibit the upbeat, hopeful character people crave.

We priests can still be a spoiled lot. While called to a life of selfless service, we are quick to insist on our rights, our prerogatives, and thus we often become petty. In 1996 something happened at the college to remind me of that. Three "crises" arose on the same day that upset me or people in this house.

The first "crisis" came when I discovered that one of the workers at the school, who was preparing a mailing for bishops, had not used the formal "office of the rector" stationery. I was upset and became curt at such an oversight! Then came the news from one of our candidates for diaconate that his retreat was "ruined" because they had been expected to wash dishes on retreat; then I find out that one of our men had rather rudely flicked the refectory lights on and off the night before, causing some of our visiting priests to become incensed. These were the three "crises." I suppose I had a right to be upset over the oversight with the letterhead; the man to be ordained had a point that to wash dishes on a retreat was a distraction and imposition one hardly needs at a time of solitude and recollection; our impatient student was perhaps legitimately put out that the priests were lingering while he was waiting for their dishes; the priests had some cause for grievance that they were treated rudely by a student childishly flicking lights. My point is that the overwhelming majority of people in the world would welcome the day when such "crises" were all they had to worry about. All this was evidence to me of our tendency to become easily aggrieved.

This was heightened that same afternoon when Sister Virginia came to visit from the convent. She was here for a few weeks of break before returning to the mission school the *hermanas* run in Angola. She had photographs to excitedly show me of the sisters caring for very poor Africans, victims of plague, tribal violence, famine. She told me how the last time she returned to Angola on the way home from the airport a band of thugs stopped the car, put a gun to each of the sisters' heads, and took all their belongings, chuckling about raping and murdering the sisters the whole time. Sister Virginia is eager to return to Angola. She exudes an upbeat, hopeful attitude . . . my three "crises" of stationery, dishwashing, and flicking lights quickly faded.

Mary, Queen of Scots, prayed: "Keep me, O God, from pettiness. Let us be large in thought, word, and deed. Let us be done with faultfinding and self-seeking. May we put away all pretense and meet each other without self-pity. And, O Lord, let us not forget to be kind."

I trust I've made my point. Notice that I have not spoken of anything particularly supernatural, of prayer, the spiritual life, orthodoxy, or faith — although such has to be the source of everything. No, I have spoken of human formation, the common, everyday traits we need to possess if we are to bring people closer to Christ by the goodness, power, and pleasantness of our personality, and the flaws and negatives that can drive people away. A few final observations that can help us.

First . . . now I can mention prayer, as we ask the Creator who gave us our human nature to continue to mold it in the image of his Son. May I suggest especially two traditions that can help us every day to advance in human formation:

• One is the morning offering: each morning, immediately upon getting out of bed, we dedicate the entire day to God, and ask him particularly for the graces we will need to attract people to him by the goodness and appeal of our personality.

• Two, at the end of the day, we practice the habit of examen: in the context of night prayer, we carefully review the day, particularly conscious of the times we may have hurt or offended people by a word, deed, or oversight, asking ourselves simply if we were that day a bridge for people to reach God or a fence to place an obstacle.

Daily honest examen keeps us sensitive about the presence or absence of human flaws.

Second . . . know yourself. Know yourself so well that you are gratefully aware of the traits in your personality that can attract people to Jesus, constantly trying to enhance those; and realistically aware of those flaws that periodically erupt and can drive people away, daily trying to refine and purge those away. Know yourself.

Third, in your drive to know yourself, you will seek counsel from others whom you trust: a spiritual director, good friends, a pastor or supervisor, a counselor, your bishop. It would seem to me an excellent idea for every priest to sit down with his pastor periodically and ask, "How am I doing? Do you have any advice? Do you notice any flaws or shortcomings?" Hopefully, this will also create a climate of trust where the pastor can ask his assistant the same thing.

As I have said before, count as a genuine blessing the friendship of one who can tell you the truth about yourself, even when that hurts. A friend who is always telling you that you're just fine and that any criticism you receive from others is unfair is not a real friend. Many of you find *Jesu Caritas* a good means of this growth in self-knowledge.

In the seminary it is our serious duty to point out areas of human formation that need attention. A spiritual director helps the directee develop the nature upon which God's grace builds. Formation advisers have the duty to point out areas where growth is needed. It is especially evident in our evaluation process. We try to do this fairly, accurately, justly. We rarely, if ever, offer criticisms on our students' prayer life, their fidelity to Church teaching, or their vocational certitude, for these important areas are usually known only to themselves, the Lord, and trusted people like their spiritual director, in whom they have confided. However, it is our duty to point out the areas of human formation where they need improvement. Most of the time I am inspired at how humbly and gratefully our students take these observations. None of us enjoy hearing about shortcomings. But, if evangelical effectiveness is a goal, if leading people closer to Jesus through the instrument of an attractive, pleasant, friendly personality is our drive, then we welcome such criticisms.

Beware of blaming the critic. "The bishop is unfair; Father so-and-so has been out to get me from the day I arrived; they don't know me. If this guy feels this way about me that's his problem." Beware of always blaming the critic. If you can't get along with the pastor, or assistant, staff, and people at one parish, there could be a legitimate grievance; maybe even a second. But when a guy is never happy and always blaming his assignment or his co-workers or his people, the problem is his, not the others'.

As we grow in self-knowledge with the help of prayer, counsel, and the direction of others, we find some things we cannot change, try as we might. I suppose we just keep trying and work on some other area of our humanity that we can improve. Some things we cannot change even if people wanted us to. For instance, some people these days will reject what I say or do because I am a white male Catholic priest of European descent. Nothing I can do about that, is there?

Sometimes there are characteristics we have that damage our evangelical effectiveness, even though they should not. Sometimes people can be narrow or misguided in some judgments about us, but, for the sake of our priestly ministry, we should still be sensitive. For instance, I suppose people should not be turned off by a priest with a ponytail, a bushy beard, or an earring, but rightly or wrongly, they are, so a priest should avoid such things. I suppose that, in the long run, people should not really care how we dress, but they do, so we're wise to be proper, clean, and in clerics when involved in apostolic and liturgical duties. It is certainly unjust for the people to prejudge a priest who is effeminate in manner, but they do, so one tries to work on that, as does one who is too gruff or overly "macho." For, as St. Paul says, "all that matters is that Jesus Christ is preached," and I will do anything it takes to achieve that goal as effectively as possible.

All I'm saying is that our personality, our human nature, our character, is one of God's greatest gifts to us. As he became incarnate in the human nature of his Son, so he becomes incarnate in our human nature. Thus our humanity can become a bridge, a door, a magnet drawing people to God and his Church. We constantly work to utilize those aspects of our humanity that attract people to salvation. And we ceaselessly try to cleanse from our humanity those dark, nasty, unpleasant traits that scare, shock, distract, or hurt people.

Fulton Sheen says that's why priests are so in love with our Lady. As in her body she allowed the Word to take flesh, so does the priest, in his person, allow the Incarnation to continue. The Word still takes flesh. Woe to us if we become an obstacle, a stumbling block, keeping the Word from taking flesh!

I thought of this whole issue of human formation recently while reading St. Paul. Paul is writing to Timothy about the qualities of an ordained minister, pointing out that he must be irreproachable, even-tempered, self-controlled, modest, hospitable. He should be a good teacher. He must not be addicted to drink. He ought not to be contentious; rather, he should be gentle, a man of peace. Nor can he love money. He must be a good manager of his own affairs, for if a man does not know how to handle his own responsibilities, how can he care for the Church? He must be well thought of to ensure that he does not bring disgrace to the Church.

As you can see, the Church has been concerned about human formation from the earliest days.

12

Stewardship of the Spirit

(Scripture selection — John 1:35-39)

It is with the account from the Gospel of St. John of the Master's invitation ("Come and see") and of the disciples' acceptance ("So they went and saw where he lived, and stayed with him") that I wish to begin because, of course, Jesus Christ is the only real reason we exist. He is the One who calls and the One who empowers us to respond to his call; he is the end for which we strive; he is the means to that end; without him, we can do nothing; with him, nothing is impossible. Everything we embark upon is for, with, through, and because of Jesus Christ.

As St. Paul wrote to the Colossians:

> He is the image of the invisible God,
> the firstborn of all creation.
> For in him were created all things in heaven and on earth,
> the visible and the invisible,
> whether thrones or dominions or principalities or powers;
> all things were created through him and for him.
> He is before all things,
> and in him all things hold together.
> He is the head of the body, the church.
> He is the beginning, the firstborn from the dead,
> that in all things he himself might be preeminent.
> For in him all the fullness was pleased to dwell,
> and through him to reconcile all things for him,
> making peace by the blood of his cross
> [through him], whether those on earth or those in heaven.
> — Colossians 1:15-20, *New American Bible*

Here is the key to our spiritual growth: a faithful, personal, loving relationship with Jesus. As Karl Rahner writes, *holiness* is "participation in the intimate union between Father and Son, led by the Spirit." Jesus Christ is the *way* to accomplish this through the *truth* he teaches and the *life* he imparts. Listen to these poetic words of Pope Paul VI:

> Jesus is Christ, the Son of the Living God. Because of him we come to know the God we cannot see. He is the firstborn of all creation, in him all things find their being. Our teacher and redeemer, he was born for us, died for us, and for us rose from the dead.
>
> All things converge in Christ. A man of sorrow and hope, he knows us and loves us. As our friend he stays with us throughout our lives; at the end of time he will come to be our judge; but we also know that he will be the complete fulfillment of our lives and our great happiness for all eternity.
>
> I can never cease to speak of Christ. He is the way, the truth, and the life. He is our bread, our living water, who allays our hunger and satisfies our thirst. He is our shepherd, our leader, our ideal, our comforter, and our brother.
>
> Jesus Christ is the beginning and the end, the alpha and the omega, Lord of the universe, the great hidden key to human history and the part we play in it. He is the mediator between heaven and earth, true God and true Man.

To know Jesus, to hear Jesus, to love Jesus, to trust Jesus, to obey Jesus, to share his life in the deepest fiber of our being, and then to serve him in his people — this is our goal. Beware, though: as Cardinal William Baum once preached at the North American College, "The danger of every seminary is to know about Jesus without knowing him, to talk about Jesus but not to him, to listen to experts speak of him without letting him speak about himself. A deep, personal, intimate relationship with Jesus Christ is the foundation of holiness!"

"Seek ye first the kingdom of God!" exhorts our Lord. The primacy of the spiritual! Stewardship of the supernatural gifts of grace, faith, mercy, prayer, sacraments, and vocation that the Lord gives

162

us! Stewardship, of course, means a responsible care for the gifts entrusted to us.

Our spiritual enterprise at the North American College is *Christological* and also *ecclesial*, growing in love for and understanding of what the Church is, what she asks, and what she needs from the men who detect a call to lead her into her third millennium. When we ponder what the Church needs from her priests, one word towers above all the rest: holiness. The Church needs holy priests. As *Pastores Dabo Vobis* so clearly states: "The priest must be a man of God, the one who belongs to God and makes people think of God. . . . Christians expect to find in the priest . . . a man who will help them turn to God . . . and so the priest must have a deep intimacy with the Lord. Those who are preparing for the priesthood should realize that their whole priestly life will have value, inasmuch as they are able to give themselves to Christ, and, through Christ, to the Father."

We aspire to a life of giving Christ to others. We can't give him unless we've got him! And that is holiness. *Evangelii Nuntiandi* says it well: "Before we evangelize, we must be evangelized."

How do we grow in holiness? How? That, of course, is our spiritual program, isn't it, the stewardship of the spirit, "the regimen of the soul bringing about the reign of God," to quote Charles de Foucauld. I propose to you a spiritual regimen, the clear expectations the Church holds for any man preparing for holy orders, a stewardship of the spirit coming not from me but from centuries of practice and learning.

I. Daily Prayer

Patient, persevering, persistent prayer, every day, is number one. Here I am not speaking of the liturgy — of the Eucharist or the Hours — but of silent, personal, private prayer, a daily period of quiet communion with the Lord, conscious of his presence, accepting his love, and returning it with praise, petition, and thanksgiving. Call it what you want: meditation, centering, contemplation — I've never seen it better described than by the great Cardinal Mercier, who wrote:

> Every day for some moments . . . close your eyes to the things
> of sense and your ears to the noises of the world, in order to

enter into yourself. There, in the sanctity of your baptized soul, the temple of the Holy Spirit, say:

"O Holy Spirit, beloved of my soul, I adore you. Enlighten me, guide me, strengthen me, console me. . . . Let me know your will."

If you do this, your life will flow serenely, even in the midst of trials. This submission to the Holy Spirit is the secret of sanctity.

Daily prayer is the foundation of this sanctity. . . . To nourish it, develop it, intensify it — this is the goal of a lifetime. Some do it beautifully early in the morning, some late at night; some come before the Blessed Sacrament, others prefer their rooms; some rely on Scripture, or devotions; some utilize the Holy Hour format — however, wherever, whenever, whatever — a daily period of private prayer is a must!

II. Daily Mass

I defer to Pope John Paul II, in *Pastores Dabo Vobis*: "To be utterly frank and clear, I would like to say once again: it is fitting that seminarians take part every day in the Eucharistic celebration, in such a way that they will take up as a rule of their priestly life this daily celebration. They should . . . consider this Eucharistic celebration as the essential moment of their day in which they take an active part, and at which they will never be satisfied with a merely habitual attendance" (No. 48).

From this daily Eucharistic meal comes a reverential awe for the Real Presence of Christ in the Blessed Sacrament and a desire to spend time before him there in visits and prayer.

III. Daily Fidelity to the Liturgy of the Hours

This is the ancient prayer of the Church most associated with those in holy orders, who have as their "job," their "office," the daily recitation of the breviary. By the time one kneels before his bishop for ordination to the diaconate, one should have a joyful attachment to the promise of daily prayer with and for the Church in the entire liturgy of the hours, our divine office. A priest who is well-known for his work with priests in trouble told me, "The first thing to go when a priest is heading for trouble is his daily office."

IV. Daily Spiritual Reading

• *Lectio divina*, daily reverent meditation upon Sacred Scripture, is first and foremost, of course;

• but I also speak of daily spiritual reading of the enduring books of our Catholic tradition, as well as interest in the burgeoning contemporary literature on the interior life;

• nor should we forget attention to the documents of the magisterium, the words of our Holy Father, the documents of the Apostolic See, the messages and pastorals of our own bishops, all vehicles of the Holy Spirit for fostering our growth in sanctity.

V. Spiritual Direction: Honest, Trusting, Fruitful, Consistent Relationship with One's Director

In some ways, this is the linchpin of all the rest, for this is where integration and interiorization begin to take place. The danger of seminary and priestly life is formalism, where we passively do things just to get by, not allowing the values of formation to sink in and become part of us. Spiritual direction can promote this interiorization, this integration.

VI. Sacrament of Penance

Regular reliance upon the mercy of God abundant in the sacrament of penance should be a priority in our lives. While how often you approach this sacrament is a good topic to discuss with your spiritual director, at least once a month seems a solid tradition of the Church. That same priest who is well-known for his apostolate to priests in trouble told me: "The second thing to go when a priest is in trouble is regular confession." That you approach confession regularly is a hallmark of sound spiritual stewardship. And a practical help to make our regular confessions more fruitful would be a daily examination of conscience, praising God for our growth, asking for healing of the faults we admit.

VII. Growing in Virtue

A tireless effort for growth in virtue and turning away from sin should be the pattern of our daily life. Obedient to the constant refrain of the Gospels, we are always in the process of conversion, repentance, dying to sin, self, and Satan, rising to new life in Christ.

This is the "paschal mystery." In practice this means growth in virtue and struggle with sin. Development in particular virtues is most appropriate.

A. Faith

I recently received a letter from a priest critical of his own seminary formation. He said that all through his years of preparation he was often asked, "Are you happy?" "Are you maturing?" "Are you open?" "How are your grades?" But never once, "Do you believe in God?" One would like to think that we can take some things for granted, and that belief in God would be one of them, but his point was a good one — the utter necessity of faith. We grow here in our rock-sure belief in God, his Son, his Revelation, and we reject doubt, cynicism, pervasive relativism, and an aimless existence that stems from a lack of faith. Remember that the Church requires an oath of fidelity from those preparing for ordination to the diaconate. That is the Church's way of assuring that her deacons and priests are men of strong faith in God and in all that God has revealed in Scripture, Tradition, and the teaching of his Church. Sometimes to examine our conscience as to whether we can indeed take that oath sincerely is a good idea.

B. Hope

A firm, joyful reliance on the utter dependability of God's promises, and a rejection of the despair, gloom, and discouragement we often face.

C. Charity

A burning love for God and his people, evident in patience, service, sharing, courtesy, generosity, and joy, and a battle against our dark side from which emerge hate, selfishness, laziness, petty resentment, and just plain meanness.

D. Simplicity of Life

Seeking to live plainly, justly, gratefully, not succumbing to the accumulation and stinginess endemic to Western society. Luxurious living and display of affluence in priests have probably been the source of greater scandal to the faithful than would be true of his succumbing to the weakness of the flesh or excessive drink.

E. Chastity

Daily striving to embrace celibate chastity, deliberately, maturely, happily, for the sake of the Kingdom, and freely surrendering all genital activity in thought, word, and deed, alone or with others, hetero- or homosexually, honestly confronting any inclinations, drives, or fantasies that threaten the wholesome, healthy, realistic purity mirrored by Jesus and expected by his Church of her priests.

F. Obedience

A childlike docility in our relationship to the Lord and his call, an attentiveness to the Church and her needs, a rejection of the smug demand for unbridled liberty so popular today.

G. Integrity

The cultivation of truthfulness, honesty, keeping one's word, avoiding deceit, shame, hypocrisy, and the drug of denial that keeps us from genuine spiritual growth. Several years ago at our graduate house in Rome, the Casa Santa Maria, Cardinal Bernardin preached eloquently at the opening Mass. He referred to those dark days of a year before when he was unjustly accused of molesting a teenager. He said, "At that moment, when all looked bleak, all the worldly honors I had — position, cardinalate, prestige, fame, Chicago — did not help one bit. In fact, they hurt my cause. All I had were two things to rely on: God's grace, and my personal integrity. They worked."

A constant growth in virtue and a struggle with sin leading to an ongoing conversion of life.

VIII. Devotion to Our Blessed Mother and the Saints

A sustaining dependence upon the "communion of saints," aware that we are members of a supernatural family not confined to the here and now, that we have the saints as examples and helpers, preeminently, especially, our Blessed Mother. Thus, a wholesome devotion to her would be an essential part of our spiritual regimen.

IX. A Holistic Formation Allowing Our Spirituality to Permeate Our Lives

You see, the spiritual life is not a tidy, isolated compartment of our existence! No, as the Holy Father says, "spiritual formation is the core which unifies and gives life to our entire being." Thus, every element of our lives is part of the spiritual arena, and growth in holiness will entail wholehearted immersion in the entire life here:

• Human and personal development. A major part of our spiritual stewardship is human development in qualities such as reliability, courtesy, promptness; the fostering of genuine friendships so essential for a fruitful priestly life.

• Academic rigor, through consistent study and research, ongoing reading and theological refinement, and the cultivation of good reading habits.

• A zeal toward our apostolic works and our assignments.

• A sensitivity to the demands of communal life, a real fraternal support for one another, just looking out for each other; a contribution through time, effort, and presence.

• Enthusiasm for retreats and days of recollection.

"The seminary," says Pope John Paul II, "should be experienced not as something external and superficial, or simply as a place in which to live and study, but in an interior and profound way. It should be experienced as a community — that relives the experience of the group of twelve who were united to Jesus."

I once was in a parish discussion group that was to ponder "married life and family." The leader set the ground rules and said, "Let's only talk about our married and family life, nothing about our jobs." One of the men, who had a tough job at the Chrysler plant said, "Why not? That's part of my married and family life! You think I'd do that if it wasn't for my wife and kids?"

Good insight! He realized that what he did, his job, only made sense because it was motivated by the love he had for his wife and children. So, everything we do comes under spiritual stewardship as it flows from our interior life, from the love we bear for Christ and share with his Bride, the Church. St. Francis de Sales articulated this principle when he insisted that holiness must happen in the work we do and place we live.

X. The Final Component in Our Spiritual Stewardship: To Keep Ever in View the Call to the Priesthood

Our goal is nothing less than a reordering of life through the sacrament of holy orders, which will configure us in an irrevocable, radical way to Christ. That we may be good, holy, happy, healthy, learned, zealous, selfless, committed priests is the drive of this house. Candidacy, lector, acolyte, diaconate are the significant steps in this journey to priesthood. I urge a commitment to the priesthood as an enduring way of life, not just as one more avocation, ministry, or job that can be set aside when frustration, temptation, or something or someone more attractive comes along! The priesthood is a call, not a career; a life, not a job; a mission, not just a ministry; an identity, not just a profession.

When, God willing, your bishop asks you before the Church on ordination day if you are ready and willing to pray, teach, serve, sanctify, and live faithfully as a priest forever, you, because of your inner relationship with the Eternal High Priest, can respond confidently, truthfully, and maturely, "I am, with the help of God!" Our spiritual development is focused on that goal of the priesthood. And this means ongoing discernment to guard against drifting to ordination simply because nothing better has come along, honestly examining the motives that drive us and the validity of our call.

Let me mention two notes of caution:

First, growth in holiness is not our accomplishment but a pure gift from God. The Lord does it, not us! One of the great heresies rampant in every seminary and rectory is Pelagianism — believing that we can earn, deserve, or achieve our salvation! Such an approach leads to discouragement on the one hand and self-righteousness or religious formalism on the other. These ten steps of spiritual stewardship I just went through are not cozy little acts we perform to produce holiness — they are simply tried-and-true ways we open up in humility to let the Lord in to do his work in, on, for, and, often, in spite of us!

Holiness is a mystery. It will always elude us. The moment we think we have it made we'd better start from scratch; the moment we want to walk tall we best get down on our knees; and the minute we think we're without sin, we've just committed the biggest one!

Secondly, "The road inward to spiritual growth always results in a U-turn outwards in love for others," to use the words of Sister Bridge McKenna. In more classical terminology, the spiritual journey *ad intra* results in a life of love *ad extra*, to others. Our stewardship of the Spirit is never a soothing benefice we cling to; rather, it inspires us to love God's people better. As Paul says, "In Christ Jesus, all that counts is faith, which expresses itself in love" (Galatians 5:6). The Jesus who calls us to spiritual ecstasy on Mount Tabor likewise invites us to the pouring out of self on Mount Calvary.

The *Suscipe* of St. Ignatius sums it up:

> Take, O Lord,
> and receive all my liberty,
> my memory,
> my understanding
> and my whole will.
> Thou hast given me all that I am and all that I possess.
> I surrender it all to thee
> that thou mayest dispose of it according to thy will.
> Give me only thy love
> and thy grace;
> with these I will be rich enough,
> and will have no more to desire.

13

Patience

(Scripture selection — James 1:2-4)

"The virtue of patience is the one which most assures us of perfection," writes St. Francis de Sales in his classic *Introduction to the Devout Life.*

The famous "Bookmark of St. Teresa" comes to mind:

Let nothing disturb you,
Let nothing frighten you.
All things are passing.
God alone does not change.
Patience achieves everything.
Whoever has God lacks nothing.
God alone suffices.

Yes, "patience achieves everything." We could meditate on patience at any time, so essential is it to genuine discipleship. In his beautiful ode to charity, which he terms the foundational Christian trait, St. Cyprian concludes by observing, "Yet, take patience away from it, . . . and it will not last! Take patience away, and it attempts to last without roots or strength."

It is a virtue central to the life of any authentic Christian, is it not? For that matter, it is necessary for success and happiness for any human being, even one without creed. All of humanity longs for it. You will only hear a few confessions before you conclude that it is perhaps the virtue that most escapes people, for all end up confessing, with a sigh, "Do I ever need more patience!" Everyone struggles for it. With customary candor the Little Flower wrote, "Restraining my impatience cost me so much that I was bathed in perspiration." Everyone extols the calm, patient person.

It is a virtue so critical for the priest. Our starting point is always that we are called to be so intimately configured to Christ through the sacrament of holy orders that we act *in persona Christi*. The tradition of the Church refers to the priest as *alter Christus*. Thus, people presume to see in us the same characteristics that made the Eternal High Priest so appealing. And high among those traits would be a patience that approaches the sublime. More than poor preaching, more than a momentary occasion of too much to drink, more than even a sexual fall, perhaps over the years the people of God have been most shocked by priests who are powder kegs, volatile, angry, dismissive — impatient.

More than ever today are there temptations against patience for the good priest. The demands made upon him, the different understandings of his ministry that people have; the expectations multiply, the resources shrink, and the faithful priest is often tempted to blow up, to lash out, to give up, to become tepid, or to leave it behind. Now more than ever is the virtue of patience critical for our vocations.

So this is the grace I hold up to you, one I ask you to think about, pray about, and grow into. Yves Congar has a book entitled *The Need for Patience*, and at the start he describes it for us:

> Patience is a quality of mind — or, rather, of soul — which takes root in these profound existential convictions: first, that God deals the cards and fulfills in us his plan of grace; and second, that for great things, certain delays are necessary for maturation. . . . This profound patience is like the sower who knows the seed will grow. . . . Those who do not know how to suffer no longer know how to hope. The man who is too busy, and who wishes to enjoy immediately the object of his desire, does not know how to attain his goal. The patient sower who confides his seed to the ground and to the sun — he is the man of hope. . . .

Now, how to approach this pivotal virtue of patience? I propose we look at it in three ways: patience with God, patience with ourselves, and patience with others.

First, patience with the Lord. Are you startled that I contend we must work on being patient with God? Be honest: in our pride, do we not really at times think we know better than God? Do we not, in surveying the mess of his creation, sometimes observe that we could do a much more competent job of running the universe? Are we not tempted to run out of patience with him and occasionally yell out, "This is no way to run a railroad"?

I remember a priest beginning a homily once at the funeral of a crib-death baby by saying, "All of us are tempted to say that God has made a terrible mistake." And are we not especially impatient with the Lord's apparent slowness in answering our prayers? I recall once bringing Holy Communion to one of the housebound of the parish, a ninety-year-old lady, right after the Berlin Wall fell, and asking her to pray for an increase in vocations. She responded, "Oh, hell, forget about that. I've been praying since I was seven for the conversion of Russia and look how long it took him to get around to that! I'm sure not going to be around another ninety years for him to take his time answering another prayer!" Boy, I was sorry I asked! But yet was she not honest in expressing a very human impatience with the Lord, one we are all at times tempted to express?

Let's admit that we do become impatient with God in our prayer. The sterility, dryness, and tedium we experience in our prayer life lead us to a discouragement that tempts us to give up. Never has a spiritual director in our seminary ever mentioned anything any of our seminarians have discussed with him, and, yet, I know the major topic each of them pours out his soul about: their impatience in prayer! I know that because it is what I used to and still do talk to my spiritual director about! We grow weary with the discipline, rhythm, and effort fruitful prayer requires, and we just get plumb tired of spending unending hours with nothing happening! We get impatient! Why in the name of God would he make something he so desires — our prayer — so difficult?

In his renowned *Life of St. Anthony*, St. Athanasius recounted an incident from the life of the great desert Father: "Anthony entreated the vision that appeared, saying, 'Where were you? Why did you not appear at the beginning, so that you could stop my distresses?' And a voice came to him: 'I was here, Anthony, but I waited to watch your struggle. And now, since you persevered and were not defeated, I will be your helper forever.'"

Sorry, but that's the way God works in prayer. Father Faber

wrote, "We must wait for God, long, meekly, in the wind and the wet, in the thunder and lightning, in the cold and the dark. Wait, and he will come. He never comes to those who do not wait."

The three essentials the Master himself taught for fruitful prayer are patience, perseverance, and persistence; so beware of that powerful temptation to become discouraged and impatient when our prayer is frustrating and dry.

Maybe that's why the older I get the more I come to appreciate and depend on two great prayers, the divine office and the rosary. Every day the priest patiently turns to his breviary. Some days, it is the only prayer, with his Mass, that he has time for; some days it is approached with less than the fervor it deserves; many times he is tempted to forget it. And yet, he patiently keeps at it, not only because he gave his word as a deacon that he would so pray daily with and for the Church in the liturgy of the hours, but because he patiently trusts that this prayer is efficacious, because through it he prays not alone, but with Christ and his Church.

And how I find myself more and more depending upon the rosary, patiently tolling away the beads, mind wandering, yes, to all the concerns and preoccupations that fill me up, but patiently joining Mary in pondering in my distracted heart the mysteries of the life, death, and resurrection of Jesus, the hinge of all history.

An article in *America* some years back contained an interview with the Confessor of the Faith Archbishop Dominic Tang, imprisoned from 1958 to 1980 by the communists in China:

> Archbishop Tang laughed when I asked him how he spent his time for twenty-two years. "Everyone wants to know that. I prayed. You had to pray. You say the rosary, counting the prayers on your fingers. You try to fill your mind with religious ideas. Otherwise, you are finished! In fact, after so many years, your memory becomes weak and you can't remember. But, everyone knows the rosary. You can say it easily. And saying the rosary includes repeating the whole life of our Lord and the Blessed Mother. . . ."

A patient prayer, the rosary is.

Then there is the impatience with the time it takes for God to answer our prayers. For him, of course, "one day is like a thousand years," while we can hardly think past the next meal. Padre Pio says, "He has promised us that he will answer every prayer, but he has not told us how or when."

We are tempted to impatience with the Lord over our prayer . . . and we can also get upset with him over the problem of evil.

We as priests are ambassadors of Christ, who is love and compassion incarnate. We preach the providence of God, a God who loves and cares for his people, who never abandons them, who holds them in the palm of his hand . . . and then we come face-to-face with suffering, especially of the innocent, and we are tempted to lose patience with him.

The North American College in Rome is right next door to the famous pediatric hospital Bambino Gesù. How often would I sit in the Blessed Sacrament Chapel praising God for his love and his goodness only to have the solitude shattered by the sound of a little baby crying out in fear and pain next door at Bambino Gesù Hospital, and be tempted to say to the Lord, "Where is your love and goodness now?"

I was a priest only three months when I received a call in the middle of the night from the police. A woman in the parish was asking for me at the morgue to come identify the body of her husband. I had just baptized their first baby a few weeks before. The husband, out of work, had succumbed to depression, taken cocaine, driven to a dead-end road, stuffed the exhaust pipe with his undershirt, left the motor running, and sat in the closed car, taking his own life. She, understandably, could not bear to identify the body. I went . . . and then I tried to console her. When I returned I could not get to sleep. That young couple, that new family shattered, that little baby without a father, that young, fragile wife with no husband — how could I reconcile this with a loving God?

Get used to that turmoil, for it can haunt you as a priest and lead you to an impatience with a God who asks trust in the midst of such darkness. And get used to futility that can come when we simply have to say, "I don't know," when one of God's people angrily demands of us, "Why did your God let this happen?"

And, when we confront the evil and immorality of the world,

the stubborn refusal of people to accept God's saving invitation, the blatant disregard for his law, the apathy and lethargy of our people toward their faith, do we not grow impatient with God, and find ourselves like the apostles asking him to rain down fire, or like the crowds begging for a sign to convince people? Yet we have a God who prefers the gentle, soft, quiet way, who never imposes himself, who invites and then waits, who compares the growth of his reign to a tiny seed. We have a God who is eternally patient.

Now, as I am considering patience with God, may I talk about patience with the Church, since we believe the Lord is alive and active in his Church? I contend that we as priests need patience with the Church. Some priests are impatient with the Church because they feel she is too slow, too plodding in renewal, too hesitant in keeping up with contemporary challenges, too cautious to take risks and leave behind outmoded discipline, doctrine, and devotion. Other priests are impatient with the Church for, in their view, being too quick to embrace new ideas, for abandoning her heritage and tradition, and for betraying the deposit of faith.

And yet the wise priest patiently trusts her, conscious of her divinity and her humanity, and, like a faithful husband, loves his spouse whatever happens. You, of course, may remember the words of Cardinal Newman:

> Trust the Church of God implicitly even when your natural judgment would take a different course from hers and would induce you to question her prudence or correctness. Recollect what a hard task the Church has; how she is sure to be criticized and spoken against, whatever she does; recollect how much she needs your loyal and tender devotion; recollect, too, how long is the experience gained in eighteen hundred years; and what a right she has to claim your assent to principles which have had so extended and triumphant trial. Thank her that she has kept the faith safe for so many generations and do your part in helping her to transmit it to generations after you.

Permit me a commercial here: the study of Church history gives you a great sense of patience with the Church. As John Tracy Ellis always said, "Simply put, Church history teaches you that she's been through it all before. You see the Mystical Body of Christ, warts and all, and you conclude that only an institution guided from above could have survived all of this." You know what Arnold Toynbee wrote in his *Study of History*? "I believe that the Catholic Church is divine, and the proof of its divinity I take to be this: that no merely human institution, conducted with such knavish imbecility, would have lasted a fortnight!"

I would like to think that Rome teaches patience with the Church to our seminarians. Yes, we see it at its finest, but we sure see it at times at its worst. Rome certainly teaches patience: remember, it is the only city in the world where *subito* (instantly), *presto* (right away), and *immediatamente* (immediately) are all translated as *domani* (tomorrow). Interesting, a bishop in the U.S. was telling me about a college seminarian in his diocese whom he wanted to send here to Rome because the young man had, in his words, a very triumphalistic, rigid, narrow concept of the Church.

"Strange," I commented, "but could not Rome only reinforce that?"

The bishop, himself an alumnus, wisely remarked, "In my experience, Rome teaches you to loosen up a bit, to laugh with and about the Church, to appreciate her long history, to learn to love her in all the earthiness and clamor of Roman life." Yes, Rome does teach us patience, and that the Church can be rather messy.

Mary Lee Settle, a novelist who won the National Book award in 1978, said that, when she became a Catholic, Walker Percy wrote her a letter of welcome and remarked, "It is a very untidy outfit you're hooking up with, but it's the one thing that will be around till the end."

We priests need to listen to what Pope John Paul II said to young people at the first World Youth Day:

> I should like to ask you, dear young people, for a favor: be patient with the Church! The Church is always a community of weak and imperfect individuals. But God has placed his work of salvation in human hands. This is indeed a great risk but there is no other Church than the one founded by Christ. He wants us human beings to be his collaborators in the world and in the Church with all our deficiencies and shortcomings.

Enough of patience with the Lord, patience especially in our prayer, in confronting evil, and in loving his Bride, the Church.

Now, patience with ourselves. Listen again to St. Francis de Sales: "Be patient with everyone, but above all with yourself. I mean, do not be disturbed with your imperfections, and always rise up bravely from a fall." Ah, well said! You see, we priests, you future priests, are striving for perfection. Studies show men entering the seminary to be some of the most noble idealists around. And, rightly so. We want to be saints. We have heroes such as Jesus, St. Paul, the Curé of Ars, St. Francis of Assisi, Don Bosco, Maximilian Kolbe. All that said, we are then ripe for the temptation to become impatient with ourselves when we fail to measure up, as we almost always do!

And yet wisdom warns us that such impatience with self leads to a discouragement that can deaden us. We fail to meet our goals so we retreat to our rooms, or get crabby, or stay in bed, or begin to drink, or find solace in the arms of an understanding woman. What is the answer? To lower our goals? No! The answer is to be as patient with ourselves as the Lord is with us, to realize his grace is more powerful than our weakness, and to admit that most of our priestly life is patiently stumbling along with his help. So, the greatest tragedy is not in our falling but in our not getting back up. Fulton Sheen says Jesus fell three times on the road to Golgotha because three represents infinity, and so there is no end to the number of times we may fall under the weight of our own crosses.

Now, let's be candid. We especially lose patience with ourselves in our struggle with inclinations to sin, especially to sins of the flesh. Satan is especially potent in convincing us that our struggle to remain pure is a losing battle undertaken only by fools, and that falls should convince us to quit trying. Thus, we lose patience in our battle with sin, whether it be chastity, temper, laziness, drink, a malicious tongue — whatever. Don't listen to him!

As Evelyn Underhill writes, "Patience with ourselves means patience with a growing creature whom God has taken in hand and whose perfection he will complete in his own time and way." And what a vicious circle it becomes! We are trying so desperately to remain sinless, to grow in virtue, and the fall comes . . . the sharp word, the morning sleep-in, the unchaste act, the temper tantrum, the unfair judgment . . . and we lose patience with ourselves, we get discouraged, we wander away from prayer and God's mercy, and sin becomes easier. Ask the recovering alcoholic about the morning after! So down on himself that the only answer is another drink! Can we not be as patient, as gentle, as hopeful, as respectful, as compassionate with ourselves as the Lord is with us?

Two helps in preserving patience with ourselves? Spiritual direction, where one whom we trust and who knows us well can keep us from impatience with ourselves, which leads to wallowing and discouragement, and the sacrament of penance, approached frequently, which effectively restores us to full friendship with our Lord and cuts short the cycle of falling further.

The mystic Julian of Norwich recorded, "I was left to myself in depression, weary of my life and irked with myself, so that I kept the patience to keep going only with difficulty . . . but immediately after this our Lord again gave me comfort and rest of soul in delight and certitude."

Patience with God, patience with ourselves . . . and finally, patience with others. Usually, of course, we approach it the other way, and consider the virtue of patience to mean just with others. I trust you see my point. Odds are we will not be patient with others if we are not patient with the Lord and patient with ourselves first.

I am told by bishops, vocation directors, and pastors that young priests have some problems being patient with people. Believe it or not, I'm even told that some of our alumni go home and get a reputation for quickly becoming impatient with the bishop, with diocesan structures, with the pastor, with the parish ministers, with the teachers at school and the DRE, with the secretary. Of course, it's always the other person's fault. So they want a new assignment . . . so they want to come back for graduate work . . . so they want some time off . . . so no one wants them . . . so they leave. . . .

Wonder why this impatience with others develops?

Well, some have "messiah complexes." The Church, especially as localized in this parish, is going to hell in a handbasket and I am here to save it. Recall that I earlier quoted Cardinal Laghi, who said he worried about priests who considered themselves the Church's messiah because, as he put it, "The Church happens already to have one!"

Then, of course, some are "know-it-alls," who grow impatient with people who do not blindly accept their ready answers to everything.

Then, naturally, some of the impatient ones are particularly aggrieved because they have studied in Rome and thus really know best, and have vests, cuff links, degrees, Italian and Latin phrases, cassocks with silk buttons, strings, and sashes, and some even capes, all to demonstrate a particularly gnostic approach that can justify an arrogant impatience with these poor parochial creatures.

Spare us! Any bishop or pastor would much prefer the man who patiently approaches his assignment, willing to learn, eager to serve, ready to bend, and earning the trust of his people before he starts changing everything.

It is no "call-to-action liberal" but our Holy Father who says that the approach of the Church today must be patient persuasion, earning the trust of people, rather than coercion and authoritarianism.

Several years ago the archdiocese of New York lost a great priest, a member of the seminary faculty, an alumnus of the North American College, at the young age of forty-two, Father Brian Barrett. After his sudden death an interesting story surfaced about a woman journalist. Seems she was covering the story of the papal visit to New York a year-and-a-half ago and was referred to Father Barrett for background in her research. She describes herself then as a radical feminist, an "ex-Catholic" who detested the Church and believed it to be the incarnation of everything she considered backward, repressive, unhealthy, and unhappy. You know the type. She unloaded all the barrels on Father Barrett.

How did he react? You know he had to be tempted to lose his patience with her. Instead, he listened, calmly answered her questions, reasonably explained Church teaching, put up with what she admitted in retrospect were insults and taunts, kept meeting with her, and never lost his cool. The result? She was in tears at his funeral; she has returned to the Church; she now cherishes her faith and loves her religion. He may have been tempted to lob a grenade; instead, he cast a fishing line, and patiently reeled her in . . . and it worked. A soul has been healed and saved.

Now, no doubt about it, you are going to meet people, pastors, brother priests, and pastoral collaborators who could prompt people like the late Mother Teresa to lose her cool! You bet you will at times have to be very firm, to correct abuses, to speak up to preserve the truth, your self-respect, and your peace of mind. All I'm saying is that it is always more laudable, preferable, and more effective if we do so calmly, reasonably, and patiently.

At times the parish priest is called to heroic patience. Hours in the confessional with no one coming; days spent in preparation for a homily and no one listening; your day planned when the pastor tells you at the last minute that you are to take the funeral at 10:00; lonely people who come up to you for a word when you're trying to meditate; servers who drop your new chalice; trying to talk to the Men's Club about a new outreach project to the unchurched when they are much more concerned about the schedule for the horse-shoe tournament; itching to speak to the parents of the First Communion class about the importance of the sacrament when they want to argue about whether or not the girls will wear veils; some dismissing you, even some of your brother priests, as too pious, too traditional, too Roman, without even giving you a chance; some, even your brother priests, forbidding you to do anything new or creative in the parish. We can rant, rave, threaten, cajole, and demand a transfer; or we can be patient, do our best, win their trust, and make a difference.

What helps us maintain our patience with others?

Humility helps: pride, you see, leads to impatience because it tempts us to think we know best and have all the answers. Humility helps us admit that these people, this parish, this assignment — these were all here long before us and will be here long after us, and we are but an instrument. You remember the night prayer of Pope John XXIII: "Well, I did the best I could. . . . It's your Church, Lord! I'm going to bed. Good night."

A sense of humor helps us keep patience with others. It's interesting that, in the Thomistic synthesis, the virtue of patience comes under hope, as does the virtue of joy. If we trust that all is in God's hands, well, it will work out in God's good time, so we might as well patiently work and learn to laugh. Maybe our plans are not the right ones anyway. Listen to this jingle of Father Solanus Casey, the Detroit Capuchin who, God willing, might soon be beatified:

We cook up plans but turn ill
with too much flavoring of self-will.
If this idea comes from heaven
it will grow like leaven.
God demands to use our powers
if we don't spoil his plan with ours.

Another help? Interpreting slights, inconveniences, and less-than-perfect situations as occasions of grace and opportunities to grow in virtue. St. Rose of Lima said, "Without the burdens of afflictions it is impossible to reach the height of grace. The gifts of grace increase as the struggles increase."

A healthy sense of original sin. Do we not believe that there is a fatal flaw in creation, that something is wrong, that, as St. Paul says, "All of creation groans in agony"? Sometimes we get impatient because we expect perfection. I remember two years after I was ordained being elected to the priests' personnel board. At my first meeting on the agenda was the case of a young priest who was asking to be moved after his second very tense assignment with a very trying pastor. I spoke up: "What this priest needs now is to be assigned to a warm, loving, wise, holy pastor." Six pairs of eyes glazed over and six jaws dropped. Finally Archbishop May broke the silence and remarked, "And where in the hell are we going to find him?" Why are we surprised that any situation in which we find ourselves is imperfect, less than ideal, flawed? We will not be assigned with a saint — and neither will they!

Another aid to patience with others? A talent for communication. You see, to remain patient, we must be able to let people know when we are hurt, or disappointed, or upset about something. For, if we do not, it will only fester and erupt. The skill comes in communicating calmly, reasonably, nonjudgmentally, a talent that we are always developing.

And, of course, a childlike trust in God's providence. "We know," Paul writes to the Romans, "that by turning everything to their good, God cooperates with all those who love him, with all those that he has called according to his purpose." His plan will ultimately prevail; he has conquered; he is Lord! How can we be anything but patient with the people and with the situations we are in?

Charles de Foucauld asked, "To be an apostle, yes, but how? To some, without ever saying to them anything about God, being patient as God is patient, being good as God is good." The greatest example of and inspiration for patience is the cross of Christ. I used to bring Holy Communion to a man by the name of Charlie Marsh. He had suffered a paralyzing stroke at a young age. People told me he had been a handsome, vigorous, active, athletic man with the world by the tail when he was felled by the stroke. I used to be amazed at his tranquility, his patience in suffering, his smile. He could only communicate by blinking. One Friday, though, as I stood near him, I noticed he was perplexed, blinking rapidly, his usual composure and smile gone. I summoned Teresa, his wife, who said, "Oh, Father, please move aside a bit. Charlie always likes to look at the crucifix on the wall and you are blocking his view."

So that explained the smile, the peace, the patient resignation. His unimaginable sufferings were united with those of Jesus on the cross; he garnered inner strength and patience from the example of our Lord's patient endurance. Should not we all, especially those of us who sense the call to be configured to the Priest who offered himself on the cross?

Many of you — especially those in Alcoholics Anonymous — know by heart the opening words of Reinhold Niebuhr's famous prayer. But listen to it as a fitting prayer on patience:

> God, grant me the serenity
> to accept the things I cannot change,
> courage to change the things I can,
> and wisdom to know the difference.
>> Living one day at a time;
>> enjoying one moment at a time;
>> accepting hardship as the pathway to peace.
> Taking, as he did,
> this sinful world as it is,
> not as I would have it.
>> Trusting that he will make
>> all things right
>> if I surrender to his will.

That I may be reasonably happy
in this life,
and supremely happy
with him forever in the next.
  Amen.

14

Simplicity of Life

(Scripture selection — Mark 10:17-31)

When I was doing graduate studies in Church history at The Catholic University of America in Washington, D.C., I used to drive back to St. Louis at Christmas and summer for a visit home. The midway point on that fourteen-hour drive was Zanesville, Ohio. Except for its "Y" bridge and the Zane Grey Museum, it was not worth much of a stop, but I enjoyed spending the night with the Dominican Fathers at their parish right off Highway 70.

I always relished a visit with a crusty but wise old Dominican assigned there, and we would usually chat for a half-hour or so after supper. The frugality of his room always amazed me: one room, which served as his bedroom and study, one closet with all his clothing, one bookshelf, a desk, a crucifix, a few religious and family pictures, a reading chair, and a lamp. That was it.

On one visit I remarked, "Your room is so plain. Where do you keep the rest of your stuff?"

"This is it," he replied.

"But it is so simple," I countered.

"Well, if I walk down to your room all you've got is your suitcase!"

"Well, sure, but, after all, I'm just passing through."

Never will I forget his reply, "Aren't we all?"

"I'm just passing through." "Aren't we all?" I sometimes wonder if my four years of graduate work were all worth it for the wisdom of that remark from that wise old Dominican.

And thus I want to address the topic of simplicity of life. I do not mind admitting to you that simplicity of life is a tough subject upon which to elaborate. Some have correctly observed that simplicity of life for a diocesan priest is not the same as the vow of poverty in a religious, since, as a matter of fact, we diocesan priests can own things, and must be concerned about material matters

185

such as bills, taxes, cars, clothes, insurance, and retirement. As the wags say, "Religious priests take the vow of poverty; diocesan priests live it!" Father Michael Curran tells me that so many parishes in Brooklyn have purchased the famous and costly vestments from the Cistercians in Spencer that it is said "the diocesan clergy has gone broke keeping the monks poor."

Anyway, you get my point: simplicity of life is easier said than done, easier to cite in violation than in obedience, vague, open to different interpretations, but — and here we all agree — crucial to every sincere disciple of Christ, essential to those who claim to act *in persona Christi* as a priest.

Maybe it would help to look closely at why simplicity of life is, in fact, so crucial. The easiest answer is that Jesus said it was. By his example — the Son of God, who emptied himself of all honor, glory, riches, and security, born in a stable, fleeing in exile, raised in utterly ordinary circumstances, without a home or profession, whose only possession was his tunic, who had nowhere to lay his head, who was buried in a borrowed tomb — by his example, and by his teaching, can you think of anything he warned us about more than riches, anything he extolled more than a simple life trusting in Providence? Jesus canonized simplicity of life.

So, I suppose that is the real reason for our desire to lead a simple life: because our Master taught us to by word and example. But we can still ask, "Why?" Why did Jesus consider simplicity of life so essential? I suggest five possible reasons.

For one, because too many possessions keep us from God. It's that practical. A life of ease, comfort, luxury, and accumulating material things distracts us from God and tempts us to think that true happiness can come from what we have and not who we are, namely children of God, made in his image, redeemed by the precious blood of his Son, destined to love him and live with him forever.

"Satan now is wiser than of yore, / and tempts by making rich, not making poor. . . ," writes Alexander Pope, realizing that riches can keep us from God. "Be not anxious about what you have, but about who you are," exhorts Gregory the Great, anticipating the modern heresy of equating worth with what we do, what we possess, what we earn, not with who we are.

This, of course, is the poverty of spirit that our Lord places first among the beatitudes: that humble, childlike recognition of our utter nothingness, our total dependence upon our heavenly Father for everything. Thus, in a spiritual way, the rich can be poor if they take their possessions in stride, do not depend on them, share them generously, and do not let them blind them to the real wealth of God, while one poor materially can be so consumed by desire for riches that he is worse off than the wealthy.

As St. Augustine writes, "A man's poverty is judged by the disposition of his heart, not by his coffers." But that is rare, isn't it, because we know that luxury, possessions, comfort, and security usually so bloat us and so choke our spirits that we merit all the maledictions the Savior heaped upon the rich, while those who voluntarily avoid accumulation and high living foster a poverty of spirit that helps them reach God. And that, in a nutshell, is the why of simplicity: because the one who practices simplicity of life is freer to reach God, the supreme possession. In the stark words of Anthony of the Desert: "The more one practices simplicity in his life, the more he is at peace, for he is not full of cares about many things. . . . But, when we cling to things, we become liable to vexations arising from them and are led away from God. Thus, our desire for many things fills us with turmoil and we wander into darkness."

As Father Robert Dillon said to me once, simplicity of life is not an end in itself but a means to an end, namely closer union with God.

A second reason justifying simplicity of life is that it fosters a solidarity with the poor. Do you realize how fortunate we are even to have the option to live simply? Most of the world is forced to! When we voluntarily embrace a simple life free from riches, ease, luxury, and possessions, we are closer to the poor of the world, who are the Lord's chosen ones. Thus, justice and a sense of passionate care for those burdened by poverty are fostered by the simple life. St. Augustine again: "Find out how much God has given you, and from it, take what you need; the remainder which you do not require is needed by others. The superfluities of the rich are the necessities of the poor. Those who retain what is superfluous possess the goods of others."

Or, listen to Tolstoy: "I am a participant in a crime so long as I have superfluous food and another has none."

A simplicity of life, then, leads to a sharing of goods and re-sources, so that all may have enough — that is justice, that is good, that is the way God wants it to be.

A third reason for simplicity of life is that it serves as a power-ful reminder that "only in God is my soul at rest," that nothing in this life, no person, no gain, and no possession will last forever or eternally satisfy us. Only God can do that, and we're asking for trouble, sorrow, and frustration if we seek true, lasting happiness from anything or anyone in this life.

A fourth reason for simplicity of life is that it encourages us to trust in Divine Providence instead of just ourselves or our posses-sions. The more we have, the more secure, comfortable, cozy, and pleasant our life, the less we count on God to give us what we really need.

And, a final reason for simplicity of life, most appropriate to the priest, is that it is a good example. Yes, there is a didactic, catechetical value to a priest's simplicity of life, as he thus teaches his people poverty of spirit and encourages them to justice.

Likewise is it a particularly gross counter-example when a priest leads a life of opulence, luxury, and comfort. When Archbishop Gaetano Bedini wrote a report on the state of the Catholic Church in the United States to Pius IX back in 1853 (the same report, by the way, which urged the foundation of an American College in the Eternal City), while praising the clergy in the new Republic, he noted three flaws: alcohol, sexual immorality, and avarice, or a selfish desire for money. Such a report, I contend, could be written today, and could certainly apply to priests in countries besides our own. Can any of us forget the scene from *Angela's Ashes* where the finest food to grace the McCourt table came when the desperate mother was able to push her way through the crowd surrounding the back porch of the rectory as the cook gave out the leftovers from the priest's table?

So, priests and future priests are impelled to the simple life not just because the Master requires it, not just because it makes it easier to reach God, not just because it promotes a more just society, not just because it reminds us that only God can ultimately satisfy us, not only because it prompts trust in Providence, but because it gives good example, and because not to do it gives grave scandal.

Having reviewed the reasons for simplicity of life, allow me now to make some observations about its practice.

Simplicity of life in practice is good not only in itself but because it undergirds the other virtues expected of a priest. I was just reading a talk Cardinal John O'Connor gave to Father Benedict Groeschel's Franciscans of the Renewal in which he stated: "Poverty is the fundamental virtue because all things flow from that: poverty of the will, that we call obedience; poverty of the desires of the body, that we call chastity; and then the obvious poverty, freedom from material possessions. Poverty is the ultimate freedom."

How true that is, that simplicity of life undergirds the other virtues expected of a priest: obedience, as we do not cling to our own wishes for assignments, our own advancement, and our own résumé and curriculum vitae, but let go of our ambition and place our future in the hands of our bishop. How I have admired some men at the college in Rome who suddenly have plans changed in mid-course, who were promised a fifth year and then had it taken away, or who were told they would come home after four, begin to look forward to that, and then be told to stay for a license; who are told to concentrate in a field they would not personally have selected, or given a pastoral year they really did not want. How I admire them when they shrug, admit disappointment, but then accept it gracefully. That obedience stems from a simplicity of life, does it not, as we try not to become attached to our own plans, designs, or ambitions.

And such detachment characterizes healthy, effective chastity as we never become absorbed in another person. We belong purely and completely to Jesus and his Church, and no other person has an exclusive claim on our love, as a husband and wife so beautifully do in matrimony.

Pastoral charity likewise depends upon simplicity of life. If our lives are cluttered with possessions, eating, drinking, shopping, expensive travel, and excessive socializing, then we lack the time, energy, and drive to pour ourselves out in generous service to our people. We find ourselves sated, aimless, going from one party to the next, one dinner out to another, one store or shop to another, too groggy to care for the souls entrusted to our care with the competence, interest, and attention they deserve. That's maybe why

Pope John Paul II refers to pastoral poverty as so necessary for a priest in his exhortation *Pastores Dabo Vobis*.

So, yes, a simplicity of life provides the freedom upon which other necessary priestly virtues can build.

A second observation on simplicity of life is that we can violate it in ways other than having too much money or possessions. We can fail to live simply in other ways.

One of these ways would be a sense of restlessness and distraction that always leaves us looking for new interests, new entertainment, new fads. We run from silence, quiet, and privacy. We cannot stand our own company. The famous quote of Blaise Pascal comes to mind: "The sole cause of man's unhappiness is that he does not know how to stay quietly in his room." I remember the first time I made a traditional eight-day Ignatian retreat as a young priest. No books but the Bible and the breviary, no mail or phone, absolute silence except for the daily meeting with the director. I went buggy! The fourth night I found myself lingering after supper carefully reading the ingredients listed on the label of the ketchup bottle.

A simple life means one that is uncluttered, uncomplicated. That does not mean such a life lacks seriousness or depth, but that it comes from within, from our ministry, not from noise, entertainment, possessions, or novelty. The priest leading a simple life longs for a quiet evening by himself in his room, and for him time alone to think, plan, pray, or read is more refreshing than an expensive dinner out and front-row seats at the theater. He likes his own company. As the old saying goes, he enjoys the "simple things of life," and longs for silence, solitude, and simple joys.

A second attitude that can violate simplicity of life is an inordinate attachment to any person, place, or thing besides Christ and his Church. A wise priest I know said about celibacy something that could just as well apply to pastoral poverty: "I know some priests who have fallen in love with a bottle of scotch or a set of golf clubs. If you're going to violate celibacy, a woman is probably more preferable."

Crude, but he had a point: no person, place, thing, hobby, pursuit, sport, friend, family member, possession, goal, or ambition should have dominion over a priest — only Christ and his Church should. Anything else violates, among other things, simplicity of life. A friend of mine, a pastor of a huge parish, finally got an older priest to help him out. The only thing he asked him to do besides daily Eucharist was take Mass at the local nursing home every Wednesday at 10:00 a.m., a time established for years that was convenient for the staff, residents, and many volunteers from the parish who assisted.

"Nope," the older priest replied. "I've had Wednesday morning tee-off time for twenty years, and I am not going to change it." Hardly correct priorities!

Thirdly, let's get practical. Let's look at concrete ways of ascertaining whether we as priests and future priests are living simple lives of pastoral poverty. The following are some areas of challenge and possible danger.

Clothes: I invite you to look in your closets, drawers, trunks, under your bed — wherever you keep your clothes — and recall what you have stored at home and ask if you dress simply. That, of course, is one of the two reasons for clerical garb; the other being the outward identification, namely that we do not need too many clothes because we have a uniform. Now, that can be violated, too, can't it? On the one hand you have fellows whose clergy shirts are so faded or whose suits and shoes are so old and dirty that they look like slobs. On the other hand you have guys who spend more on cassocks with water-silk sashes and cloth-covered buttons, on gold cuff links and a half-dozen tailor-made vests than their fathers would on their best suits. Both extremes are wrong.

We need enough clothes to be clean, presentable, comfortable, and healthy. We handle sacred objects, we are present at the most important events in people's lives, so we owe it to them to be clean and presentable. The Talmud teaches that "poverty does not mean dirt." Do not mistake simplicity in dress with sloppiness and unkemptness. Yet we avoid flashy, ostentatious dress, both informally and in clerics.

People will give us a lot of clothes as priests, and we gratefully accept them and, if appropriate, use them. You get so many, though, that sooner or later you just have to give some away. The real danger is not in the clothes we are given, but in what we are tempted to buy. Simple, clean, presentable — these are the important adjectives.

Be careful, too, about overly expensive vestments. Every parish should have beautiful solemn vestments, usually one set for Sundays and feast days, another for weekdays. I think every priest is entitled to a special vestment for his first Mass, that he then might use for special occasions the rest of his priesthood. I don't mind telling you, though, that it does bother me when men here buy very expensive vestments, in every liturgical color, and then go home to their first assignment and ignore the vestments that the parish already has, thus coming across as a bit supercilious and fussy. In general, parishes, not priests, buy vestments.

Cars are another trouble spot for priests. On the one hand, you need a dependable, comfortable, durable car, for a priest spends a lot of time in one. On the other hand, a luxury car owned by a priest can be scandalous. When Monsignor Yarrish and I worked at the Apostolic Nunciature in Washington, I was impressed by the guidelines issued by the Secretariat of State that papal representatives were not to be in cars considered "luxury" by the country in which they were assigned, which for us means a Cadillac, Lincoln, or Mercedes. If it is scandalous for the papal nuncio to own one, it certainly is for a parish priest. Of course, today some priests drive jeeps or pickup trucks that are nearly as expensive. Yes, cars can tempt our simplicity of life.

Vacation and travel are also problem areas. Every priest deserves a vacation now and then, and travel is one of the legitimate perks we have. But I think you will agree with me that many priests give scandal not only by how many vacations they take, but by how luxurious and exotic they are.

Going out to eat: a good friend of mine says that priests know the finest restaurants. I'm afraid we have that reputation. In one way, a fine meal out at a nice restaurant with good friends is perfectly acceptable. It is a legitimate, healthy source of relaxation and enjoyment for us. The problem comes if we do it too often, and if we begin to prefer the expensive places. In general, you should not go out to eat more than one evening a week.

Machinery: a contemporary temptation to simplicity of life comes with what I call "machinery" or gadgets; VCR's, TV's, stereos, elaborate computers in constant need of upgrading. It just seems that priests and future priests often get addicted to what women call "male toys," always buying the latest gadget and equipment. Of course, what can happen is that the technology (computers, telephones, e-mail) that was supposed to save us time so we can better serve God's people devours our time and becomes a distraction to the simplicity of life we long for.

There are exceptions, but I have never met a priest who owned property — a cabin, condo, apartment, place in the country, a home, or a boat — who did not admit that if he was not careful, it could begin to interfere with his priestly ministry. Property takes time, money, taxes, repairs, and attention, all of which can be detrimental to simplicity of life. True, I know of some priests who have very modest places that are affordable, easily maintained, and generously shared with others. These, though, are the first to admit that you have to be careful about property. Such a caution also applies to memberships in clubs. With more and more men becoming priests after a lay career, the ownership of property becomes a real question of concern.

A seventh and probably most dangerous threat to pastoral poverty is money. We know how the Master has warned us about the threat of money. It has ruined more good priests than booze or sex. We can become money-hungry selfish bachelors whose pursuit of the "good life" makes evangelical poverty a sham. Thus, a cultivation of the proper use of money is a necessity for a man preparing for the priesthood. May I list a few questions you should be asking yourself now to make sure that you are not serving mammon rather than God?

Are you in debt? I'm talking about stores and shops, phone bills, credit cards — a quick way to have money enslave you is to get in debt. Certain debts, such as college tuition or car payments, are unavoidable. Just make sure you are paying them off in a timely, responsible, consistent fashion.

Do you live within your means? A few years ago a man came to me at the college for financial help for Christmas travel. He explained that he had no money for travel, and could I help. I was happy to do so, and have a limited fund for such purposes. "How much do you need?" I asked him.

"Oh, about twelve hundred dollars."

I was shocked. "Where are you going?" I inquired.

"Turkey," he replied. Now that is living beyond your means. I was happy to give him three hundred dollars for a less glamorous trip, say to Florence or Siena. But, if you have no money, you don't go to exotic places. If you're behind on your phone bill, you stop making phone calls. We live within our means. If we have a constant battle living within our budget, that indicates a fiscal immaturity that will harass our resolve to live in pastoral poverty.

Do you find yourself doing things just for the money, or ingratiating yourself with people in the hopes of gaining a benefactor? People are generous with priests, and, if not careful, we can find ourselves courting people whom we believe can be financially beneficial to us and avoiding those who are not.

A final threat to evangelical simplicity is excess. Our simplicity of life is intended to increase our pastoral effectiveness, our joy, and our zeal, not to dampen it. Our Catholic tradition savors a good time, celebrations, a passion and zest for living, food, drink, arts, entertainment, music, a prudent use of God's many good natural gifts. Our evangelical poverty, then, never turns us into somber, puritanical crabs who live to make sure nobody else is having a good time. So a few caveats about possible excesses in the area of simplicity of life:

In his talk referred to earlier, Cardinal O'Connor warns against a lack of authenticity in the pursuit of poverty. "Even poverty can become a sham," he says. "Even poverty can become a cause of pride, of arrogance, of vanity. 'I am poorer than you are, and so I must be holier than you are.'" Yes, how true. Genuine simplicity of life by its nature would not draw attention to itself, would not show off.

Nor would it damage our health. You may think it a practice of poverty not to buy a new coat or new shoes, but it is hardly so if your feet get wet and your chest frozen and you end up in bed with a bad cold. Your laudable attempt to be temperate with food, drink, and sleep is counterproductive if you end up weak and sick.

And your admirable efforts not to go out too often, to be careful about too many videos, too much TV, or too many vacations, would backfire if you turned into a moody, carping, reclusive bore.

Simplicity of life by its nature avoids excess, and leads to a healthier, more effective, more joyful life.

I bring these observations on various aspects of simplicity of life to a close by mentioning what we can do to foster it, conscious that we too often dwell on what to avoid, what we should not do. Yes, there are positive aids to develop simplicity of life.

One is plain, raw generosity, as we give away the money, clothing, and possessions we do not need. A good priest-friend of mine every New Year's Eve sits down with his checkbook and writes checks to different charities until he has but one hundred dollars left. Now, he is not irresponsible about it, because he makes sure all his debts are paid, has a savings account to take care of his annual vacation, to help pay for his next car, and to take care of an emergency. That's just prudent stewardship. But, he gives away the excess every year. That's his way of fostering simplicity of life. One man here told me that, if he goes out more than one night a week, he has promised to give the same amount he spends at the restaurant to the local soup kitchen. Such practices enhance simplicity of life.

A second help to maintaining pastoral poverty is in periodically asking yourself if you are beginning to count on certain possessions or habits of comfort. Material goods are fine as long as we do not become dependent upon them. So, ask yourself if your worth, your inner peace, would be shattered if you had to part with something.

They say when the stock market crashed in 1929, the atheists jumped out of windows, and the people of faith went back to work. A blessing we priests have is that we move often, and, when we do, we usually clear away those things nonessential. I was once complaining about packing up and moving when a brother priest commented, "It sure beats a fire." A priest I know will only move with him what fits in his car — the rest he gives away. The Missionaries of Charity must be able to fit all their earthly possessions in their one cloth bag. We are not Missionaries of Charity, but we are called to the simple life, and thus periodically we should take inventory to see if our life is becoming too cluttered, our minds too dulled, or our souls bloated by too many riches, comforts, and possessions.

Make sure you remain close to the poor. Yes, it is easy for me to visit with wealthy benefactors, but tough to see the man at the gate who is looking for a job. Some priests love black-tie dinners with the Knights of Malta but scoff at the fish fry with the Knights of

Columbus. A good priest makes more time for the poor than he does for the rich, and is really helped by them, as his attempt to live simply is promoted by his genuine love for those who yearn to be accepted only for who they are and not what they can do for him. Likewise does frequent contact with the needy help us to appreciate what we have, and prod spoiled consciences to live more modestly in keeping with the Gospel.

And, as a final help, cultivate friendships with salt-of-the-earth laypeople who help you keep your feet on the ground. My family does that. When I visit my sisters and brothers and their families I realize how good I got it. They could never go out for dinner as often as I do, or travel like I do, or shop like I can — all in moderation, of course. They are on lean budgets with bills, tuition, repairs, and doctors to pay. No wonder my brother-in-law works two jobs so his wife and six kids can have a decent life. And every Sunday they take from what they need, not from the extra but from the essential, and put that money into their envelope to support the Church they love so that we priests can live high on the hog and complain about the tough life we have. You make sure as a priest you have two or three wholesome families where you feel at home and where you are brought back to earth. They keep us sane and simple.

Every Christmas Eve I notice an Italian man at our Mass at the North American College. His suit was obviously bought twenty years and forty pounds ago, and never cleaned since; his tie has evidence of last Christmas Eve's cannelloni on it; he has the Mass prayers all wrong and knocks us all off key with his attempts to sing the Christmas carols at Mass; he knows no one here by name . . . yet, he is here every year, on top of the world, happy as can be, right at home, as he comes to Mass and joins us for dinner. To tell you the truth, I was getting a bit irritated with him.

After all these years I finally asked him who he was, and he explained that he lives on the side of the hill, along the steep steps down from Sant'Onofrio, and that he has been coming here to the college on Christmas Eve for eleven years, ever since his wife and daughter, the only family he had, died. This, he smiled, was his Christmas, and here he felt welcome and at home, the men always warm and courteous. How simple can you get? God forbid our lives would ever be too cluttered, too complicated, too fussy, or too distracted to appreciate someone like that. Forgive me, but welcoming a man like that is the college at its best. That's simplicity of life.

You probably know the following by heart, but allow me to read it again to help us focus on our model, our motive, for simplicity of life: Jesus.

> He was born in an obscure village,
> the child of ordinary people.
> He grew up in a small town in a carpenter shop
> until he was thirty.
> Then for three years he was an itinerant preacher.
> He never wrote a book.
> He never held an office.
> He never had a family or owned a house.
> He didn't go to college.
> He did none of the things one usually associates with
> greatness.
> He had no credentials but himself.
> He was only thirty-three when the tide of public opinion
> turned against him.
> His friends ran away.
> He was turned over to his enemies
> and went through the mockery of a trial.
> He was nailed to a cross between two thieves.
> While he was dying his executioners gambled for his clothing,
> the only property he had on earth.
> When he was dead, he was laid in a borrowed grave
> through the pity of a friend.
> Nineteen centuries have come and gone,
> and today he is the central figure of the human race
> and the leader of mankind's progress.
> All the armies that ever marched, all the navies that
> ever sailed, all the parliaments that ever sat,
> all the kings that ever reigned, put together,
> have not affected the life of man on this earth as much
> as that One Solitary Life.

15

Joy

(Scripture selection — Philippians 4:4-7)

As a priest assigned in Washington, D.C., I used to have the privilege of assisting occasionally at the Gift of Peace House, in the northeastern corner of the capital, a hospice for dying AIDS patients conducted by Mother Teresa's Missionaries of Charity. On Good Friday, 1989, I was celebrant of the Liturgy of the Lord's Passion for the sisters, volunteers, and patients. After the assembly had venerated the cross, two sisters led me upstairs so that the bedridden patients could kiss the feet of our Lord on the cross.

As I went from bed to bed, I noticed one emaciated man in the corner who seemed agitated, and kept beckoning to me to come to him. As I began in turn to approach his bed, the sister halted me, warning that this man was unusually violent, hateful to all, and had actually attempted to bite the attending sisters a number of times. Of course, you realize the consequences of being bitten by one with AIDS. However, the poor man kept signaling for me to come near. What was I to do? What would any priest do? Slowly, cautiously, I approached, and carefully extended the crucifix, which he grasped and kissed — not the feet, I remember so vividly — but the face of the crucified Lord. He then lay back down, exhausted.

The next day, Holy Saturday, the sisters called to tell me that the same man had asked to see me. I went, and, again, in company with two of the sisters as "bodyguards," approached him. As I got nearer he whispered, "I want to be baptized!"

I moved a few inches closer, and, expressing satisfaction, asked if he could explain to me why he desired to enter the Church. "I know nothing about Christianity or the Catholic Church," he said, with the little bit of strength he had left. "In fact, I have hated religion all my life. All I do know is that for three months I have been here dying. These sisters are always happy! When I curse them, they look at me with compassion in their eyes. Even when they clean up my vomit, bathe my sores, and change my diapers, they are smiling; when they spoon-feed me, there is a radiance in their eyes. All I know is that they have joy and I don't. When I ask them in desperation why they are so happy, all they answer is 'Jesus.' I want this Jesus. Baptize me and give me this Jesus! Give me joy!"

Never as a priest has it brought me more satisfaction to baptize, anoint, and give first Holy Communion to someone. He died at 3:15 on Easter morning.

"Joy," wrote the French philosopher Léon Bloy, "is the most infallible sign of God's presence." Faith, hope, love, humility, zeal, penance, fidelity, chastity, penance, and joy — these are all virtues critical in the life of a priest. At first glance, joy might not seem to rank up there too high in the pantheon of priestly virtues, but I exhort you to look again. A priest without joy is an oxymoron, but, my brothers, as you well know, "their name is legion," I am afraid.

When I was an assistant at Little Flower Parish back in St. Louis, I met with our parish vocation committee and asked them what we priests and nuns in the parish could do to encourage young people to consider a vocation to the priesthood or religious life. One crusty old guy spoke up, "Well, you can begin by being happy! Show us you love your work and enjoy your life! Be joyful!" Not bad advice.

None other than Andrew Greeley wonders if the major reason for the decline in vocations is simply that we priests and religious have turned into crabs, worried about the future, overwhelmed by work, complaining about everything, fretting about our lives, feeling sorry for ourselves, and taking ourselves way too seriously. Who wants to join an outfit such as that?

I remember being a new student at the North American College in October, 1972, when the cardinal-vicar of Rome, Angelo Dell'Acqua, had the opening Mass for the seminary academic year at St. Peter's Basilica. As he looked out at thousands of priests, sisters, and seminarians, he concluded his homily by saying, "Now I have a favor to ask each of you." We expected some heroic sacrifice or great exhortation to sanctity and scholarship. Instead, he asked, "As you walk the streets of Rome, please smile" — a favor that, as you realize, has yet to be granted.

"If the world saw our happiness," wrote St. Madeleine Sophie

Barat, "it would, out of sheer envy, invade our churches, houses, and retreats, and the times of the Fathers of the Desert would return when the solitudes were more populous than the cities."

Yes, joy is what most often attracts people to the Church. Catholics are not Puritans. Chesterton has defined a Puritan as "one who lives in mortal fear that someone somewhere might be having a good time!" I remember once preparing a young couple for marriage; she was Catholic, he was Presbyterian. He at first showed absolutely no interest in the Church, but, after a couple of months, he stopped to see me and told me he wanted to find out more about the Church. "Why?" I inquired, figuring it was some teaching or practice of the Church that may have affected him.

"Well, I've gotten to know Deidre's family so well since we got engaged and, well, they seem to enjoy life, they are so happy." Good Catholics usually are.

Once I was taking a trip through Germany with my first pastor after he had retired. We started in the north of Germany and, by day three, we entered the south, Bavaria. Now, the two of us had gone incognito, and the tour guide had no idea we were priests. As we entered Bavaria, she said, "You'll notice a big change now. Up north, people work hard, there is a lot of industry, the folks are more somber, and life looks drab. Down here, look at the flowers, the painted homes, the chubby, smiling people, lots of kids, good food, dancing, song, and lots of beer." She concluded, "The north is Protestant, the south is Catholic."

Remember Chesterton's great jingle?

> Wherever a Catholic sun doth shine,
> There's plenty of laughter and good red wine.
> God grant that it be ever so,
> Benedicamus Domino!

Now, please keep in mind that, when I say joy, I mean that interior peace about which St. Paul speaks that gives rise to an exterior happiness. I do not mean some giggly, unrealistic, Pollyannaish mania. These people get on your nerves and usually deep down are not at peace. Joy makes us carefree but never careless. A pastor told me about his assistant, a very irresponsible man

201

who laughed a lot, not showing up one Friday morning, meaning the pastor had the two scheduled morning Masses and then the funeral the assistant was supposed to take. When the guy finally showed up he explained that he had just been carried away by joy out in the countryside and decided to spend the night and enjoy nature. The pastor told him to go back out to the country because he didn't need him around anymore. Genuine joy is realistic, responsible, prudent, deep, and reasonable, not some hollow, empty-headed, childish put-on.

It makes sense that if the Church is joyful, its shepherds, its pastors, its priests had better be men of joy, for, if we are not, we make the "good news" a lie. If we as priests are to be joyful, we better find out how to get there.

So, let me ask, where does this joy come from? What is the source of our joy? Of course, joy comes from the Lord, who plants it in the heart of the believer.

Thus you know that St. Paul lists joy as one of the fruits of the Holy Spirit, a grace, a charism given by God. I could spend a long time giving a list of the ways God is the source of our joy, but let me concentrate on four.

First is the conviction that God loves us. As St. Ignatius recognized in his spiritual exercises, the first step in all growth in holiness is the recognition of God's overwhelming love for me, completely unmerited, totally undeserved. My second grade teacher taught us to pray every day: "Sacred Heart of Jesus, I place all my trust in thee! / Sacred Heart of Jesus, I believe in your love for me!"

I was in the middle of preparation for this chapter on joy when we came to the Office of Readings for the Tuesday of the third week of Easter, where St. Augustine speaks of Easter joy and its source: we cannot love unless someone has loved us first. Listen to the Apostle John: "We love God because he first loved us." The source of our love for God can only be found in the fact that God loved us first. "The love of God has been poured into our hearts."

"Sacred Heart of Jesus, I believe in your love for me!" That profound conviction that God loves us can cause nothing but joy. The priest is constantly aware of God's infinite love for him, and is eager to convince others of the fact that God loves them as well. To be every moment of our lives fully convinced of God's love for me, to bask in it, to accept it, to express gratitude for it, and to return it in love to God is, of course, the secret of real joy.

A second source of joy flows from this conviction of God's unconditional love for us, namely a belief that he actually dwells within us through the gift of sanctifying grace.

I was a priest for only eight months when I got the toughest convert I've ever had. The parish was holding a mission, and on the third evening a man about my age approached me. He introduced himself as a professor of mathematics from nearby Washington University, and he expressed an interest in Catholicism. Well, for six months I intellectually wrestled with him, going through instructions, knock-down-drag-out fights to all hours of the night during our weekly sessions. Finally, when I completed all the instructions, at our last meeting, he said to me: "You know, there's one point of Catholic teaching I can't accept at all."

"What is it?" I asked, presuming it was going to be one of the regulars, like the Real Presence, the sacrament of penance, the role of our Lady, or the teaching authority of the pope.

How surprised I was when he went on: "Way back at the beginning, you taught me about something called 'sanctifying grace.' I must have misunderstood you because I thought you explained that sanctifying grace means that the very life of God actually dwells in the soul of the believer, that we literally share in God's life. I obviously misunderstood you, because that would just be too good to be true."

"You understood me perfectly well," I replied. There was a man who fully appreciated the gift of sanctifying grace.

If we not only believe that God loves us passionately, but actually dwells in our soul, you tell me how we can be anything but joyful. To be gratefully aware of God's indwelling then becomes a real source of joy. He will never extinguish that life; only we can do it by mortally offending him, and then that sanctifying grace can be restored simply for the asking through the sacrament of penance. Thus the deep joy of a good confession.

That supernatural life, imparted in baptism, must, like natural life, be nourished and cared for, and that is done through prayer, practice of virtue, and the sacraments. A great source of joy is daily worthy reception of the Holy Eucharist. St. Ephrem realized this back in the fourth century when he wrote: "In Your sacrament we daily embrace You and receive You into our hearts; we have had Your treasure hidden within us ever since we received baptismal grace; it grows ever richer at Your sacramental table. Teach us to find *joy* in Your favor."

That we here would have God's own life within us fanned into a flame through our participation in the Eucharist first thing each morning is a genuine blessing, one that would, God willing, be a source of joy all through the day.

So, a second cause of joy is a humble, grateful, awesome, constant awareness of the indwelling of the Trinity, sanctifying grace, deep within our soul. You tell me how we can be mean, spiteful, depressed, if we really believe that at the core of our being God is living with us? As Abbott Marmion wrote, "Joy is the echo of God's life within us."

The third font of joy is a trust, a hope in Divine Providence. If, as is our rock-sure belief, the Lord is omnipotent, all is in his fatherly hands, Jesus has conquered sin, Satan, and death, and, as St. Paul teaches, "all works together for those who have faith," why would sorrow, distress, and setbacks extinguish our joy? The flame may flicker, the winds may threaten to blow it out, but, ultimately, all is in his hands, and all will work out according to his plan. A simple, childlike trust in his Providence gives rise to a joy, a tranquility that no sorrow can dispel.

This is why we are so inspired by the joy often evident in those who, from a human point of view, should be in desperation. Wait until, as a priest, you are struck by the interior joy you detect in the poor and the sick. I suppose it has to be because, without any human resources, they have to exhibit total trust in Divine Providence. You will bring Holy Communion to sick people who, in the midst of agonizing pain and infirmity, radiate an interior serenity and happiness. You will visit people who literally have no idea where their next meal is coming from, but yet are people of joy. And, then, you will come into contact with wealthy, powerful, strong, healthy people who are catty, petty, angry, and unhappy.

Back home in St. Louis there is a group of physicians who each summer spend two weeks in Haiti. I remember once convincing a pediatrician in our parish to go. He did, and, when he returned, he was beaming. When I asked him what impressed him most, he answered immediately, "The joy of the people! We went into the most destitute conditions I ever saw: mud shacks, families crowded into them, and sick children, and yet the people were happy! They welcomed us and shared with us the little they had. And here, at home," he concluded, "we have so much and seem so sad." Again, that joy has to have its source in a trust in Divine Providence, since they have no one else to hope in.

The final font of joy is prayer. The vocabulary of trust in Divine Providence is, of course, prayer. Think back to our opening passage from Scripture: "Present your needs to God in every form of prayer and in petitions full of gratitude."

Now, prayer is a source of joy in two key ways. For one, since, as has been mentioned, joy is a virtue, a charism, a gift from the Lord, well, then, if we don't have it, or if we desire more of it, we ask for it through prayer.

Secondly, though, the conviction that we can approach God for mercy, help, and direction is a great boost to joy, is it not? That we can give over to God our anxieties and worries removes a serious reason not to be joyful. What do we do with the myriad of naturally valid reasons to be fretting, sullen, and unhappy? We submit them to the Lord in prayer, leaving them to his care, and then, we can be joyful. This seems to be what Charles de Foucauld had in mind when he wrote: "O God, how good you are to allow us to call you 'Our Father.' What gratitude, what joy, what love, and, above all, what confidence this should inspire in me. And as you are my Father and my God, how perfectly I should always hope in you."

Well, as I said, I could expand on sources of joy, but I had better go on to things that can sap our joy. There are many threats to the joy that should exude from Christ's priests, you know, and stay with me now as I try to mention a few of them.

A real peril to joy is self-pity. Priests today can swim in self-pity, especially with all the crises around us. In 1996, with a grant from the Lilly Foundation, the National Catholic Education Association issued an interesting study called *Grace Under Pressure, What Gives Life to American Priests*. That study demonstrated that priests indeed can feel besieged by the demands made on them from above, by bishops and the diocesan bureaucracy; from below, with their people expecting so much and becoming more critical; from society in general; and even from within the ranks, as the numbers of priests dwindle. One could start to feel sorry for oneself as a priest, to become burdened, to wonder why one ever got into this, to think of ourselves as martyrs, being taken for granted, worked to death, unappreciated. That's self-pity!

That, of course, hardly causes joy. That's when we get grumpy, listless, and burdened. Poor me! Of course, the problem is that the me becomes the focus, I become the center of my thought and energy instead of Jesus and his people. Put Jesus first, then others, then yourself, and therein is joy. Self-pity, of course, inverts that and puts the self first.

A second temptation to joy that is very common to priests is worry. Lord knows there's plenty to worry about in the priesthood, because there are souls at stake. Even the usual problems like finances and personnel are enough to worry the most saintly pastor. Our worries can preoccupy us and turn us inward, taking the joy out of our lives.

I remember a woman telling me she considered worry a sin. Never having heard that before, I asked her to explain. "Well," she replied, "I figure I sin against faith if I worry too much. Jesus told us not to be anxious, not to worry, that our heavenly Father knows what we need and will take care of us. When I worry, I am not trusting his promise." What a wise woman she was! Worry is a sin against faith, and can destroy joy. So you see priests who just act like they have the weight of the world on their shoulders. They can't take any time off, they can't relax, they can't go on retreat, because there are just so many things to get done and, of course, it all depends on me!

I once heard Cardinal Bernardin describe how he went into the office of the archbishop of Chicago for the first time the day after he was installed. There was a thick file that had not been opened since Cardinal Cody, his predecessor, had died. The file was marked "Confidential: crises which must be handled immediately." Well, as Cardinal Bernardin remarked, "The file of emergencies had sat there for six months unopened and the Church in Chicago had survived just fine." I once had a pastor who hardly ever went on vacation. When he would finally go away for a week he would usually come back early and then frantically ask how everything had gone in his absence, and almost get mad that everything had gone so well. Yes, cemeteries are filled with people who believed the world could not go on without them. Priests especially can fret and worry that all depends on them, mostly because they want it to and need that control. But can that kind of worry ever take a toll on joy!

I know I have some worriers reading this: money, vocation, problems at home — we can find dozens of reasons to worry. And, as Jesus said, it won't add one cubit to our span of existence. And when we worry too much, other people become a nuisance, a bother, and we hardly exude joy.

A third threat to joy especially common to priests is the heresy that our happiness depends upon something outside of ourselves.

Thus, we lose joy if we feel we were passed over for an assignment we wanted; we become sullen if the pastor says no to a particular project or request we had; we get down if our sermons do not arouse universal interest and applause. . . .

Joy does not depend on acclaim, advancement, promotion, recognition, fame, prestige, or power. Joy can never come from without — it can only come from the Lord, who plants it deep inside. If our joy is contingent upon affirmation, success, or career, it is planted in sand and will never endure.

Actually, our joy as a priest should have nothing to do with where we're assigned, what we're doing, or any external reward or recognition we get. It only depends on who we are, not what we do or have. We are beloved of the Father, configured to his Son, alive with his grace, sealed with his promise — everything else is gravy. If we're counting on anything or anyone outside of the Lord to cause our joy, we're setting ourselves up for a fall. The saddest men in the priesthood are those who longed for titles, acclaim, and advancement, and never got them, or those who got them and then realized they still lacked joy. Oh, yes, those things may bring pleasure, but, remember, pleasure is not joy! As C. S. Lewis says in his masterpiece on joy: "Joy is never in our power, and pleasure is. I doubt whether anyone who has tasted joy would ever, if both were in his power, exchange it for all the pleasure in the world."

A fourth danger to joy — again, unfortunately, quite common among priests — is complaining. Priests can really be like children when it comes to griping. I once heard Archbishop John May say after a priest council meeting, "Some guys would have complained about the menu at the Last Supper." You will quickly discover that there are two kinds of priests: those who work hard, try their best, are not afraid of risk or failure, and then those who sit back and complain, pointing out how it should have been done. In other words, you've got the guys playing hard on the field, and then the guys criticizing on the sidelines. I hope to God you are among the first group.

If you, please God, are in the first group, be prepared for carping and petty complaints from group two. As you may have heard, clerical envy at times becomes an epidemic among the presbyterate, with the more insecure, less zealous, less joyful priests threatened by the more confident, hardworking, happy guys. Priests, of all God's people, should show joy. Think about it: at the core of our being we are intimately configured to the Eternal High Priest. He has a twinkle in his eye for us because he has called us by name to act in his person in loving his Bride, the Church. Not only has he flooded our soul with sanctifying grace like all the other baptized, he has also intensified that with the powerful grace of holy orders, impressing upon our identity an indelible seal marking us one of his priests. In addition to who we are, his chosen priests, look at what we do: the most noble of work! Each day we perform miracles of changing bread and wine into our Lord's body and blood, forgiving sins in his name, and representing him to others. Our ministry instills in so many of our people an awe and reverence we admit we do not deserve, yet they share with us their most private problems and want us near when they are in need. No wonder Lacordaire could exclaim, "My God, what a life!" No wonder St. Maximilian Kolbe could answer the Gestapo commandant with such tranquility, "I am a Catholic priest." No wonder people expect us to be men of joy.

Priests, especially parish priests, have to be "people persons." We are enlivened by people, we see God's image in them, we enjoy their company, and they are attracted to us because we exude a joy, a serenity. So, as I said before, a crabby priest is an oxymoron. Yet, how often do we hear our people say about priests, "Oh, I'm afraid to bother him!" "Oh, he always seems so busy." "Oh, he only has time for the rich ones." "Oh, he walks right by and doesn't even say hello." "Oh, he turned his back on me." "Oh, he blew up at me and really chewed me out."

A mean, unfriendly, crabby priest is a scandal, as much as a drunk or a philanderer. In fact, maybe worse, because at least drunks and philanderers are usually smiling! No matter what the polls say, you won't meet too many people who have left the Church because of its teaching on women's ordination; you'll sure meet a lot who have wandered because of priests without joy.

What an icon of joy our priestly commitment makes us! I know it is becoming a cliché, but think of how "countercultural" our promises make us:

• To a world that believes you cannot be happy without immediate sexual gratification, with whomever, wherever, whenever you want — we pledge lifelong celibate chastity!

• To a society which holds that, without the license to do what you want, when you want, where you want, you can't be fulfilled — we promise lifelong obedience to one man!

• To a culture that thinks fulfillment comes in constant buying, hoarding, shopping, accumulating — we commit to a simplicity of life on around a thousand dollars a month!

• To a world that is pragmatic and utilitarian, judging worth by what is produced — we vow to waste time daily praying with and for the Church!

• To a society which holds that we take care of ourselves first and never compromise our comfort and convenience — we pledge to serve others in sacrificial love in union with the crucified one!

And yet we are joyful! Because joy comes not from orgasms, license, buying, producing, or selfishness, but from pure love, committed responsibility, simplicity of life, prayer, and generous service.

Everyone in the seminary daily asks himself: Is the Lord calling me to be a priest? Or, if you already are one: How is the Lord calling me to be a better one? Joy had best be part of that discernment: Am I a person conscious of being loved by God, grateful for his life within me, confident of his saving help, and thus at peace with God, myself, and others, so much so that it causes me a joy that others note? If I'm not, I should not be a priest.

"Joy is the infallible sign of God's presence." I conclude by turning to the "Cause of Our Joy":

Mother benign of our redeeming Lord,
Star of the Sea and portal of the skies,
Unto your fallen people help afford —
Fallen, but striving still anew to rise.
You who once while wondering worlds adored,
Bore your Creator, Virgin then as now,
O by your holy joy at Gabriel's word,
Pity the sinners who now before you bow.

Part Two

Living the Priestly Life

16

The Eucharist in the Life of the Priest

(Scripture selection — John 6:35ff)

"History — Mystery — Majesty." You have heard those words before, have you not? They were made famous by the renowned liturgical scholar Pius Parsch in his meditation on this season of Advent, to describe the threefold coming of Christ: (1) in history, as the baby at Bethlehem; (2) in mystery, through grace; and (3) in majesty, as judge at the end of time.

Yes, the Lord comes to us in "history, mystery, and majesty," and it is the middle one, mystery, about which I want to speak to you. This coming in mystery is as real and as potent as his coming in history and in majesty.

The Lord comes to us in mystery, invisibly, quietly, calmly, simply, in dozens of ways daily. The one I want to address is his coming to us in the Eucharist. "The mark of a Catholic," wrote Fulton Sheen, "is the willingness to look for the divine in the flesh of a babe in a crib, and the continuing Christ under the appearance of bread and wine on an altar."

While a recognition of this truth, that Jesus comes to us in mystery in the Holy Eucharist, is essential to all in the Church, the priest especially must exude an awe about this mysterious presence, a profound faith in its reality, a constant hunger for this heavenly food, a ready desire to savor his presence in this sacrament, and an exuberance about telling others of this sacred gift. Simply put, a passionate love for the mysterious presence of Jesus in the Eucharist is the driving force in the life of a priest. As the Second Vatican Council bluntly puts it, the Eucharist is "the center and root of the whole priestly life" (*Presbyterorum Ordinis*, No. 14).

It would be profitable for us briefly to review the teaching of the Church on the Eucharist. Obviously, one of the most important courses taken in the seminary is the tract on the Eucharist, where you systematically consider our Eucharistic doctrine. Here I only want to review the basics, really, although perhaps in more elaborate words, what we were taught in preparation for our first Holy Communion. For the basics I go to — where else? — the *Catechism of the Catholic Church.*

The *Catechism* begins its beautiful article on the sacrament of the Eucharist by citing *Sacrosanctum Concilio*: "At the Last Supper, on the night before he died, our Savior instituted the Eucharistic Sacrifice of his body and blood. This he did in order to perpetuate the sacrifice of the cross throughout the ages . . . and so to entrust to his beloved Spouse, the Church, a memorial of his death and resurrection: a sacrament of love, a sign of unity, a bond of charity, a paschal banquet, in which Christ is consumed, the mind is filled with grace, and a pledge of future glory is given us" (No. 1323).

Maybe I should stop right there! Continuing to quote the council's Document on the Sacred Liturgy, the *Catechism* tells us that the Eucharist is "the source and summit of the Christian life. . . . For, in the blessed Eucharist is contained the whole spiritual good of the Church, namely, Christ himself" (No. 1324). In brief, we are taught, "the Eucharist is the sum and the summary of our faith" (No. 1327).

Going through the names we give this mystery, the *Catechism* reaffirms that the Eucharist is the supreme act of praise and thanksgiving, wherein Christ feeds his people in a sacred meal, within a community that is the visible expression of the Church, as a memorial of the passion, death, and resurrection of the Redeemer, and as the renewal of the everlasting, infinitely meritorious sacrifice of the Son to the Father on the cross.

This central action of the Church is liturgy in its purest form, which, although having experienced cosmetic changes, has remained essentially the same since the time of Christ, with the immutable elements of assembly, priest, Word, bread and wine, and sacrament:

• the assembly, the community, is essential, as every Mass is ecclesial, for the Church, an action of the entire Church (on earth and in heaven) in which the assembly participates fully and sincerely;

• the ordained priest is indispensable, in that he acts *in per-*

sona Christi, representing the Lord who is both the sacrifice and the one sacrificing;

• the proclamation of the Word is essential as God himself continues to speak to his people as the Scriptures are proclaimed;

• the bread and wine are critical in that, at the consecration, they become, really and truly, the body and blood of Christ, again offered to the Father, and communicated to his people as food for the soul, remedy for sin, an intimate communion with Jesus, and a pledge of future glory (cf. No. 1391ff);

• and that presence of Christ remains in the Blessed Sacrament, wherein he is really and truly present, body, blood, soul, and divinity.

Enough of our catechism lesson, although it is never really over, is it?

Now to the main course . . . what does all this have to say to us as priests and future priests? I want to dwell on the corollaries of our Eucharistic faith, seven practical implications it has in the life of priests and seminarians.

First of all . . . I ask you: Do you really believe what the Church believes about the mystery of the Eucharist? My brothers, perhaps the greatest pastoral challenge we will face as parish priests is to rekindle in our people a childlike, vibrant faith in the wonder of the Eucharist, and, we can't give it unless we got it! Do you have it?

• Do you believe that the Mass is the greatest of all prayers, that as a priest there is nothing better you can do for and with your people than celebrate Mass?

• Do you believe that our Lord is really and truly present in the Most Holy Sacrament of the altar, there to be adored?

• Do you believe that, as a priest, you will nowhere act more intimately in the person of Christ than when you offer Mass, and that to do so reverently, attentively, sincerely, and daily, is the hallmark of our sacerdotal life?

What I am asking, I suppose, is that you ponder now the questions the bishop will ask you on ordination day or, if you have already been asked them, to renew your response:

• "Are you resolved to celebrate the mysteries of Christ faithfully and religiously as the Church has handed them down to us for the glory of God and the sanctification of Christ's people?"

• "Are you resolved to unite yourself more closely every day to Christ the High Priest, who offered himself for us to the Father as the perfect sacrifice?"

And, in those haunting words addressed to us when he gives us the chalice and paten: "Accept from the holy people of God the gifts to be offered to him. Know what you are doing, and imitate the mystery you celebrate. . . ."

I suggest to you that a very important part of your discernment of a priestly vocation is your love of the Eucharist. Do you fully accept the Church's doctrine on the Eucharist? Do you now love the Mass, participate fully every day, look forward to it, and find yourself attracted to our Lord's Eucharistic presence? If not, this could be a sign you seminarians are not intended to be priests, because, again, as the Second Vatican Council teaches, "The Eucharist is the center and root of the whole priestly life." And so, the first corollary flowing from our faith in the mystery of the Eucharist is simply, "Do you really believe it?"

The second implication for our priestly life is that the celebration of the Eucharist, the Mass, must be the center of our life. As the old wish goes, "Lord, help me make the Mass, not just a part, but the heart of my day."

You have heard me tell the story of Dominic Tang, the courageous Chinese archbishop who was imprisoned for twenty-one years for nothing more than his loyalty to Christ and his one, true Church. After five years of solitary confinement, in a windowless, damp cell, his jailers came to tell him he could leave it for a few hours, to do whatever he wanted. Five years of solitary confinement, and he had a couple of hours to do anything he wanted! What would it be? A hot shower? A change of clothes? Certainly a long walk outside? A chance to call or write family? "What will it be?" asked the jailer.

"I would like to say Mass," replied Archbishop Tang.

A hot topic today is "the spirituality of the diocesan priest." Even the pros admit it is a nebulous, ill-defined, new topic, with a variety of worthwhile opinions on just what "the spirituality of the diocesan priest" is. But all agree on one thing: it has to be centered on the daily celebration of the Eucharist for the priest's people.

What a practical approach to the spirituality of the diocesan priest that is! We make our daily Mass the heart of the day. That means we prepare for it, by meditating on the readings beforehand, by a spirit of prayer and recollection prior to Mass, by a reverent, sincere celebration of the Mass, and by a period of thanksgiving afterwards. If we do that, we're on our way to "the spirituality of a diocesan priest," then realizing that we bring that Christ whom we have offered up and received to our people, in our ministry, throughout the day.

Pope John Paul II wrote: "The spirituality of all diocesan priests is linked to the Eucharist. Here they obtain the strength to make the offering of their lives together with Jesus, high priest and victim of salvation. Through the Eucharistic sacrifice, celibacy is confirmed. From the cross the Lord speaks to all his priests, inviting him to be, with him, signs of contradiction."

About ten years ago my mom had serious surgery, and, only three days later, had to undergo a second operation. As you can imagine, we, my brothers, sisters, and I, were very worried as we waited for word upon completion of this second procedure. The surgeon finally came out to give us the good news, thoughtfully explaining what he had done. Soon over the hospital's P.A. system came the announcement, "Mass begins in the chapel in ten minutes."

"Excuse me," the surgeon said, "that's my cue. If I don't make Mass I'm not much good for the day." How much more should a priest be able to say that?

John Clifford, the American Jesuit who spent three years in a Shanghai prison, wrote in his book *In the Presence of My Enemies*, "I had not said Mass, or received Holy Communion, for 888 days. No one but a priest can fully realize the significance of that deprivation."

Again I ask you seminarians if daily Mass is the heart of your day. If you dread it, if you are not consistent in your attendance, if you are passive and sullen — if it is peripheral to your day and not the heart of your day — that is a sign you are not called to be a priest.

At the celebration of his golden jubilee of ordination, the Holy Father preached: "In the span of fifty years of priesthood, what is still the most important and the most sacred moment for me is the celebration of the Eucharist. My awareness of celebrating *in persona Christi* at the altar prevails. Holy Mass is the absolute center of my life and of every day of my life."

Point number three: our faith in the Eucharist, and our recognition that the Mass is the heart of the day, then flows to a continual desire to savor our Lord's Real Presence in the Eucharist through frequent prayer before the Blessed Sacrament.

The former archbishop of San Francisco, John Quinn, loves to tell the story about the arrival of Mother Teresa and her Missionaries of Charity to open their house in the city. Poor Archbishop Quinn had gone to great efforts to make sure their convent was, while hardly opulent, quite comfortable. He recalls how Mother Teresa arrived and immediately ordered the carpets removed, the telephones, except for one, pulled out of the wall, the beds, except for the mattresses, taken away, and on and on. Explained Mother Teresa to the baffled archbishop, "All we really need in our convent is the tabernacle."

I received a letter not long ago from Brother Randal Riede, the beloved former librarian of the college, who recently retired. Needless to say, his adjustment to a new life, at his age, after twenty-six years here, was difficult. But he wrote, "I am happy here. I have my room, my books, and the chapel close by."

How we as priests and future priests should savor time visiting with our Lord — our Savior, our pastor, our be-all and end-all, our best friend — who is present to us in the Blessed Sacrament! How we should never pass him without at least saying "hello."

Nor do we forget to savor our Lord's presence to us within, after we have received him in Holy Communion. Pope St. Pius X said, "Remember, this side of heaven, there is no way to be closer to Jesus than by worthily receiving him in Holy Communion."

The newest doctor of the Church, the Little Flower, writes, "Our Lord does not come from heaven every day to stay in a golden ciborium. He comes to find another heaven, the heaven of our soul in which he loves to dwell." There's the secret! And it's no secret, because we want to spend our lives telling others about it!

Conscious of our Lord's Real Presence among us, we want to savor it, within ourselves, and as he remains alive in the Most Blessed Sacrament.

The fourth corollary: the Eucharist belongs to Christ and his Church, not me. Remember what the Curé of Ars said: "All the good works in the world are not equal to the Holy Sacrifice of the Mass, because they are the works of men, but the Mass is the work of God.

Even martyrdom is nothing in comparison, for it is but the sacrifice of man to God, but the Mass is the sacrifice of God for man."

The Eucharist is the action of Christ and his Church, not mine! The mystery of the Eucharist is that we are absorbed into the infinite act of praise, atonement, satisfaction, and pleading of the Son to the Father! Yes, we participate fully and attentively, but only to make the more sincere our union with the Son, for the Mass is his work, the Eucharist his presence. St. Ambrose writes, "When it comes to this venerable sacrament, the priest no longer uses his own language. It is Christ who consecrates."

One of our fifth-year priests articulated his understanding of this very well during my recent interview with him. He recounted how he had so cherished daily offering his own Mass, as the sole celebrant with his congregation, after his ordination over the summer, and, then, how difficult it was to return here to the college to be only one of dozens of concelebrants every day. Then it dawned on him in prayer that, really, Jesus is always the only presider, the real principal celebrant, at every Mass, and we always concelebrate with the one, Eternal High Priest. The Mass, the Eucharist, belongs to Christ and his Church, not to me.

Now, let that sink in, for it has practical implications.

For one, that means we are not free to tamper with the Mass, to alter it to conform to how we think it should be, because the Mass is never selfishly personal, but Christological and ecclesial. Thus, we are attentive to the rubrics, proper, reverent, and careful. We are stewards, not owners, of this ineffable gift.

So, I say to you:

• If you believe you can change the words and rubrics of the Mass, except where there are the legitimate options at the discretion of the celebrant . . .

• If you believe that the priest does not have a unique, indispensable role at every Mass, substantially different from the laity . . .

• If you believe that the liturgical norms of the Sacramentary, the guidelines of the legitimate liturgical authorities, our bishops and the Holy See, are easily overlooked . . .

• If you believe you have a gnostic insight into the way the Eucharist should be celebrated, and will help your people get used to a radically new liturgy of the future by giving them previews of coming attractions, grasping at every fad and trend that comes along . . .

. . . Then it's time for some serious reorientation, because the Eucharist is not mine, it belongs to Christ and his Church.

That means we fully embrace the way the Eucharist is to be celebrated now, in the United States of America, not the way those on the left hope it will be celebrated after Vatican III or those on the right long for the way it was celebrated in 1959!

So, I say to you:

• If you do not fully embrace the genuine liturgical reforms of the Second Vatican Council . . .

• If you do not believe that the Mass of Paul VI is valid . . .

• If you are not fully committed to the Mass in the vernacular, facing the people, with full participation of the faithful, including women, in legitimate liturgical roles . . .

• If you feel unable to celebrate Mass with contemporary music, lectors, offertory processions, extraordinary ministers, the sign of peace, and Communion under both species . . .

. . . Then it is time to do some serious soul-searching, because the Eucharist belongs to Christ and his Church, not me; I as a priest am the steward, not the owner. The Church does not need futuristic priests who ignore and discard liturgical law and rubrics to fashion their own shows, or traditionalist shock troops who arrogantly dismiss the providential reform and renewal that has come about in the Church in the last three decades, or who snidely dismiss those whose approach may be different from their own.

This means that, really, issues of taste are secondary. We all have liturgical tastes. This house has about, oh, one hundred eighty different ones.

• Some are huffy if we do not have Gregorian chant at every Mass, while others turn up their nose at any song composed before "On Eagle's Wings."

• Some whine at the Spanish Mass, while others roll their eyes when we use some Latin.

• Some want cassocks and surplices, while others want jeans and cutoffs.

• Some want fiddleback chasubles while others want Spencers.

Fine . . . different liturgical tastes will always be with us. But, if we begin to gauge the value of the Eucharist by how it conforms to our taste, we have forgotten the principle that the Eucharist belongs to Christ and his Church, not to me; I as a priest am the steward, not the owner; and a patient appreciation for the different tastes, needs, and styles of liturgy, as long as they are legitimate, is a necessary virtue for a priest.

The fifth corollary: the great pastoral challenge for us today is to renew in our people a deep faith and profound love for the Eucharist.

Of all the frightening polls that we hear of these days, has any statistic been more chilling than that of the Gallup poll several years ago indicating that only twenty-nine percent of Catholics receiving the Eucharist on Sunday believe that it is really and truly the body and blood of Christ? That is not due to intentional heterodoxy or stubborn resistance to Church doctrine; it is because we as priests, and the other catechists of the Church, have not effectively taught proper doctrine.

Saints such as Francis de Sales, Charles Borromeo, Peter Canisius, John Vianney, and Don Bosco would tell us that all genuine renewal in the life of the Church begins with the Eucharist. Thus we, who will be parish priests in the new millennium, must set as a major pastoral goal to foster love for the Eucharist: an understanding of the Mass, and a full participation in the Liturgy, and a faith in the Real Presence of our Lord in the Eucharist, whom we receive at Mass and whom we adore in the Blessed Sacrament.

How do we do that? You know as well as I do: by word and example.

By word, as we teach clearly, cogently, and attractively the Church's belief in the Eucharist, never passing up an opportunity provided in our homilies, school and CCD visits, and RCIA classes to explain the faith of the Church. I know a pastor who has a wonderfully developed RCIA program, with trained lay catechists to take every lesson except for the two on the Eucharist, which he rightly claims for himself. In each of the three parishes I have served, the pastor admirably reserved for himself the preparation of the children for their first Holy Communion. By our word can we renew Eucharistic vitality in the Church.

And, perhaps more importantly, by our example. Do our people see us offer Mass with joy, reverence, and preparation, or do we become sloppy, either flippant with the rubrics, or robotlike in what should be a warm, inviting style of presiding?

• Do they see us genuflect reverently, spending time in prayer before the Eucharist, bringing Communion frequently to the sick and housebound even when we have a loyal corps of extraordinary ministers, encouraging silence in Church, promoting Eucharistic devotion, and feeding our people with the Bread of Heaven at every Sunday Mass, even those we do not celebrate?

• Do they see us treat the sacred species with tenderness, carrying the Blessed Sacrament properly in pyx, burse, with a stole, careful about the remaining Hosts?

• Do they hear us remind them about the necessity of the sacrament of penance before reception of Communion when one is conscious of serious sin, and the proper observance of the Eucharistic fast, as minimal as it is?

• Do they know that we consider Sunday Mass, with a properly prepared liturgy, a first-rate homily, good music, with full participation of the people, as a priority in our pastoral plans?

Our example can foster or destroy Eucharistic piety, for any priest worth his salt has a renewal of faith in the Eucharist as a very high pastoral goal.

Corollary six: the Eucharist is by its nature public, social, and communal, constantly calling us beyond ourselves in sacrificial love for others. Never can the Eucharist become a tidy, reclusive, cozy, private time of selfish comfort. While celebrating Mass, or while in prayer before the Blessed Sacrament, we are ever mindful of the needs of God's people.

Yes, you bet the Eucharist soothes, consoles, comforts, refreshes — but that is to strengthen us for generous service to God's people. Even the word "Mass," as you know, comes from the Latin dismissal, "*Ite missa est*" ("Go, you are sent"). We are not called to be contemplatives who spend hours a day in front of the Eucharist, as appealing as that on occasion is. We are called daily to offer the Eucharist, and root our day in that mystery, precisely so we can be zealous pastors of souls.

Our daily Mass, our moments of silent visitation with our Eucharistic Lord, recharge our spiritual batteries to serve God's people more effectively. You wonder how the Holy Father gets his energy to persevere through his daily punishing schedule, still internally vigorous while his body deteriorates? You have the answer if you have ever attended his morning Mass, for, when you enter, he is kneeling in prayer before the tabernacle, and has been, we are told, for an hour, and then reverently offers his Mass. His prie-dieu is overflowing with prayer requests from all over the world as he takes the needs of God's people with him and renews Calvary at his Eucharist.

I was not a priest very long when I was called to the hospital by the parents of a little ten-month-old infant who had fallen down the basement steps while crawling. The baby was not expected to live, and, as you can imagine, the young parents were distraught. After spending time with them, I explained that I had to leave and get back for noon Mass. I'll never forget the words of the dad, "Father, please put our little baby on your paten when you say Mass."

We do bring all the needs, sufferings, hurts, and struggles of our people with us to Mass. And our love of the Mass and our time spent in the Real Presence of the Eucharist inspire us to serve our people better. Often have I quoted Father Walter Burghardt, S.J., who claims that the words the priest utters at Mass — "He blessed the bread, broke it, and gave it" — characterize as well our priestly ministry, as we bless, are broken, and given in love and service to our people.

One of our alumni had this printed on his ordination card, called "The Prayer of the Chalice": "Father, to Thee I raise my whole being, an empty vessel. Accept my emptiness, and fill me with Thyself, that Thy precious gifts may radiate through me and overflow the chalice of my heart into the hearts of all whom I meet this day, revealing to them the beauty of Thy joy and wholeness, and the serenity of Thy peace which nothing can destroy."

When the English College in Rome celebrated Martyrs' Day, I would always stop to visit their chapel, moved unfailingly by the depiction behind the altar of those alumni of the English College, who went back to England as newly ordained priests almost certain of martyrdom; I venerated the relics below the main altar. For the first time I heard the story from my host that every time word would reach the college in Rome that another of their alumni had been martyred, the seminarians would gather in the chapel and sing the *Te Deum*. Then he pointed out what I had never noticed before: that the altar holding the tabernacle was actually a butcher's block, symbolizing the block upon which those martyrs were gutted and quartered. Forgive me for being so graphic, but, as he celebrates each Mass, as he kneels before the tabernacle, the priest indicates his willingness to pour himself out in loving service to his people, to place his life on the butcher block.

The Vietnamese Jesuit Joseph Nguyen-Cong Doan, who spent nine years in labor camps in Vietnam, relates how he was finally able to say Mass when a fellow priest-prisoner shared some of his own smuggled supplies. "That night, when the other prisoners were asleep, lying on the floor of my cell, I celebrated Mass with tears of joy. My altar was my blanket, my prison clothes my vestments, but I felt myself at the heart of humanity and of the whole of creation."

The Eucharist constantly calls us beyond ourselves in sacrificial love for others.

And my final point: the Eucharist is the sign and cause of unity, and woe to those who make it a source of division.

Two hundred years ago, a beautiful young Episcopalian woman accompanied her husband, a merchant, to Italy, leaving four of their five children at home with family members. They had sailed for Italy, hoping that perhaps the change in climate might help her husband, whose failing business had evidently affected his health adversely. Tragically, he died in Livorno. The grieving young woman was warmly received by an Italian family, business acquaintances of her deceased husband, and she stayed with them for three months before she could arrange to return to America.

The young widow was very impressed by the Catholic faith of the family, especially their devotion to the Eucharist: their frequent attendance at Mass, the reverence with which they received Holy Communion, the awe they showed toward the Blessed Sacrament on feast days when the Eucharist was carried in procession. She found her broken heart healed by a hunger for this mysterious presence of the Lord, and, upon returning home, requested instructions in the faith. Soon after being received into the Church, she described her first reception of the Lord in the Eucharist as the happiest moment of her life.

I was in St. Peter's Square on September 14, 1975, when Pope Paul VI canonized this woman, Elizabeth Ann Seton, our first native-born saint. The Eucharist for her was a sign and cause of union with God and the Church.

Just a few years earlier, another event happened on the same continent. A disciple of Voltaire wrote him in Paris with a problem. As much as he wanted to become an atheist, curse God, hate the Church, and renounce his faith, as Voltaire was exhorting, the young man confessed that he could not, because he still felt a strange attraction to the Eucharist.

How, he asked Voltaire, can I get over this unenlightened, superstitious belief in the Real Presence of Christ in the Eucharist? Easy, replied Voltaire. Keep receiving Communion; in fact, go five and six times a day. As you do, say to yourself, "I do not believe; I hate God; this is superstition." Not only that, counseled Voltaire, go out and commit dozens of mortal sins, but keep going to Communion, deliberately wanting to destroy your faith and curse your silly God. Four months later, the proud young man wrote back to say it had worked, that he was now a committed atheist. That young man used the Eucharist to divide — that is, to sever — his union with God.

The Eucharist is the sign and cause of unity, and woe to those who make it a source of division. You know the latter can happen today. The liturgy, questions of Eucharistic praxis, can become the battleground, with parishes, religious communities, and, yes, even seminaries, torn asunder by fanatics on either side who place their own taste and preference above the unity of the Church.

St. Bernard tells us that, just as a worm attacks a healthy tree at its strongest section, Satan attacks us where virtue and grace are most evident. Virtue and grace are most evident for priests in our love for the Eucharist, so, watch out, because that's where Satan will strike.

St. Peter Julian Eymard warns: "Satan wages incessant warfare on the Eucharist. He knows Jesus is there, living and substantially present. So, he tries to efface the Eucharist in us: for, in his mind, this decides the struggle."

The great social activist Dorothy Day observed: "Mass filled my heart with a sense of love for all, even bigots, racists, bad priests, selfish laypeople alike. We are all united, as husband and wife in marriage are united, by the deepest spiritual bond, so that we become 'one flesh.' "

Because the Eucharist is the sign and cause of unity, and woe to those who make it a source of division.

One of the seminarians who gives tours of St. Peter's told me of an interesting incident. He was showing around a group of Japanese tourists who knew absolutely nothing of our faith. With particular care did he explain the great masterpieces of art, sculpture, architecture, and finally concluded at the Blessed Sacrament Chapel, trying his best to explain quickly what it was.

As the group dispersed, an elderly man, who had been particularly attentive, stayed behind, and said, "Pardon me. Would you explain again this Blessed Sacrament?" Our student did, after which the man exclaimed, "Ah, if this is so, what is in this chapel is a greater work of art than anything else in this basilica."

It is this masterpiece, this work of art, that is entrusted to us as priests. We, more than anyone else, must value and appreciate its worth.

> O Sacrament Most Holy, O Sacrament Divine!
> All praise and all thanksgiving, be every moment thine!

17

Priestly Identity

(Scripture selection — Matthew 4:18-22)

Most of you know the inspirational story of St. Maximilian Kolbe, but I trust that you, like me, never tire of hearing it. Recall that fateful day at Auschwitz when the Nazi prison guards assembled the concentration camp inmates in rows, and, at the commandant's order, randomly chose ten helpless men for execution in retaliation for a recent escape. Remember how one of those chosen, a husband and father, cried out to be spared death for the sake of his family. Picture the stillness when Father Kolbe spoke up, "I wish to take the place of that man."

Imagine the sneer of the commandant as he asked, "Who is that Polish swine?" And recall again the reply of Maximilian Kolbe: "I am a Catholic priest."

"Who are you?" snickered the commandant! Father Kolbe did not reply:

- I am Maximilian Kolbe . . .
- I am a Pole . . .
- I am a human being . . .
- I am a friend of his . . .

His response was simply and humbly: "I am a Catholic priest."

In the eyes of God, in his own eyes, in the eyes of God's Church and his suffering people, Maximilian Kolbe's identity was that of a priest. At the core of his being, on his heart, was engraved a nametag, which marked him forever a priest of God. That identity could not be erased by the inhuman circumstances of a death camp, or the godless environment of Auschwitz, or by the fact that Father Kolbe was hardly "doing" the things one usually associates with priestly ministry, or that the people around him had mostly lost any faith or recognition of the supernatural they may have had before they entered that hell hole.

That identity hardly depended upon the acclaim of those around

227

him or was lessened by the doubts and crisis he may personally have experienced in such a tortured setting. That identity came from God, and was imbedded indelibly within, born of a call he had detected early on from the Master to follow him, and sealed forever by the sacrament of holy orders. So conscious was he of his priestly identity that he could boldly answer the sneer of the Nazi commandant and simply state what he knew to be the central fact of his personal definition, "I am a Catholic priest."

"The priest," we read in the Decree on the Ministry and Life of Priests (*Presbyterorum Ordinis*) from the Second Vatican Council, "shares in the authority by which Christ himself builds up, sanctifies, and rules his Body. Therefore . . . the sacerdotal office . . . is conferred by that special sacrament through which priests, by the anointing of the Holy Spirit, are marked with a special character and are so configured to Christ the Priest that they can act in the person of Christ the Head" (No. 2).

The priesthood is a call, not a career; a redefinition of self, not just a new ministry; a way of life, not a job; a state of being, not just a function; a permanent, lifelong commitment, not a temporary style of service; an identity, not just a role.

We are priests; yes, the doing, the ministry, is mighty important, but it flows from the being; we can act as priests, minister as priests, function as priests, serve as priests, preach as priests, because first and foremost we are priests! Being before act! *Agere sequitur esse*, as the Scholastics expressed it. Father William Byron, the former president of The Catholic University of America, is fond of saying that "we are human beings, not human doings, and our basic dignity and identity comes from who we are, not what we do." This is true as well of the priesthood.

On the day before I was ordained a priest, I went to confession to a Paraclete Father in St. Louis. He asked me what I looked forward to in the priesthood. Of course I answered, predictably, "Offering Mass, hearing confessions, serving people in a parish," and so on.

"Excellent," my confessor responded, "but enjoy as well being a priest. You know, if you were in an automobile accident the day after your First Mass and were paralyzed completely, meaning you could not ever do any of the things ordinarily associated with priestly ministry, you would still be a priest." And then words I'll never forget, he said, "Spend time every day acknowledging that priestly identity, rejoicing in it, nourishing it, thanking God for it — and then what you do as a priest will be all the more effective and rewarding, because it flows from who you are." Now that's what I mean by priestly identity.

Listen to what Archbishop Rembert Weakland said to the National Conference of Priests in England and Wales in September of 1996:

> I am, with regard to the priesthood itself and its sacramental character, an "ontologist." I believe that something happens when one is ordained that assures the validity of the acts when that person functions in the name of Christ and his Church. Such a difference does not make the person any better than anyone else, but it does assure the validity of the sacraments that a priest performs. . . . In this we differ from so many Protestant denominations. . . . I have slowly come to see the wisdom of "orders" to assure order among God's people.

Or, as Cardinal Joseph Bernardin spoke in May of the same year: "We priests are not dispensable functionaries; we are bridges to the very mystery of God and healers of the soul. When we claim this priestly identity unapologetically, we not only find ourselves, we also provide the Church and our culture with the sustenance they require."

You get my point. In our Catholic understanding, priestly ordination is a radical, total reordering of a man in the eyes of God and his Church, bringing about an identity of ontological "reconfigurement" with Christ. This priestly identity is at the very core, the essence, of a man, affecting his being and, subsequently, his actions.

Enough of theory. How about some consequences of that priestly identity?

Well, because as priests we are configured to Christ at the very core of our being, our priesthood will have the same characteristics as that of the Eternal High Priest. Two especially are worthy of our consideration: our priesthood is forever, our priesthood is faithful.

"When a man says 'yes' to the priesthood," says John Paul II, "that 'yes' is forever."

In practice, my brothers, this means we cannot "leave" the priesthood or quit being a priest, any more than your father can stop "being" your father. The priesthood is forever.

Now most of us know a priest who has left the active ministry. The Church's insistence on the perpetual nature of priestly identity, and my dwelling upon it, is in no way a judgment upon those many men who have left priestly life. Two of the most eloquent explanations of the eternal dimension of priestly identity I have ever heard came from two friends of mine who have both been dispensed of their priestly obligations and are now active and prominent laymen in the Church. So do not interpret my words as some chastisement of these good men.

But, no matter how many leave, no matter how many criticize, no matter how many scandals there may be, the priesthood is still forever. It is a complete, lifelong commitment to Christ and his Church.

I hope this is obvious to you, but we can take nothing for granted: if any of you look at the priesthood as less than a lifelong, absolute pledge of one's whole being to Christ and his Church, as simply a ministry that can be left if one becomes frustrated, or a productive way to spend some years in service to people until one wants to pursue another career, please realize that such is not the mind of the Church!

How else can I say it? The priesthood is forever! How we live the priesthood, where we are assigned, what we do — all these things will certainly change, but our priestly identity will never change. The priesthood is eternal.

If that frightens you or causes you awe, good! A seminary exists to make sure that you can freely, deliberately, joyfully say the "yes" that lasts forever. God forbid anyone would take that lightly!

It is good for me to be up front about one of the great temptations of seminary life, namely to drift into the priesthood. Our decision for priesthood, our conviction that the Lord is calling me to serve him and his Church forever as a priest, must be clear, enthusiastic, deliberate, and free. We do not become priests to please Mom, Grandma, the bishop, the diocese, or anybody else; we become priests because we have prayerfully and rationally discerned God's call, we have carefully tested that call, and we now freely and joyfully embrace it. To sustain a lifelong commitment to our priestly vocation will be next to impossible if we simply float into it. We do not become priests simply because something better has not come along. If we do, guess what? Something or someone better will come along one day, and then we're in trouble.

How can it happen that a man will go through the seminary and then, a few years after ordination, leave? That happens, as you well know. Why? Because issues are not faced in the seminary, such as serious doubts, sins, emotional problems, personal difficulties — and they are bound to surface later.

That's why seminaries have spiritual directors, psychiatrists, formation advisers, clear community expectations, annual evaluations, retreats, supervised pastoral service, etc. — because the call to priesthood is so total, so forever, that one must be confident and clear about it.

Everything we do at the North American College is directed to the priesthood. We begin the year with ordination to the diaconate; the presence and example of devoted priest-faculty members, fifth-year men fresh from ordination, priests on sabbatical; the ministries of lector and acolyte; the closing banquet when the vice-rector reads the list of those leaving "to preach the Gospel" — constant focus on the priesthood.

"When a man says 'yes' to the priesthood, that 'yes' is forever."

A second characteristic of our priestly identity is fidelity. You know by heart Mother Teresa's famous dictum, "The Lord doesn't ask us to be successful; he asks us to be faithful."

I will always recall the words that Paul VI spoke to my class after diaconate ordination: "Be faithful, always be faithful."

We are faithful to our priestly identity no matter what the circumstances. This may sound Pollyannaish, but the value of our priesthood does not depend on where we are assigned, who our pastor is, or what type of ministry we are engaged in. Pastor Ignotus, the famous anonymous columnist for the London *Tablet*, meditates: "The priest is blamed for many failings. He visits rarely, preaches badly. He is anti-intellectual. The sociologist details his defects. 'Men, not angels, ministers of the gospel,' Newman heads a sermon. This consoles. For the priest there is no such thing as success, no gold, silver, or bronze. He just plods on and, when the going gets rough, there is very little he can do. Except, possibly, have a good cry."

Fidelity will be easy when our priestly lives are happy, interesting, invigorating. Ah, but the sorrow, loneliness, frustration will come, and then can we be faithful? Yes, if we know that our fidelity is not to a job, a career, a function, an assignment, but to a call, an identity, a Person, namely Jesus and his Church! It is not based on achievement, reward, or fulfillment.

In one of the parishes to which I was assigned, there was a couple I recall vividly. When I knew them they were already in their late forties, but twenty years before that, only about five years into their marriage, she had developed crippling rheumatoid arthritis, which left her twisted, physically useless, gradually confined to bed or a wheelchair.

He was a handsome, vigorous man, very successful as a stockbroker. For over twenty-five years he was faithful to her constantly. Every morning he got her out of bed, bathed and dressed her, helped her with breakfast; every lunch break he was home for a visit and to take her for a walk in the wheelchair. Every evening he helped her with supper, read to her, dressed her for bed. He could have left her; he could have had numerous affairs; on his business trips out of town how he must have been tempted to seek the sexual satisfaction she could not provide. Never! Always faithful! Not to what she could give him or do for him, but faithful to her, to his vocation, to his identity as a husband and father!

At times in our priesthood we will experience a dryness, a confusion, a doubt, a fatigue, a frustration, a loneliness, an anger — and that's when fidelity is proved. Our Spouse, the Church, may at times seem crippled and useless, a drain; our Master, Jesus, may occasionally seem distant, aloof, absent. We are still faithful. As St. Thomas Aquinas prayed:

Give me, O Lord, a steadfast heart which no unworthy affection may drag downwards.

Give me an unconquered heart which no tribulation can wear out.

232

Give me an upright heart which no unworthy purpose may tempt aside.

Bestow on me, O Lord my God, a faithfulness that may finally embrace you!

So we are faithful; we are priests at the core of our being; there is no "day off" or vacation from priestly identity, no sabbatical or retirement, no "office hours," because our priesthood is not some external imposition but an internal identity that has captivated us from head to toe.

As rector, I am always getting suggestions regarding what I should tell the students at the seminary as future priests. One priest-friend at home, a very fine, savvy priest, advised me to exhort them to be *duro* (you know from that word that he is obviously an alumnus). Now, by *duro*, he explained, he does not mean strict, rough, mean. No, he means tough, determined, dogged, persevering. He is on his diocesan personnel board and he says he is flabbergasted at the number of guys who come complaining about assignments, feeling they are not being used properly, wanting a change, needing time off, requiring a special assignment, tired of the demands. "Whining," as he calls it. Now, I know him well enough to realize that he recognizes priests need compassion and understanding, and he provides it in abundance, by the way. But I think he may have had a point in calling us to be more *duro*. That could be another word for faithful: we keep at it, day in and day out, not allowing the setbacks and frustrations to get us down. Our pastor may be a crab, our people unresponsive, our assignment less than ideal. That's when fidelity is the key.

"Be faithful! Always be faithful."

Now this is a lofty call. To embrace our priestly identity, to live it with confidence, humility, conviction, and gratitude, to acknowledge that it is forever and that it is faithful — that is a plateful and inspires awe and maybe even trepidation. Thus we need to be cognizant of the helps that we have in our priesthood, the supports to nurturing our priestly identity.

The first, no surprise here, is prayer. Prayer of course is predicated on the belief that by ourselves nothing is possible, while, with him, nothing is impossible. Prayer is built upon the trust that God never calls us to something without supplying the grace to do it. Listen to what the archbishop of Cincinnati, Daniel Pilarcyzk, recently said to the priests of the diocese of Pittsburgh at their convocation:

> If the priest is to lead his people into contact with the presence of the mystery of God, which is what holiness is, then the priest himself has to be in touch with the presence and mystery of God. He has to be familiar with God in the deepest part of his being. This is what we call prayer. Put most bluntly, a priest without a deep prayer life is condemning himself to a career of superficiality in that aspect of his ministry which is, at the same time, the most demanding and the most satisfying.

Let's get a little more practical about this prayer that is so essential to bolstering our priestly identity.

The divine office is a prayer particularly priestly. What a spirit of solidarity comes from realizing that every day we are united with our brother priests of the Church universal in this anthem of praise and petition! On the occasion of the thirtieth anniversary of *Presbyterorum Ordinis*, Pope John Paul II said, "Prayer, in a certain sense, creates the priest. At the same time every priest creates himself constantly through prayer. I am thinking of the marvelous prayer of the breviary, the divine office, in which the whole Church, through the lips of her ministers, prays together with Christ. . . ."

The greatest of all prayers, the Eucharist, is where we experience our priestly identity most intimately. Is there ever a more powerful moment of configuration with Christ, of acting *in persona Christi*, than when we say, "This is my body; this is my blood"? Notice we do not say, "This is *his* body"; no, we say, "This is *my* body! This is *my* blood!" We are Christ!

"The priest is a man of the Eucharist," continues the Holy Father in that same exhortation cited above. "In the span of nearly fifty years of priesthood, what is still most important and the most sacred moment for me is the celebration of the Eucharist. My awareness of celebrating *in persona Christi* at the altar prevails. Never in the course of these years have I failed to celebrate the Most Holy Sacrifice. If this has occurred, it has been due entirely to reasons independent of my will. Holy Mass is the absolute center of my life and of every day of my life."

Flowing from that would come our prayer before the Holy Eucharist. I once heard a woman psychologist, addressing priests, say how rewarding she felt it must be for a priest to pray before the Blessed Sacrament. Every man, she said, needs to see something he has brought about, created — most men have that joy when they see their child. A priest has that when he beholds the Eucharist. Here is a life he has procreated, brought about with God's help. Prayer before the Eucharist is a powerful boost to our priestly identity.

Another help for us priests is prayer in union with Mary, the Mother of the First Priest. Cardinal Szoka's moving words about our Lady in the life of a priest during his homily at the North American College a few years ago on December 8 reminded us of this. As our natural lives and identity were formed and nurtured in the womb of our earthly mother, so is our priestly life and identity fostered under the care of our heavenly one.

Another way to guard our priestly identity is to develop strong friendships with brother priests.

The companionship and support of our "comrades in arms" is an inestimable help in vivifying our own priesthood. Of course this presumes you keep the company of good, wholesome priests, not cynical, wavering ones. In fact, avoiding priestly company is usually a sign of trouble. Father Stephen Rossetti, who has done pioneer work in clerical problems, says that an indication that a priest is headed for trouble is that he is reclusive, a loner, especially uncomfortable in the presence of his brother priests.

We priests can bring out the best in one another. When we visit, share a drink, meal, day off, or vacation, discuss things, let off steam with one another, challenge one another, ask a brother if something's bothering him, or pray together, we enhance one another's priestly identity. Events such as support groups, days of prayer, study days, priests' retreats, convocations, confirmations, forty hours, deanery meetings, priests' funerals and jubilees, or just plain get-togethers — these are all good ways to build up our common identity as priests.

The art of developing and maintaining genuine friendships is one we hope is part of our life at the college.

Examine your conscience: Do you have real friends in the priesthood? Do your friends drag you down or bring out the best in you? If you were in trouble could you share that with a trusted friend? Can you discuss topics like prayer, theology, vocation, fears, worries, with a good friend?

One priest you may not consider a friend, but one whom you as a priest should love, trust, and stay in touch with, would be your bishop. The intimate bond between a bishop and his priests is a theological necessity, which is to be a human reality as well. There is not a bishop I know who does not have the welfare of his priests as a top priority. As I have in the past, I encourage you now to remain in close contact with your bishop. An older priest I respect told me that twice each year — at the conclusion of his retreat and on the anniversary of his ordination — he would write the bishop a very personal letter, just reviewing his life and renewing to him his priestly promises. An excellent idea! Closeness with our bishop is a good insurance in protecting our priestly identity.

And, even though I am stressing healthy friendships with brother priests, let me not exclude good ones with the laity. They keep us on the ground. In general, our people have never had an "identity crisis" about the priesthood. They love and cherish priests, and value our ministry. While we always have to be careful about having favorites in a parish, we can and should, as we go along, cultivate close associations with people who bring out the best in us and see deep down in us that indelible mark of priesthood.

So many things can whittle away at our priestly identity that sometimes it is in jeopardy and we don't even realize it. Thus we need the guidance of someone who knows us well, who can warn us of danger, who can encourage us when we fall. So is a trusted spiritual director a real blessing in nurturing our priestly identity, as is the grace and mercy that comes from regular celebration of the sacrament of penance.

A fourth guarantee of priestly identity would be, and this might seem somewhat generic, a way of life appropriate to priests. Under this rubric I would list such safeguards as clerical dress, a comfort in being called "Father," simplicity of life, avoiding plush restaurants and places of entertainment, and the temptation for fancy and extravagant clothes, cars, vacations; retiring for the day at a proper time, a disciplined way of life. Common sense, perhaps, but all practical ways to protect our priestly identity.

I suppose all of these safeguards pale when we conclude with the most important aspect of fostering our priestly identity: a close, intimate relationship with Jesus. We are only priests because of our call from him and our union with him. Especially are we called to be united with him on his cross. Here, of course, he was most the priest, and we are most priests when we share in his suffering. This can be physical — we think of priests who have been tortured and imprisoned because they were priests, or priests who are sick in mind or body. This can be a spiritual suffering, as men struggle with dryness in prayer, wrestle with sin, fight temptation, or confront doubt. This can be emotional suffering caused by loneliness, inadequacy, discouragement, or the heavy burden that comes when good priests suffer with their people. The presence of the cross is not a sign that something is wrong with our priesthood, but that something is right with it! The classical writers called this "victimhood," as the priest, like Jesus, takes upon himself the sins, worries, and cares of his people, knowing full well that he will stumble a lot more than three times going up the hill of Calvary.

I have spoken about priestly identity; I have urged a sense of confidence and gratitude for our priestly vocation; I have listed some ways to safeguard and foster this identity, this "pearl of great price" that we cherish in holy orders. Now a word of caution.

While dreading that whole sense of the watering-down of priestly identity, an apologizing for the unique call of holy orders, a sense of nervousness that recent years have generated in priests who have heard so much about the so-called "identity crisis," we equally dread the other extreme: the arrogant insistence on prestige and power that history has called clericalism. Clericalism is a deplorable vice in the Church.

Clericalism speaks of privilege, prerogatives, special treatment, being served rather than serving; it prefers sacristies to streets, and is usually more concerned with cuff links and cassocks than care of souls. Clericalism does not indicate a sense of confidence in one's priestly call but rather such a lack of confidence in self, God, and vocation that one must prop up one's weak identity with externals and pettiness.

What I ask you to do is contemplate the difference between clericalism and priestliness — one is a vice, the other a virtue. You know the difference, because you have seen both. I call you to priestliness, not clericalism. When, with Maximilian Kolbe, you say to yourself, to your people, to your God, "I am a Catholic priest," we say that gratefully, humbly, confidently, never arrogantly, and we say it, not expecting to be served, but expecting — like Father Kolbe — that it will lead to sacrifice for and with our people.

And it all started not with us, but with that call, that whisper from the Master to "Come, follow me," that call all of you hear, that call all of you are discerning and translating, that call which will become audible on ordination day, that call you will answer, please God, every day of a long and fruitful priestly life. As the Holy Father Pope John Paul II said to newly ordained priests, a few years ago, "Up to the evening of your life remain in wonder and in gratitude for that mysterious call which one day echoed in the depths of your spirit: 'Follow me!' "

Allow me to conclude with an old poem attributed to St. Norbert:

> O priest, who are you?
> Not through yourself, for you are drawn from nothing.
> Not for yourself, since you are mediator of humanity.
> Not to yourself, for you are married to the Church.
> Not your own, for you are the servant of all.
> You are not you, for you are God.
> Who are you, then?
> You are nothing, and everything.

18

Sacrament of Penance

(Scripture selection — John 20:19-23)

Since I heard his story for the first time from Sister Bosco in second grade, I have always had a devotion to Blessed Damien the Leper. Over this past Lent I reread his biography, *Holy Man*, by Gavan Daws, and was moved yet again.

Try to guess what was the heaviest cross Father Damien bore.

• Was it his quarter-century away from family and home in Belgium while he labored as a missionary in the then very primitive Hawaiian Islands? No . . .

• Was it his sixteen years isolated on Molokai where he zealously served the most scorned and forgotten of all, the lepers? No . . .

• Could it have been the misunderstanding he experienced at the hands of his own religious superiors? No again . . .

• It must have been the extreme physical suffering he bore when he himself contracted leprosy. (Will we ever forget the story of his poor leprous housekeeper accidentally spilling the tea kettle on his legs while Father Damien was saying his office, falling to her knees to apologize, until they both realized he had felt nothing from the scalding water, thereby knowing that he, too, had the dreaded disease . . . and then the following Sunday instead of beginning his sermon with his usual "My beloved lepers," he said, "We lepers . . .")

• Was it that physical anguish — which was so bad that he had to put his cassock on over a wooden frame to keep it from touching his bloated, poisoned body, the image captured in his sculpture in the U.S. Capitol — surely that was his heaviest cross? . . . Guess again!

• Well, then, it must have been the emotional anguish caused by the malicious charges by critics that he had contracted the disease through sexual immorality? No!

The heaviest cross Damien the Leper had to carry, according to his own testimony, was the impossibility of frequent confession, since no other priest could come upon the island of Molokai. Can you imagine? With all his suffering, the worst he bore was missing the sacrament of penance. You've heard what he would do, haven't you? He would wait on the dock with his lepers as the dreaded ships would come to bring supplies and more victims, and he would yell up at the captain, asking if a chaplain were aboard. Periodically there would be; but, more often than not, the priest would not be allowed to leave the ship. So, Father Damien would yell his confession in Latin or, if the priest could comprehend, in his native Dutch, and then receive absolution from the deck of the ship. In his words, "That sacramental absolution meant more to me than the tea, tobacco, clothing, food, or letters being brought ashore."

Is it mere coincidence that our Lord gave us this sacrament as one of his first gifts after his resurrection? According to the Evangelist, it was that very first Easter Sunday evening when Jesus imparted to his Church the forgiveness of sins, sharing with his first priests the power to pardon sins in his name. His first gift upon his resurrection! He did not say, "I promise you eternal life!" — although he certainly did win that for us. Nor did he proclaim, "I have conquered Satan for you!" — although he accomplished that too. No, what he most wanted to give his Church was mercy for sins, and share with his priests the power to absolve them. "Peace I give you! Whose sins you shall forgive, they are forgiven them, and whose sins you shall retain, they are retained." According to the Council of Trent, that is the moment of the institution of the sacrament of penance.

Francis de Sales observes that every mother shows her love to her baby in three ways: feeding, cleaning, and correcting, and thus did the risen Savior impart to Mother Church the mandate to cleanse in baptism, feed in Eucharist, and correct in penance.

I know some will brand me hopelessly naïve because of this observation, but I detect in the Church today a grassroots movement calling us all to a profound appreciation of the Lord's mercy. In the midst of the crisis, crime, immorality, violence, hatred, injustice, and evil of the "civilization of hate," or "the culture of death," God's people are again recognizing the overwhelming power of his mercy. This should not surprise us, as almost all now acknowledge that the loss of a sense of sin is the beginning of the decline of faith, and is the major religious problem of our time. H. Richard Niebuhr, criticizing much modern theology, observed, "A God without wrath brought men without sin into a kingdom without judgment, through the ministrations of a Christ without a cross."

In one of his last public addresses, during the presidential prayer breakfast at the White House, Bishop Sheen remarked that Catholics used to be ridiculed for believing that one human person, our Lady, was free from sin; now, he remarked, the Church is criticized for believing that only one, and not everyone, is without sin! The Little Flower writes that a humble recognition of our own sinfulness, and an acceptance of God's mercy, is the beginning of all growth in holiness. That self-taught psychologist, Ignatius of Loyola, claims that the road to perfection begins with the acknowledgment of God's love, the admission of our unworthiness of it, due to sin, and then the acceptance of his merciful love as an unmerited gift.

I just finished the autobiography of Billy Graham, who says that all faith begins with the recognition that we need salvation, we need redemption because of our sins, and then acceptance of the mercy of God available in Christ. That's what he preached on his famous crusades. I have been intrigued by the amazing popularity of the Divine Mercy devotion, how so many of you have found consolation and challenge in the mystical revelations given the recently canonized Faustina, all boiling down to our Lord's burning desire to shower us with his mercy.

This explosion of interest and craving for mercy, this recognition that we need it, is generating genuine renewal in the Church, and — here is where I will be dismissed as naïve — will, I predict, slowly lead to the rediscovery of the beauty and power of the sacrament of penance. How we need it!

When the history of postconciliar Catholicism is written fifty years from now, scholars, I am convinced, will point out as a casualty of the Second Vatican Council the near disappearance of the sacrament of penance. There are those of us who well remember lines so long that to wait an hour for confession on Saturday afternoon was not extraordinary, when lines literally stretched out to the street as penitents waited for the sacrament, especially during

Advent and Lent. Frequent confession was common, annual confession the minimum. That sacrament was almost more associated with Catholic folklore than reception of the Eucharist.

But no more! Even sincere Catholics will admit they have not been to confession in years; some parishes have actually stopped scheduling confessions. Pope John Paul II himself observes that "the Communion lines get longer, the confession lines shorter."

I remember once hearing the first confession of a little boy who was obviously very nervous, and, at the end, I said, "You did so well! It will be much easier next time."

To which he replied, "You mean I have to do this again?" I'm afraid many never do it again. Devotional historians of the future may conclude that this could have been the Lord's way to purify the sacrament of penance from the mechanical routineness, and tendency to scrupulosity and gloom that at times characterized preconciliar days. But I pray, and my gut tells me, that the destructive and discouraging decline may be over.

In my years as rector at the North American College, I have been blessed with hearing a lot of good news, from increased enrollment, to a balanced budget, to impressive physical improvements. But the best news I ever heard came several years ago when our spiritual directors said to me, "You know, there are so many men going to the Jesuit confessor on Monday evening that he's down there until close to 9:00 p.m. We think we should begin assigning one of the spiritual directors as a backup man on Mondays." Now that's the best news I've heard!

My point is that I think we are turning the corner, that all over the Church we detect a groundswell of a renewed reliance on this powerful sacrament, and that I am now speaking to the men who will be the agents of Divine Mercy, the sacramental reconcilers of the Church in the third millennium. So it would make sense to speak to you of the sacrament of penance from two angles: you as a confessor, and you as a penitent.

First, each of you priests and future priests as a confessor. Do you seminarians ever think of yourselves as confessors? You should . . . you should dream about it, relish it, prepare for it. It is one of the greatest joys of priesthood.

I received a letter from one of our alumni, Father Jim Hauver, known as "joggin' Jim" from Duluth, Minnesota. Listen to his observations on his first year of priesthood:

> The actual experience of priestly ministry has been at once challenging, humbling, and awe-inspiring. The celebration of Mass, the very center of a priest's life, is now the absolute focus of my own spiritual life. And how can I describe the joyous and humbling experience of pastoral ministry: anointing and bringing Communion to an elderly patient near death, but profoundly trusting in the Lord's mercy; hearing the confession of a penitent returning to the sacraments after years away from the Church; giving absolution to a tortured soul longing for forgiveness for an ancient sin. Yes, there have been difficulties, but I wouldn't trade my priesthood for all the wealth and splendor of the world.

Let me approach the priest as confessor in three ways, all "c" words: the confessor as Christ, the virtue of compassion, and the necessity of confidentiality.

I can only speak for myself, although I have heard scores of brother priests say the same thing, but I never feel more a priest than when hearing confessions. We believe, as Pope John Paul II has so eloquently taught, that the essence of priesthood is "configurement" to Christ as the head and shepherd of the Church to such an intimate degree that we actually act in his person. Never do I feel more *in persona Christi* than in the confessional. Our people know that they are not confessing to a priest but to our Lord. We stand in his place. We are his ears, his words, his forgiveness! Christ is the minister of the sacrament, and we act in his person, and how awesome and humbling that is!

An alumnus was telling me how he and his classmates went to see Padre Pio some forty years ago while seminarians here. They waited for hours in line to go to confession to him, but never got in. The next morning after Mass, they met him, and this young seminarian told Padre Pio how disappointed he was at being unable to confess to him. The great priest shrugged and said, "Go to confession back in Rome. It's the same thing!" He wasn't being rude — he was being realistic! Christ is the confessor; we priests are only his instruments.

Now that gives us much-needed confidence. I often hear seminarians say how the thought of hearing confessions makes them nervous, and that's certainly understandable. But they shouldn't be. Christ does the work; he is the confessor. The sacrament works in spite of us! The grace of God's mercy flows through us. The sacrament works.

So every priest has stories about things he said in the confessional that have no logical explanation, of people that come up to him and recount helpful words he said to them in confession of which he has absolutely no memory. Do not be surprised. We are acting *in persona Christi.*

So it is that the major message we proclaim in the beautiful sacrament is not a proposition, not advice, but a person: we proclaim Christ! As confessors, we are not theologians, although Lord knows a sound knowledge of theology, especially a good grasp of solid moral theology, is called for. As confessors, we are not psychologists, although insights from that helpful discipline are valuable. As confessors, we are not social workers, or friends, or advice columnists, although elements from each of those roles would be beneficial. As confessors, we are Christ, and so the major thing we say is, "Our Lord loves you very much; Jesus now completely forgives all your sins; your sorrow for sin moves his Sacred Heart; heaven is rejoicing because you have returned; Jesus is happy because you have accepted his invitation to repent and have made his cross worthwhile; Jesus never loves us more than when we tell him we're sorry."

Not much theological profundity there, not heavy on psychology, social work, or practical advice — but watch the tears, hear the sighs and the sobs. It is Christ who works in the sacrament, not so much us, and to assure the penitent of Christ's love and mercy is the main task of the confessor.

Periodically you find yourself trembling as you contemplate the grandeur of the sacrament. How dare I! How dare I say, "I absolve you from your sins!" I am claiming to be Christ. Tremble indeed, for that is exactly what you are claiming, to act *in persona Christi.* Get out of the way and let him work in this marvelous sacrament.

Now, that having been said, Jesus does act through us, so our skill, our part, is necessary, too. The qualities we bring as a confessor can, therefore, make it easier for the penitent to meet Christ in the sacrament, or it can make it harder. God forbid we should ever block out Christ. He is there in the sacrament. If he is not discovered therein, it is either the fault of the penitent or the confessor. God forbid it be ours!

The most essential attribute we need as a confessor is compassion, which, of course, means to "feel with" our penitent. A confessor who is brusque, rushed, crabby, impatient, distracted, disinterested, distant, or cold can hardly attract people to the compassionate Christ.

We use the term "hearing confessions" purposefully. The "matter" of the sacrament is the confession of sins by the penitent. We are most helpful in listening. Every muscle of our body is taut so intently do we listen. It is an active listening. We give the penitent the impression we have all the time in the world, that his or her confession is the most interesting thing we have ever heard, that his or her anxiety, pain, and struggle are mine as well. That's compassion.

If we yawn or doze, if we read *Sports Illustrated* or keep checking our watch, if we seem bored or far away, that is not compassionate. Just to listen intently and lovingly is half the battle. We often say more by how we listen than how we speak.

The first time I heard confessions in Italian taught me that. I perhaps understood half of what the penitent was saying, but I listened intently, maybe even harder, since I was trying so much to comprehend. When it was time for me to respond, Lord knows I could hardly say much, probably in very childlike language, then the words of absolution. But the penitent was crying and kissing my hands! I guess I was successful in showing compassion or maybe I had let an ax murderer off with three "Hail Marys"!

We are compassionate as confessors because, again, we are acting in the person of Christ. Remember, he never lost his temper with sinners, only with those who felt they were not! Never, ever, get angry with a penitent. You will regret it for the rest of your life. That does not mean you are not firm, that you do not rebuke, challenge, correct, and even admonish. But all of this can be done compassionately. In fact, people want us to take their sins seriously, because they do, or they wouldn't be there.

So, compassion can mean pointing out the horror and destruction of a sin. "Neither do I condemn you. Now go, and sin no more!" as Jesus said. But he never tried to talk people out of their sins, either. He knew that owning up to sin was the first step toward salvation. Billy Graham says the preacher's job is to convict people, to move people to be so convinced of their sins that they view themselves as convicts waiting for a sentence from the Eternal Judge.

And then our job is to give the sentence: You are forgiven! Sometimes, we priests, in an effort to be compassionate, make light of penitents' sins, or explain them away. Let our people have their sins. I just finished a book by Mary Cantwell, who recalls an incident from her life in the 1960s. Her husband had left her with two children, and she, in her troubles, began to lust after another man who was married. Although she never physically sinned with him, she had a sensitive conscience, raised as she was a Catholic, and confessed these lustful thoughts to a priest, who told her she was neurotic and apologized on behalf of the Church for making her so. She then went to another priest, who dismissed her sin as nothing. As she points out in the book *Manhattan, When I Was Young*, at this lonely, crucial juncture of her life, she deeply needed absolution, but was denied it and then drifted from the Church. Our job is not to explain sin away but to forgive it.

Part of compassion is taking upon ourselves the sins of our people. As you know, that is at the heart of the biblical understanding of priesthood. "Lamb of God, you take upon yourself the sins of the world." Jesus said, "Give me your sins, as many, as horrible, as ugly, as vicious, as embarrassing, as they are. Give them to me. I'll take care of them for you!" So do our people look to their priests to be compassionate in taking upon themselves the sins of their people. So there is nothing more exhausting than being a compassionate confessor. We take upon ourselves the sins of our people. They love to unburden themselves to us!

In an article by our former spiritual director George Aschenbrenner, S.J., he observed: "[The priest's] vocation is bathed in confession of all sorts. People confess and expose their hearts to him in intimately personal ways. . . . He sometimes feels submerged, almost to sinking, in the ugly and grimy details of the evil and suffering that drench the lives and families of his people. Fatigued and frustrated feelings [make the priest] begin to question, 'Why do they bring this all to me?' "

Padre Pio's biographers observed that his stigmata often "acted up," or hemorrhaged, in the confessional. Makes sense, I suppose. Every priest worth his salt bleeds with his penitents. His heart goes out to them in love and compassion. He takes those sins with him to the altar, to his own prayer, in his own acts of penance.

A confessor is compassionate because he is acutely aware of his own sins. A man yelled out to the Curé of Ars as he was leaving the confessional, "You must be a saint because you are such a good confessor." "If I am a good confessor," replied Vianney, "it is because I am a great sinner."

I hear the confessions of Indian sisters here in Rome every other week and want to take the purple stole off my shoulders and put it on them — I am aware of my own grievous sins as I hear those of these humble sisters. And so the priest is compassionate, as he knows his sins to be as many and as grievous as those of the person's he is hearing.

The confessor represents Christ, is compassionate, and thirdly, would die rather than break the confidence of the seal.

I hope I do not have to dwell on this. The seal of the confessional has a legendary sacredness and inviolability about it. A good confessor doesn't even speak of what he has heard, even generically, in the confessional. He would not even acknowledge that a person had been to him for confession. Scrupulous discretion and prudence are called for to protect the seal.

The stories of brave priests defending the seal are numerous. I just came upon one about a Father Pierre, to whom the parish gardener confessed that he had murdered a woman in town, and left Father Pierre's bloodstained cassock near the scene of the crime. Sure enough, all of France was shocked when Father Pierre was arrested, convicted, and sentenced to the dreaded Devil's Island, saying only at his trial, "I am innocent of this crime." There he lived a horrid life, physically and spiritually, as he was despised by the prisoners who viewed him as worse than them, a murdering priest. Yet, his charity began to win them over, and one day he was called to help a notorious prisoner who was dying.

As he looked into the dying man's eyes he whispered, "I am your friend. Can I help you?"

The man looked up at Father Pierre and said, "I am the gardener who murdered the woman." The gardener called other prisoners around, "Father Pierre is innocent. For over twenty years he has suffered because of me and he has never revealed the secret. Please now tell the officials of my public confession of guilt." With that, he quietly made another confession to Father Pierre, was absolved, and died in peace.

When Father Pierre, by the way, was offered his freedom, he chose to remain as chaplain to the prisoners. There are many such stories, and we need to hear them lest we ever be tempted to violate that sacred seal.

So much for the priest as confessor. . . . How about ourselves as penitents? You know there is an old saying that the best way to be a good confessor is to be a good penitent. Unless we love and frequent the sacrament, we probably will not be a Christ-like, compassionate confessor.

To one serious about Christian discipleship, the regular celebration of the sacrament of reconciliation is a real gift. A love for the sacrament — along with a reliance upon its mercy and grace, and a celebration of it at least once a month, if not even more frequently, but at least once a month — is essential. If such does not now characterize your spiritual regimen, see that it soon does; if you as seminarians cannot seem to make the sacrament of reconciliation a consistent part of your spiritual life, question your call to the priesthood. The growth in virtue, humble dependence upon the Lord, and constant interior renewal, the result of ongoing conversion of heart, all essentials for priesthood, are difficult even with frequent confession, but impossible without it!

When the man who was to become Pope St. Pius X, Giuseppe Sarto, was appointed bishop of Mantua, he found his diocesan clergy lazy, rebellious, and scandalous in their immorality. The Holy See told him that his main duty would be the spiritual renewal of his priests. Now, nearby bishops had tackled the same task by suspending priests, publicly castigating them, and transferring many of them from the parishes where they had pastored for years. So, when Bishop Sarto first met with his clergy, they were particularly resistant and unfriendly, suspecting he was about to lower the boom.

Instead, the wise future saint said, "Brothers, I'll make a deal: before you leave this room, I want every one of you to promise me to my face that you will do three things: celebrate Mass every day, pray your office daily, and make a good confession monthly." The priests breathed a sigh of relief, feeling they had all gotten off easy, and made the promise. When Sarto left ten years later to become patriarch of Venice, the diocese of Mantua had been revitalized, led by a zealous clergy striving for holiness.

Today we speak so glibly of biblical terms such as "conversion, metanoia, reconciliation, renewal." For us those are not fluffy clichés but real actions that occur at a precise moment in the sacrament of penance. Billy Graham said that all the success of his huge crusades came down to that one moment, what he termed his "decision for Christ," when, at the end of his final sermon, he would invite people to come forward to him and his ministers, bow their head, renounce their sin, and publicly accept the salvation of Jesus. That's our sacrament of reconciliation, just that we don't have a choir singing when it's all going on.

When I was in the seminary, at a day of recollection, the former bishop of Springfield, Illinois, Joseph McNicholas, said to us, "If you make a sincere confession at least once a month, you will be a faithful priest." At the time I thought that simplistic, but now I wonder if indeed it is true. Think about it: at least once a month, you carefully examine your life, using the Gospel, the commandments, and appropriate priestly virtues as your guide, then honestly admit your sins and bring them to a brother priest in all humility, there to express sorrow and a heartfelt desire to amend your life, finally to receive encouragement, direction, and, most importantly, the unfailing mercy of Christ and transfusion of his life — Bishop McNicholas had a point! It would be difficult to get on the wrong track, to drift, to fall into dangerous habits if we are faithful to confession.

All of you have experienced the power of the sacrament; most of you can point to it as a decisive occasion of God's grace. Every year as I read the autobiographies of our new men, I am struck by how much the sacrament of penance has helped them toward the priesthood. So many have personal stories of moments of crisis, doubt, and searching when they indeed met the mercy of Christ through the ministry of a priest in the confessional.

Just a few observations about the role of the sacrament of penance in your spiritual life now.

Perhaps the reason why confession is so integral to a vibrant interior life is that it fosters the virtue of humility, which is the key virtue for those seeking perfection in discipleship. It is hard work, embarrassing work, and, yes, humiliating work recalling our sins, owning up to them, and admitting them to another human being. It is a real exercise in humility, and therein is its value.

A seminarian told me that a turning point in his life came when he heard a retreat master say, "The theme of contemporary self-help is 'I'm okay — you're okay!' The theme of this retreat will be, 'I'm an ass — you're an ass!' "

So much contemporary pseudo-spirituality is built around a faulty understanding of the principle "God loves me just the way I am." Well, he does, yes . . . but, he loves me so much that he doesn't want me to remain just the way I am. . . . He is constantly calling forth the good, the light, the truth he sees in me to conquer the evil, the darkness, the sham that is also there. And the sacrament of penance is one of the most powerful ways he accomplishes that. But it takes humility to admit that we do indeed have evil, darkness, and hate within . . . but we cannot be perfect unless we are humble.

When those of you into exercise know a particular muscle, bone, or section of your body is weak, flabby, or injured, you do specific exercises to strengthen that area. Well, our "humble muscle" is weak, and the sacrament of penance can strengthen it.

A priest I know compares the sacrament of reconciliation to golf. He explains that, in every other sport, you can blame someone else for your failures: the pitching was lousy, the goalie was slow, the fish just weren't biting, the defense was lacking. In golf, there is no one to blame but you. So golfers will bore you to tears telling you how their slice is bad, their putting terrible, their low irons need work, and practice incessantly to improve their admitted weaknesses. So is the sacrament of penance one area where we can blame no one else; for a few pivotal moments it is God and me, my soul, our relationship, my sins.

I once went to confession and was griping about the other assistant until the wise confessor stopped me and said, "This is your confession, not his." Humility — "I'm not okay . . . matter of fact, at times, I'm an ass."

Flowing from that is the absolute necessity of honesty in the confessional. Lying, rationalizing, soft-pedaling, sidestepping in the confessional is as silly and dangerous as lying to your physician: you're only hurting yourself. St. Margaret of Cortona wrote, "Hide nothing from your confessor. A sick man can be cured only by revealing his wounds." St. Augustine remarks, "Lord, the depths of a man's conscience lie exposed before your eyes. Could anything remain hidden in me, even though I did not want to confess it to you? In that case, I would only be hiding you from myself, not myself from you."

That's why the Church insists on an integral confession: specific, blunt, thorough. No generic stuff like, "Since my last confession I have failed to love." Whoopee! No. It is: How? When? Where? As Chesterton said, "Sin is one thing we do not do in the abstract." "Since my last confession I have failed in chastity." Not good enough! How? Where? When? With whom? How often? Is the Church hung up on numbers and specifics? No! It is just that she wisely knows that honesty demands specifics, and the essence of the sacrament is honesty! Thus the value of a regular confessor, or of making confession part of spiritual direction — honesty is easier.

A real help to making the sacrament of penance the anchor it should be in our lives is the daily examen. This used to be a constant part of the seminary *horarium*: every day the whole house would gather in the chapel for time to review the day so each man could see where he had sinned. Thus weekly or biweekly or monthly confession would naturally flow from a recollected life where we were constantly seeing where we were hurting our beloved. Night prayer from the liturgy of the hours is a natural time to do this, and is actually built into the rite, as you know.

I remember once having the sixty-fifth wedding anniversary of a couple in the parish. At the reception I asked them their secret. "Well," the husband replied, "when we got married, Father Toolen told us that every night before we went to bed, we should kneel down next to each other at the side of the bed, say the Our Father together, then apologize to one another for any hurt we may have caused the other that day. No matter how tired, how angry, how upset we were, we were never to go to bed without saying 'I'm sorry' if we knew we had hurt the other. And we've done that!" There — that's daily examen.

I believe the Lord is calling us, priests of the new millennium, to be not only good confessors but aggressive apostles of this sacrament. The good news is that Jesus gave the Church a gift on the very evening of his resurrection, a gift by which he wants to share with all of us his victory over sin, and that gift is called the sacrament of penance. We must catechize about, preach, and promote this wonderful gift.

A prominent Jewish psychiatrist in St. Louis lived in the neighborhood of my first parish, and he would often walk on the parish grounds. One night the pastor and I were taking an after-dinner stroll, and we met up with him. He asked us about an article he had recently read documenting the sharp decline in the use of the sacrament of penance, and the two of us regrettably had to agree, sharing with him some observations as to why people were no longer frequenting the sacrament. As he got to the end of the parking lot and turned to go home, he said with a chuckle, "Well, a decline in confession is good for my business. If that sacrament ever really caught on, I'd be out of a job. People pay me well to do what you guys do in confession, and I can't even forgive their sins, all I can do is help them live with the results!"

I'll never forget that! What a great prize we have in the sacrament of reconciliation, yet how unfortunately shy we are about promoting it. How frustrating it is that we have a cure for sin, the deepest conflict in the human heart: Divine Mercy. And, yet, people ignore it.

We priests are often like an old doctor I once knew who had begun organizing health clinics in Haiti in the 1950s. He told me the greatest frustration he and the other physicians experienced was in offering medicine and cures but having people not take them. "We had a shot for typhoid, dysentery, a vaccination for smallpox, polio, and measles; we would see children dying of those diseases and yet we could not convince people to come for the cure. They were afraid, they felt they did not need it, or they felt they could handle it themselves. We were so frustrated because we had the medicine and they would not come!"

Just like us today: we have the medicine from the Divine Physician to heal the wound of sin, and often no one comes. So we must explain, encourage, invite, and coax. We are not snake-oil salesmen! We have a product that works! Fight the trend to cancel hours scheduled for confessions, with the bulletin announcement "Confession available by appointment." Come on! We cancel them because the people don't come; the people say they don't come because we cancelled the times!

We must be creative! I know a pastor, for instance, who hears confessions at 2:45 each Friday afternoon because that's when parents come to pick up the children at his school. When people are going into the hospital for surgery, we ask them if we can hear their confession. If they are shy or scared, we offer to walk them through the sacrament.

When they sit in the parlor and tell us how spiritually listless they are, how their faith seems dead, we ask them how long it has been since their last confession. We are not afraid to be bored silly sitting in the confessional for an hour with no one coming. My first pastor described it as "fishing," hours without a nibble, but then the big one comes. We have a product that works and we need to promote it like any successful salesman!

Not only does the sacrament take something away, it gives us something, namely an increase in God's life. As Jesus taught us in the Gospel, "My Father and I shall come and make our home with you!" Second only to the Eucharist is the sacrament of penance in the transfusion of grace it gives to the soul. Then what our Lord promised is ours, "Peace I bequeath to you, my own peace I give to you, a peace the world cannot give, this is my gift to you!" Thank God that you have been called to minister this sacrament of inner peace. Don't do it unless you are a devoted client yourself.

19

The Liturgy of the Hours

(Scripture selection — Luke 18:1-8)

When I was a parish priest back in the archdiocese of St. Louis, I was called once to the hospital room of a parishioner. He was in his mid-sixties, a very wealthy, prominent, and influential businessman. When I got there, he was sitting up in bed, looking very healthy, surrounded by his five sons, all of whom were in business with him. He proceeded to inform us that he had to undergo very delicate, life-threatening brain surgery to relieve an aneurysm that the doctors had diagnosed as ready to burst. Careful, competent man that he was, he then began to assign each of his son's duties.

"Al, you are an attorney. I want you immediately to review my will to make sure everything is up-to-date and in order. Michael, you're an accountant, so go over the books and assure me that there are no gaps or danger signals. Larry, as my investor, review the portfolio and determine that everything is stable and in order. Joseph, you take care of your mom and sisters. They will be very upset, and you are closest to them. You stay in touch with the doctors, and keep the family posted. And Tony, as my insurance expert, see that I am fully covered during recuperation, and take care of all the expenses."

They were all breathless and taking notes, and I was the only one left. I said to him, "And what am I to do?"

Immediately twelve eyes glared at me, all surprised that I had even asked such a question, and Leo, the father, quickly responded, "Why, Father, you pray, of course!" — as all the sons nodded in agreement, astonished that I had even to ask.

"Why, Father, you pray, of course." It was one of those pivotal, memorable moments we all have in our priesthood, when a fundamental truth so obvious it had escaped us hits home. In the eyes of our people, we as priests are the official pray-ers; our people count on us to pray with them and for them. Perhaps the most common request we as priests receive is, "Father, please pray for me."

They will constantly take us into their confidence, entrusting to us their special intentions. And we find ourselves replying dozens of times every day, "I will pray for you." Never should that be a hollow, trite, throwaway line. Even though we admit our prayers might not be the best, even though we constantly urge our people to pray themselves and not just count on us, and even though we confess that they are often far holier than we are, we know that as priests we have a sacred duty to be the official pray-ers of our people. "Why, Father, you pray, of course."

The official pray-ers. . . . Yes, our office in the Church is to pray. I want to focus precisely on the divine office. We call it "the office" because it is our duty, our job in the Church, to pray daily with and for the Church.

"Are you resolved to maintain and deepen a spirit of prayer appropriate to your way of life and, in keeping with what is required of you, to celebrate faithfully the liturgy of the hours for the Church and for the whole world?" Those of us already in holy orders answered yes to that at our diaconate ordination; those not yet will, please God, hear the bishop pose that question before too long.

By our unswerving response to that interrogation, we do become the official pray-ers of the Church, co-intercessors with Jesus before his Father. Thus the divine office becomes an intimate part of our priesthood. Corny as it sounds, we call our breviary "the Mrs." because it is as close to us as a wife, and we are rarely without her. Our breviary is like our glasses; we are lost without it.

As the Code of Canon Law describes it, "The Church, fulfilling the priestly function of Christ, celebrates the liturgy of the hours, whereby hearing God speaking to his people and memorializing the mystery of salvation, the Church praises him without interruption and intercedes for the salvation of the whole world" (No. 1173).

So, we owe it to our people to be faithful to our divine office, for we pray for them as we say the hours. As a boy growing up, I remember seeing our pastor, Father Callahan, often saying his office. Years later, when he died suddenly, I was executor of his estate, and I took for myself his breviaries for my own use. I use them —

rebound — to this day. As I looked through the well-worn pages of those four volumes, how moved I was to find so many holy cards and slips of paper with prayer intentions written on them . . . the holy card of my ordination, the one from my father's death, those of dozens and dozens of deceased brother priests of the archdiocese of St. Louis, the anniversaries of the sisters in the parish, slips of paper about gall-bladder operations, miscarriages, marital problems, unemployment . . . all taken to daily prayer as that good pastor fulfilled his divine office to pray with and for his people.

Those of you who have been privileged to attend the Holy Father's morning Mass noticed the same thing. In his prie-dieu is his breviary, overflowing with letters, cards, lists, slips of paper, and notes, all with prayer intentions. As he says his office he holds all of them up to the Lord.

George Weigel told me that at one meeting with Pope John Paul II he gave him a note from his wife asking the Holy Father to pray for a friend of hers. About six months later when George introduced Joan to the Holy Father, he asked her, "And how is your friend?" That's how seriously he takes his divine office to pray daily with and for the Church in the liturgy of the hours.

As the archbishop of Omaha, the Most Reverend Elden Curtiss, wrote to his priests on Holy Thursday, 1998, "In our role as co-intercessors with Christ on behalf of his people, we priests have accepted the obligation to celebrate the liturgy of the hours daily. The Church holds us to this obligation out of love for us and for the people we serve."

So, we owe it to our people to be faithful to the divine office. . . .

And we owe it to ourselves, to our priesthood, to be loyal to the daily office. At the risk of oversimplification, the fervor and fruitfulness of our priesthood is in direct proportion to our fidelity to the liturgy — that of the Eucharist and that of the hours.

Now, I hardly shock you when I tell you that some priests do not consider the breviary essential. You know yourselves that some today are quite blunt in admitting that they do not pray the office. Maybe this is an understandable reaction to the scrupulous ritualism with which some priests used to say the office; maybe it is part of a cultural reaction against anything mandatory.

We need not get into a "blame-game" or wag fingers at priests who say they do not pray the liturgy of the hours. We can thank God that, as a matter of fact, today there is a great resurgence in appreciation for the office, even among laypeople, and even priests who do not say it, admit that as a regret, and not as a boast.

Pragmatically, we have seen the data that tell us that a negligence in the breviary is usually the first sign that a man's vocation is in danger. Experience tells us that those who say, "Well, I don't say the office, but I do other prayers every day," are usually deceiving themselves. It has become clearer and clearer that a priest needs the daily office for his survival!

Thus is Holy Mother Church wise in mandating it. As a rector, I must be clear about that duty to candidates for ordination: as a deacon and priest you promise solemnly to pray the entirety of the office daily. Only a serious reason — sickness, for instance — would dispense from this duty. "Not enough time" is not such a serious reason! This pledge binds us under pain of sin. If you do not intend to keep the promise, don't make it — don't get ordained. By your third year of major seminary, if you are not praying the entire office habitually, if you do not love it and look forward to it, take that as a sign that you should postpone ordination until you do. May I quote from paragraph 29 of the "General Instructions of the Liturgy of the Hours"?

> Bishops and priests, therefore, and other sacred ministers, who have received from the Church the mandate to celebrate the liturgy of the hours, are to recite the whole sequence of hours each day, preserving as far as possible the genuine relationship of the hours to the time of day. They are to give due importance to the hours which are the two hinges on which this Liturgy turns, that is, Lauds as morning prayer and Vespers; let them take care not to omit these hours, unless for a serious reason. They are also to carry out faithfully the Office of Readings, which is above all the liturgical celebration of the Word of God. Thus, they will carry out daily that duty of welcoming into themselves the Word of God. That the day may be completely sanctified, they will desire to recite the middle hour and *compline*, thus commending themselves to God and completing the entire "Opus Dei" before going to bed.

Many of our students pray the entirety of the office every day from the moment they arrive at the college — bravo! For those who are developing the habit, I would think it fair to expect a first-year man to pray morning and evening prayer every day — which is obviously easy, given the blessing we have of daily lauds and vespers beautifully done in common — and compline (night prayer). By the second year I expect seminarians to work in the Office of Readings and midday prayer, so that by the third year they are praying the entirety of the office daily.

I urge you seminarians and priests to speak often to your spiritual directors about how they are integrating the liturgy of the hours into your daily spiritual regimen. Part of your discernment for priesthood should be how faithful you are to the office. If you dread it, if you can never complete it, or if you find it onerous and burdensome, the Lord may be telling you not to get ordained.

And here's a good test: How do you do on your day off? Funny enough, most priests can complete the office on their busy days, but find it tough to say it on days off or vacations.

So, let me repeat it: to pray the entirety of the office daily is a grave duty for every transitional deacon and priest. Only a very serious reason can excuse us from missing one of the hours. Careful fidelity to our divine office is necessary for the survival of our priestly vocations.

But, come on now, the divine office is certainly more than a legalistic burden that we're frightened into just to survive and to stay out of sin. In fact, it was just such an attitude that led to the unfortunate rejection of the breviary by some priests in recent years.

We have all heard of Cardinal Richelieu, who began his office for the concluding day at about 11:15 p.m., finished it at midnight, then began the next day's, saying it in forty minutes, and then announcing that he was free for the next forty-seven hours.

When I went to my diaconate assignment in England, the housekeeper led me to the pastor's study, where he was saying his breviary. I paused, impressed, until a few minutes later, he slammed it shut and bellowed out, "Thank God I got that damn thing out of the way for the day!" Not quite what the Church has in mind, I'm afraid.

No, for us, the liturgy of the hours is an act of love, not just of duty — a responsibility we enthusiastically embrace and savor; and it is not just an act of survival but an unparalleled way to deepen our spiritual life. Let me mention some genuine spiritual rewards that flow from a faithful reliance upon this great prayer.

The first and most valuable spiritual fruit of fidelity to the divine office is union with Jesus. Certainly union with Christ is the goal of all prayer. My contention is that the liturgy of the hours is second only to the liturgy of the Eucharist on the list of efficacious ways to achieve this sublime goal of union with Christ.

I contend this because the divine office is indeed the prayer of Christ. When we pray the liturgy of the hours, we are intimately united with Jesus in his infinite and eternal praise, atonement, and supplication to his Father. Not only do we pray with Jesus, we pray through him, realizing that he is the perfect mediator, our way to the Father; and we pray to him as the only begotten Son of God, "God from God, light from light, true God from true God, one in being with the Father." St. Augustine explains it far better than me: "[Jesus] prays for us as our priest, he prays in us as our head, he is the object of our prayer as our God. . . . We pray to him as God, he prays for us as a servant. We pray then to him, through him, in him, and we speak along with him and he along with us."

Or, as your old favorite, St. Fulgentius of Ruspe, reminds us: "[Jesus] is at once priest and sacrifice, God and temple. He is the priest through whom we have been reconciled, the sacrifice by which we have been reconciled, the temple in which we have been reconciled. He alone is priest, sacrifice, and temple. . . ."

You see how Christocentric the liturgy of the hours is, how union with Christ is so beautifully evident in this great prayer?

Christ prays especially in the psalms. I must admit that the older I get, the more I appreciate the psalms. They cover every emotion. In the daily life of a priest, he will experience a gamut of emotions: when he grabs his breviary to snatch some moments of prayer, he may feel terribly tired, maybe angry, perhaps confused, at times discouraged or sad, other times joyful and exhilarated, then again sick or anxious. In the psalms of his office he unites with Jesus in expressing all of these emotions to the Father. Listen to a selection of excerpts from the office of just one day, and tell me that a priest cannot say these with Jesus from the bottom of his heart!

- "I am worn out with longing for my God!"

- "In your great love rescue me from sinking!"
- "Come close to my soul and redeem me!"
- "I have reached the end of my strength!"
- "Have mercy on me, God, in your kindness!"
- "How good is the Lord: eternal his merciful love!"
- "My God, my God, why have you forsaken me?"
- "Lord, do not leave me alone!"

I reckon every one of you has expressed such sentiments to the Lord; you certainly will as a parish priest. You will find that union with Jesus in praying the psalms in the office is particularly consoling in times of struggle, discouragement, anger, or temptation. To express that in union with Jesus praying the psalms of the divine office has infinite value. As St. Ambrose observed: "Though all Scripture is fragrant with God's grace, the psalms have a special attraction. In them, not only is Jesus born for us, he also undergoes his saving passion, he lies in death, he rises again, he ascends into heaven, he sits at the right hand of the Father."

A consciousness that, while praying the office, we are in union with Jesus can help us fight the boredom and discouragement that often come in our daily desire to be faithful to our office. You see, the efficacy of the office does not depend on what we get out of it, does it, because, in the long run, we're not doing it — Jesus is, and we are in union with him in praying the liturgy of the hours. While this should never give us an excuse to be sloppy, irreverent, distracted, or perfunctory in our recitation of the office, it sure encourages us when the daydreaming and ennui come — as they do.

Secondly, the office brings us a union with the Church. "Hence, all who perform this office," teaches the council in its Constitution on the Sacred Liturgy, "are not only fulfilling a duty of the Church, but also are sharing in the greatest honor accorded to Christ's Spouse, for by offering these praises to God, they are standing before God's throne in the name of the Church, their Mother" (No. 85).

When I left the North American College in June, 1976, to return home, I got a cheap fare through Air India, and I was ecstatic to find that Mother Teresa was on the same flight. Of course I visited with her during the trip. As she left, I said to her, as thousands of others had, "Mother, please pray for me!"

She tapped the breviary I was holding and said, "We pray for each other when we pray this!" She was right — we are in solidarity with all the Church all over the world, in this endless chant of praise, supplication, and contrition from all God's people. The liturgy of the hours is thus exquisitely ecclesial. You may be saying it in some out-of-the-way hotel room, with no one around, and yet you are surrounded by the Church as you do so.

Especially — and this is the third spiritual fruit blossoming from the divine office — are we in union with our brother priests as we pray the office. I remember one of our alumni, who had been gone perhaps two or three years, returning for a visit. He joined us for corridor evening prayer, and left his breviary in my room. Not knowing whose it was, I later on opened it to find the name, and was so moved to discover tucked in the cover the list of all his classmates from here typed on a card by then well worn from use. The fraternity of priests is a theme so oft encouraged these days.

That we need the support and encouragement of one another is so true. In friendship, on vacations, in Jesu Caritas groups, through confessors and spiritual directors, just in getting together and staying in touch, we priests can support each other. But never should we forget that daily union we have with one another in our common prayer of the office. As you daily recite it, be reverently conscious of your brother priests, especially those sick, lonely, suffering, tempted, or in trouble. Recall that at the moment you are praying, you are united with hundreds of priests throughout the world praying the same words.

I propose that such a union with priests is of special value to diocesan priests. Not that religious are immune, but they have institutional safeguards built in to counter the isolation that can at times weigh upon the diocesan priest, who needs every help available to keep him united with his brother priests.

A recent alumnus ordained only two years told me how, on his day off each week, he drove the seventy miles to the closest priest for the sacrament of penance, for evening prayer together, and for a good meal, conversation, and a good night's sleep. That was the high point of his week. We may be physically distant from our brother priests in the diocese, but we are in close spiritual union with them through the liturgy of the hours.

Much is written today about the "spirituality of the diocesan priest." I am far from an expert on this, but something tells me that our spiritual life as diocesan priests must be grounded daily in the liturgy of the Eucharist and the liturgy of the hours, or it will be very shallow. Sometimes we dismiss the immense value the breviary has for our spirituality. How often, when hearing the confessions of brother priests, do we hear, "My spiritual life has been very shallow. Oh, I say my daily Mass and office, but that's it." Wait a minute! That ain't bad!

In the spirituality of the diocesan priest, to offer our daily Mass with reverence and joy, and then to pray our office with fervor and care, is the very core of our relationship with the Lord. Our daily meditation and examen can take place naturally within the plan of the liturgy of the hours. Rather than be dismissive of that foundation — "Oh, all I manage to get done is my Mass and office" — we should be grateful we at least have that cornerstone, and make sure it is done with thought, attention, and piety.

One of my pastors once said, "I don't need one of these spiritual gurus as an assistant. Had one once and all he did was go on retreats, workshops, desert days, and support-group overnights. Never got much parish work done. Hell, just give me a good guy who says his Mass and office every day!" I don't know if I'd get that skeptical, but he had a point. You will find, brothers, that as parish priests, if your daily prayer does not revolve around your Mass and office . . . it's probably nonexistent.

A fourth gift the liturgy of the hours offers us is union with eternity. "When you come to the office, it is as if you were dropping in on a conversation already in progress — a conversation between God and men which began long before you were born, and will go on long after you are dead." As that quote from Evensong in Coventry Cathedral indicates, the liturgy of the hours powerfully unites us with eternity.

For one, all of heaven joins us in the recitation of the office. Our Lady, the saints, the angels, our ancestors in the faith, and the entire communion of saints are always invisible but major participants all the same in the Church's liturgy, which shares in the eternal worship of heaven.

Two, as the liturgical documents remind us, the liturgy of the hours is meant to sanctify the parts of our day, particularly morning, midday, evening, and before bed. As far as possible, then, we should honor the integrity of the hours, avoiding praying the entirety of the office at one sitting, for instance — although that is sure preferable to missing any part of the whole office. My point here is that the liturgy of the hours reminds us poetically of the eternal rhythm of God's time, that all of the efforts and moments of our hectic day are directed to eternity, to the Lord of all time and space, and that the hours do insert our — at times cockeyed — schedule into the eternal rhythm of God's design.

Peter Levi, in his work *The Frontiers of Paradise*, comments about monks chanting the office that "monks are behaving 'as if' constancy were possible in this world. At any visitor's first entry into a monastery, time seems to stand still. This new time scale involves a tranquil, unhurried, absolutely dominating rhythm. This liturgical sense of time is the greatest difference between monastic life and any other."

Lord knows we parish priests are hardly monks, with a predictable daily schedule, but perhaps because of that do we need all the more that rhythm of the day the hours provide, keeping us united with God's eternal plan.

Three, the liturgy of the hours reminds us of the eternal truth that, ultimately, all depends on God, not us. All is in his providential hands; all does not ultimately depend upon our efficiency, productivity, and utility. Yes, sometimes we can consider our breviary "a waste of time," and, it is — as long as we remember Thomas Merton's definition of prayer as "wasting time with the Lord."

When we get back to our room at night it might be much more "productive" to return a few phone messages, write out a sermon, or shine our shoes — but we instead pray compline, thus uniting with eternity, acknowledging that this use of time is in the long run much more critical than anything else we can do. How "countercultural"! The Presbyterian poet Kathleen Norris, who writes so movingly about monastic life, notices this when she observes, "The monks' ability to maintain a schedule centered on the liturgy of the hours sets them apart from the rest of us, and, over the years, submission to liturgical time can develop a playful patience that is very much at odds with worldly values."

You see, our fidelity to the office reminds us that, in the end, eternity trumps the temporal, and that sanctifying the day with periodic prayer acknowledges the greatest revelation of all, that God is more powerful than we are, that his Son, Jesus, is Lord. Kathleen Norris again: "Liturgical time is essentially poetic time, oriented toward process rather than productivity, willing to wait attentively in stillness rather than always pushing to get the job done."

Four, the office unites us with eternity by reminding us of the value of perseverance in our prayer. Our prayer must be eternal; it must keep going. You know you can never stock up on food, eating a lot, say, on Monday so you don't have to eat the rest of the week. No — we have to eat daily — thank God. Same is true of breathing. I don't take ten deep breaths and then say, "Good, that's over for a while. I won't have to breathe for a couple of hours." Same is true of sleeping, exercising. Same is true of prayer! It must be constant, it must be ongoing, it must be persevering. As Abraham Joshua Heschel writes:

> Prayer is not a stratagem for occasional use, a refuge to resort to now and then. It is rather like an established residence for the innermost self. . . . A soul without regular prayer is a soul without a home. Weary, sobbing, the soul, after roaming through a world festering with aimlessness, falsehoods, and absurdities, seeks a moment in which to gather up its scattered life . . . in which to call for help without being a coward. Such a home is prayer.

And, I might add, such a prayer is the breviary. When Jesus teaches us about prayer, he tells us its two most essential qualities are faith and perseverance. We are never done with the office. We might "catch up," but the next hour is not far away. And well it should be, because we must be persistent, unrelenting in our prayer. It goes on for eternity. And the liturgy of the hours reminds us of that.

The divine office is a duty and a gift. It is one of the great assets of our priesthood. Not to be faithful to it is sinful, silly, sad, and tragic. To be faithful to it is an infinite blessing, uniting us with Jesus, his Church, our brother priests, and eternity.

Martin Buber, in the *Tales of the Hasidim*, writes:

Imagine a man whose business hounds him through the streets and across the market place the livelong day. He almost forgets there is a maker of the world. Only when the time for prayer comes does he remember, "I must pray." And then, from the bottom of his heart, he heaves a sigh of regret that he has spent his day on vain and idle matters, and he runs into a side street and stands there and prays. . . . I tell you, God holds him very dear, and his prayer pierces the firmament.

That man is you, the priest . . . that prayer is our divine office. I conclude with the prayer recommended to us before the office:

Lord God, I offer this divine office to you, together with the adoration and praise of the angels and saints in heaven, as well as that of all the priests of your Church and all other consecrated souls. I present to you, heavenly Father, through the Immaculate Heart of Mary, this chorus of prayer, made holy in the Sacred Heart of Jesus and made one with his most holy prayer. May all the words of this prayer be acts of pure love, adoration, thanksgiving, satisfaction, trust, and surrender to your holy will. Let this prayer be for my weak self a spiritual communion, an act of humility, and of perfect self-denial; and may it be a sacrifice of praise and glory to you, O Blessed Trinity. Amen.

20

Parish Priesthood

(Scripture selection — Mark 4:26-29)

I heard it from the man himself, George Lodes, a priest of my home archdiocese of St. Louis, who, while in Rome in 1962, had the privilege of an audience with Pope John XXIII. He recalled that there were about ten others priests in the *sala*, and he was last in line to greet the pontiff. Each of the priests before him introduced himself to John XXIII, told him what he did as a priest, and then knelt to kiss the fisherman's ring.

"I am a university president," the first one reported, and then knelt to kiss the pope's ring; "I teach in a college," the next said, genuflecting for the *baciamano*; "I am a hospital chaplain," declared the next, dutifully genuflecting; "Holy Father, I am chancellor of my diocese," the next said, then knelt to kiss the ring.

Well, reported my brother priest from St. Louis, as Pope John came to him he felt rather lowly, for, so he thought, his priestly work was hardly as exalted as those nine before him, so he almost inaudibly whispered, "Holy Father, all I am is a parish priest."

Whereupon, to his consternation Pope John genuflected before him, kissed his hands, and stood to say, "That's the greatest priestly work of all!"

A parish priest . . . the greatest priestly work of all . . . the Scripture citation mentioned at the beginning of this chapter is from Mark's Gospel about the man scattering the seed and watching the harvest grow. The field for the seed is the parish; the harvest grows in the parish.

When the judge asked the infamous thief Willie Sutton why he robbed banks, he replied, " 'Cause that's where the money is." When they ask us, "Why do you want to be a parish priest, we can respond, " 'Cause that's where the souls are!"

The parish priest is on the front lines of the Church. We can talk about all the programs, all the movements, all the initiatives, all the goals; we can talk about evangelization till we're hoarse, and none of these things amount to a plate of polenta if they are not implemented in the parish, led by the holy and zealous priests. No wonder Pope John said that being a parish priest is "the greatest priestly work of all!"

Now, don't get me wrong: parish priesthood is not the only area of effective ministry. I would sure be depressed if I believed that, for of my nearly twenty- four years as a priest (at this writing), only eight have been as a full-time parish priest. Certainly the work my brother priests on the faculty do so well is immensely noble, and they are not parish priests; certainly the priestly ministry of priests in advanced theological study at our graduate house, the Casa Santa Maria, and priests who labor for the Holy See — all of this has priceless value. But I'd bet my bottom lira that every one of those men who are diocesan priests would rather be a parish priest if he had his way, which, of course, he doesn't, that every one of them looks forward to the day he can return to it; and that every priest, of every different religious order, in every array of priestly ministry, will tell you of his high regard for the men who bear that sacred title of pastor, men who come in direct contact with the people of God every day as parish priests.

As I often say to the seminarians in Rome, the seminary there, like every diocesan seminary, exists to form good, holy, effective parish priests. If they are not excited about spending the rest of their lives as parish priests, they should be elsewhere. Will some of them end up teaching? Yes! Will some of them end up doing graduate work? Yes! Will some of them end up working for the Holy See? Yes! Will some of them end up as chaplains or heads of diocesan or national offices? Yes! Will some of them be in seminary work? Yes! But they shouldn't count on it! And, if they do end up in those other apostolates, it's only because they were darn good parish priests and would have preferred to have remained so!

Some priests, vocation directors, and even bishops say to me, "I'm reluctant to send men to Rome to study because then they think they're too good for parish work. They come back expecting that, after a couple years treading water in a parish, they'll be sent back for degrees, and then have office jobs or career assignments." Now, all I can tell them is that such a view is completely contrary to all the North American College stands for, and that our men here want nothing more than to be faithful parish priests, that their highest ambition is to be pastors.

I use the word "excitement" to characterize what should be your posture toward parish priesthood, because, far from being a constraining ministry, it is the most challenging and expansive in the whole Church. A good parish priest is pastor, confessor, hospital chaplain, social worker, administrator, teacher, preacher, financial planner, psychologist, neighborhood activist, health care specialist, organizer, development director, canonist, legal expert, cantor, marriage and family counselor, homeless advocate, gerontologist, baby-sitter, employment agency worker, youth director, sacramental minister, etc.! It is one of the most exciting forms of life possible.

I just read an article written by a diocesan priest, Father Richard Antall, as he concluded a parish assignment. Listen to his observations:

> Parish priesthood involves a man in so many different lives. My ministry . . . placed me in the vortex of changes in a small town with social problems such as immunization, health care for the poor, family fragmentation, alcoholism, and violence. . . . I was there for it all — the hospital, the morgue, the jail, the courtroom, the family home saddened by grief. . . . Parish priesthood is so public, yet intimate. At marriages, baptisms, conversions, and confessions, the life of a parish priest involves him . . . with so many people. This is another reason for priestly celibacy — we priests need room in our hearts for everybody.

You see, each parish is a microcosm of the Church universal, presenting all the joys, challenges, and sorrows of life.

And more and more bishops are saying that their diocesan clergy must be first and foremost parish priests. The days when a diocesan priest can be freed up for full-time teaching, or study, or diocesan administration are coming close to an end. Men who have such duties usually carry them out in addition to parish assignments. A bishop knows, of course, that pastors are of primary importance, and that he cannot afford to take men away from such an essential and noble apostolate. All this is my way of saying it again:

be ready, willing, and eager to spend the rest of your life as a parish priest.

So we need to examine our consciences: on your part, do you have any secret desires for special consideration, extraordinary assignments, or any type of ministry outside of a parish? If so, you are setting yourself up for disappointment. Do you think that your education makes you "too good" for parish priesthood? Good God, I hope not! Is there any kind of clerical ambition or careerism that will eventually make you restless serving in a parish? Better deal with it now.

On the part of the North American College we must examine our consciences to make sure we are preparing our students well for parish priesthood. That is why the programs in homiletics, pastoral counseling, and presiding at the sacraments are so vital. That is why we insist on second and third summers in a supervised parish assignment. That is why we hold all accountable for an apostolate. That is why your advisers and spiritual directors point out to you behavior that would diminish your evangelical effectiveness in a parish. That is why when advancing you each year in our evaluation sessions, we as faculty members find ourselves asking questions like: If I were a pastor, would I want this man as my associate? If I meet one of this man's parishioners five years from now, would he shake my hand and thank me for helping prepare him, or would he punch me in the nose and say, "How did you ever let this guy through?" Or, if my sister were dying in the hospital, would I want this guy to tend to her as her parish priest? Because, again, everything we do here has as its goal the formation of good, effective parish priests.

Let me get specific, down to some meat-and-potato observations about the life and demands of parish priesthood.

First, the mission of a parish priest is first and foremost sacramental. By that I mean that his main work is to administer the sacraments with faith, reverence, and sincerity.

On the frieze around the former main altar of our chapel at the North American College, you see captions accompanying scenes of a priest celebrating the sacraments. The planners of this chapel wisely wanted us daily to look at that priest administering the sacraments to remind us that we are here in preparation for doing just that the rest of our lives.

"All the visible realities of our Redeemer have passed over into the sacraments," writes Pope St. Leo the Great. Do you believe that? A parish priest must have immense faith in the power of the sacraments, and believe there is nothing he can do to help his people more than to give them the sacraments.

Now let that sink in, because sometimes today you hear a warning that parish priests are being "reduced" to sacramental ministers. Funny . . . I always thought the joy of our vocation was in being "elevated" to being sacramental ministers! Granted, there is legitimate cause for caution lest a parish priest become robotic, mechanistic, a mere functionary in his celebration of the sacraments. But, if we believe in the utter power of the sacraments, if we are convinced that there is nothing better we can do to assist our people than to bring them the sacraments, that will not happen. We are most a pastor when we are administering the sacraments.

I once resided in a parish where the pastor boasted that he had shared so much of his ministry with laypeople, a good idea, until he went on to elaborate, that:

• he had a corps of lay ministers bring Communion to the sick, so he never went;

• he had laypeople prepare couples for marriage, so he only had to show up for the ceremony itself;

• he had laypeople instruct parents of infants before baptism, which was celebrated only once a month;

• he had laypeople preside over Communion services two days a week instead of Mass;

• he had his nonordained pastoral associate preach at all the Masses one weekend a month so he was free of homily preparation;

• he had laypeople trained to do wake and communal services . . . all of this, he beamed, "so he as pastor could be free to attend to the really important matters."

Am I the only one who sees the irony here? Lay ministry, a genuine blessing in today's Church, is intended to do the opposite: free the pastor to attend to the sacraments! Yes, properly trained and commissioned laypeople can and should assist the parish priest, but can never replace him. Why? Because our main duty is sacramental!

Listen to these rather blunt words from the respected Jesuit theologian Jean Cardinal Danielou:

271

All of a sudden, poor pastors no longer know what to do! They had become priests to distribute the sacraments, and they were quite right! It is indeed for this reason that we become priests. . . . But now they have been told that it is the "word" which is the only important thing and the sacraments are secondary. They have been informed with scholarly airs that sacraments are mere rituals, vestiges of the Old Testament and of paganism, reeking of superstition. And so, they try to become as useful as they can, in doing their therapy, in building houses, in teaching sociology, and, of course, in streaming out words without stop.

But, how is this going to change the world? How is this going to change life? Jesus Christ did not come to make speeches. He came to change life. He changed it by his death and resurrection. . . . It is by the sacraments that his life is communicated. And it is by the priest that the sacraments are given.

At the seminary, we prepare men for a life where the most important service they will perform for their people is to daily — especially on the Lord's day — celebrate the Eucharist for them, sometimes even two or three times a day; where the most effective service you can perform for the sick is to anoint them; where you can do nothing better for a family than to baptize their babies; where you can do for the burdened soul what no one else can, namely forgive their sins in the sacrament of penance; where you can be of no greater aid to the dying than by bringing Viaticum. Don't aspire to the parish priesthood unless you believe this!

You seminarians should begin now by daily renewing your faith in the power of the sacraments, by daily rejoicing in the life of God within you given in baptism, by frequently tapping into the gifts of the Spirit given you in confirmation, by daily savoring the Holy Eucharist, by frequently approaching Divine Mercy in confession, and by yearning for "configurement" to Christ in holy orders. Ours is the mystical trust in the sacraments that Newman described when he wrote:

We approach and, in spite of the darkness, our hands or our head or our brow or our lips become, as it were, sensible of the contact of something more than earthly. We know not where we are, but we have been bathing in water, and a voice tells us it is blood. Or we have a mark signed upon our foreheads, and it spoke of Calvary. Or we recollect a hand laid upon our heads, and surely it had the print of nails in it, and resembled his who with a touch gave sight to the blind and raised the dead. Or we have been eating and drinking, and, it was not a dream surely, that one fed us from his wounded side, and renewed our nature by the heavenly food he gave. . . .

That is the sacramental life we are mandated to impart as parish priests.

A parish priest has a love for souls. *"Habeo curam animarum,"* goes that beautiful old "job description" of the pastor . . . "I have the care of souls." "Give me souls — keep all the rest!" pleaded Don Bosco.

To shepherd the souls of our people to heaven . . . the role of a pastor. Romantic? I suppose. Outmoded? I hope not!

A parish priest has a love for souls. He sees beyond bodies, good looks, clothes, defense mechanisms, social status, external appearances — and gazes at the soul. He develops a sixth sense that allows him to detect those in spiritual distress. And he has favorites, whom he searches out and spends time with: those whose souls are dark due to ignorance or doubt, and who thirst for the light of Christ, and the teaching of his Church; those of the poor, whose souls are particularly cherished by him "who had nowhere to lay his head"; children, whose souls are so tender and eager to be properly formed; those who are sick and whose souls are heavy with pain and that piercing question, "Why?"; those whose souls are wounded by sin or by having drifted from the faith; souls empty and fallow, sated by the lust and luxury of our age; the souls of the elderly and forgotten, which bounce to life when someone bothers to stop and chat and show interest. These are his favorites.

"Doctor of the Soul," as Victor Frankel called the priest. "Didn't you see that brazen lady, immodestly clad, all made up, approach you for help?" the stern prior asked of Solanus Casey. "No, sorry, Father. I only saw a soul in need."

The barber said to me the other day, "Monsignor, you and I are lucky. We'll always have work, because they'll always be hair and always be souls."

The parish priest is a hard worker. Notwithstanding all the tragic headlines today of clerical sexual misconduct, I contend that what scandalizes our people far more than anything we do is all that we do not do! The major temptation of a parish priest is not sex, booze, or money, but laziness. One pastor told me, "We'll never get all the work done that people expect us to, so why even start? Fix a drink and turn on the TV." Many priests follow this old saying: "I know it's said that hard work never killed anybody, but I figure, why take a chance?"

So we show up at a parish as their new priest with sleeves rolled up ready to work hard. So it is not good to ask your pastor right off the bat what day off you have; so it is not good to start off by telling him what weeks you already have slated for your vacation; so it is not wise to outline for him what you will not do in the parish.

A few particulars here: a parish priest has to be a self-starter. You see, in most parishes you have a bottom line of duties such as daily Mass, Saturday confessions, scheduled weddings and baptisms, two or three organizations you're supposed to look after, and a number of Communion calls. Other than that, you have to have the initiative and drive to make your own work. And there are tons of that to be done! There is no end to the work that an energetic, creative, self-starting parish priest can do!

I cringe when I hear an associate pastor say, "My pastor won't let me do anything!" Sometimes I hear pastors say of their assistants, "He does all the minimum stuff I ask of him, but, that's all. If there's nothing scheduled for him, he goes out or closes himself in his room." The parish priest is never satisfied with just the minimum requirement: he is a self-starter who sees what needs to be done and does it.

A parish priest is a "general practitioner." How can a guy show up in a parish and say, 'I don't go to nursing homes!' " or, "I'm no good around the sick," or, "Teenagers drive me crazy — I'm not doing anything with them." Parish priesthood is inclusive: nothing is alien to us. We spend hours waiting in the confessional — and hours waiting for a meeting to end. We clean up messy domestic arguments — and overflowing urinals in the cafeteria bathrooms. We take out Holy Communion — and groceries for a shut-in. We close out lives at funerals — and close up the parish hall after a meeting. Nothing is above us, and nothing below us, because we're the general practitioners.

A parish priest is willing to be inconvenienced. A retreat director once told me that putting on the Roman collar is like putting on a sign saying, "Please bother me." A priest was in the airport in his collar waiting to board his plane when another man in sports clothes came up and introduced himself as a priest, too. "I never wear my collar when I travel because people keep bothering me, always coming up and wanting to talk."

"I know," the other one said; "that's why I wear mine."

Days off, vacations, time to take care of your legitimate, spiritual, and human needs are so important for a parish priest precisely because, while in the parish, you are always "on duty," always inviting inconvenience and bother. New priests often comment how they have trouble making the transition from seminary life to the parish. While both are demanding, the seminary is rather predictable and scheduled, while parish life is spontaneous and surprising.

In the parish you may look at your calendar and say: "Boy, no appointments or meetings today; I can work on my homily," and one phone call or someone at the door can change that. But we never look at people as an intrusion, because a parish priest is willing to be inconvenienced.

I have a theory that, these days, the most precious commodity we have is time. Convenience is a god; to save time, our constant goal. How countercultural, then, for a priest to be called daily to "waste time" with God in prayer, and to "lose time" and be inconvenienced by the demands of his people! "Stay with the task whether convenient or inconvenient," Paul writes to Timothy as proclaimed in the liturgy of the word.

One of the best compliments a parish priest can receive is, "He acted like he had all the time in the world, like I was no bother whatsoever."

Parish priesthood is countercultural not only because we expect and invite inconvenience, not only because we do not worship the pagan idol of convenience and are willing to "waste time" with our God and our people, but also because we freely surrender much personal liberty and are willing to be "tied down," to be bound, wedded to our parish. That's why you must be very judicious in accepting commitments outside of the parish, for your primary duty is to your parish. In a society that values "blocks of time," "free weekends," and "country escapes," the parish priest is often tied down, expects to be, and wants to be.

A parish priest knows the power of presence. Because we're here in the business of forming good parish priests, I always keep my ears open to hear what people are saying — positive and negative — about their own. I may be wrong, but I find their major criticism to be: "We don't see him that much . . . he's just not around."

People want to see their priest; they want to chat with him, shake his hand, get to know him. They expect him to be there at pivotal times such as births, weddings, sickness, trouble, and death. They even expect him to be there at less pivotal times such as meetings, basketball games, bingo, picnics, and socials. They never forget it if you actually visit their homes, a pastoral practice of enormous value that is now unfortunately being forgotten.

So, a good parish priest is a real Cal Ripkin, who is there, in the lineup, day after day, one who agrees with Woody Allen's observation that "half of success is just showing up."

The effectiveness of priestly presence. . . . No, you don't have to be a bubbly extrovert, but you do have to be friendly, approachable, present. The parish priesthood needs no recluses, no more priests who run away from people, or hide in their rooms, or in the sacristy, or become addicted to their TV or computer. Even hardworking, affable guys these days can let the crush of meetings, committees, programs, or projects keep them locked inside bureaucracy, aloof from most of the people in the parish. One popular pastor told me, "We need street priests, guys on the playground, in the homes, all around the parish, because people love to see their priest."

A parish priest must be internally strong and confident, because, while his ministry brings much joy and affirmation, he often serves as a lightning rod, attracting much criticism in a polarized Church.

A respected pastor I know well, an alumnus of the North American College, tells me, "We've got too many priests who are fragile, who get crushed when someone criticizes them or argues with them, who pout when the pastor offers correction, who whine because no one ever thanks them. We need thick-skinned fellows who are strong inside, confident about what they're doing, and ready to take the heat."

He's got a point. You see, parish priests are on the front line of combat. Those to the far left don't like you because you represent the institutional, patriarchal, oppressive Church; those on the far right can't stand you because they believe parish priests have capitulated to the modernists.

One guy told me that on the first Sunday after altar girls were allowed, one woman backed him up against the wall for, in her words, "allowing such an abomination," while another came up and proclaimed that such trivial condescension insulted her and she would never be happy until a woman was celebrating Mass, not serving it. He got it from both sides! You certainly have to have an interior sense of self-worth, confidence, and strength in your priesthood to remain at peace and unscathed on the front lines.

As I have said before, parish priests receive a lot of affirmation from their people, but don't count on it, don't get addicted to it, don't tether your priestly effectiveness to it. And, let me approach something delicate: don't always expect your brother priests to serve as the best models for you. Priestly fraternity and support are a real blessing for us, but, ultimately, if our essential affirmation does not come from the Eternal High Priest, we're setting ourselves up for a fall. One of the struggles I most hear recounted by our alumni is dealing with brother priests, even their pastors, who do not share their zeal, noble ideals, or vision.

One priest I know well was first assigned to a large parish with a pastor, a fellow associate, and two priests in residence who had another diocesan job. He relished the appointment because he envisioned a rich priestly camaraderie.

After a few weeks he found the one priest passed out drunk on the steps; he kept hearing commotion from the other priest's room only to find out that often he invited the seventh- and eighth-grade boys over for wrestling matches on the floor and then had them all shower in his bathroom; the other resident was a fine man but would only talk to him during commercials because he watched TV most of the time.

Thank God he had a wise pastor who told him, "Quit feeling sorry for yourself. Your priesthood does not depend on anyone but Christ. You can do three things: one, get judgmental, depressed, and cynical about your situation, which would be a mistake; two, figure that you might as well quit trying to be a good priest, lowering your standards to those of the ones around you; or, three, love the men you're with, help them as much as you can, and don't let your priesthood depend on the example or support of anyone except Jesus."

Some of you guys will quickly be assigned by yourself, far away from a brother priest. It will be necessary to nurture solid priestly friendship and structure time for sacerdotal fraternity. I recently received a letter from one of our alumni, Father Antonio Dittmer, telling me how happy he is as a parish priest, but commenting, "The great adjustment is going from an atmosphere where one hundred fifty peers support me to one where I live with a seventy-year-old priest, a staff of women all over fifty, and very few people my own age." Of most importance is to nurture your own interior life, staying healthy, holy, strong, and confident in your identity and vocation.

To repeat, a parish priest must be internally strong and confident, because, while his ministry brings much joy and affirmation, it also brings criticism, rejection, and sometimes less than helpful support and example from brother priests.

All right, that's some of the meat and potatoes of parish priesthood. Let's get to the *dolce*.

Do you think that I have presented a too blunt, realistic, sobering picture of parish priesthood? Good! Then my words have been a success. In justice we must make sure seminarians know what they're getting into; it is a tough, demanding, difficult, at times tedious, humanly unrewarding life. Know that! Do not be surprised when loneliness, boredom, fatigue, doubt, criticism, scandal, and lack of gratitude and affirmation come.

But, my brothers, parish priesthood is also the most exhilarating, rewarding, meaningful ministry there is, because it allows you to bring God to your people and your people to God. All the warnings I have issued in this chapter notwithstanding, there is no other work in life where more good is done, more graces channeled, more souls saved, than parish priesthood. You all know that. Rereading the autobiographies of our new men as I prepare to meet with them in the weeks ahead, I am again moved by how many point to the direct influence of a happy, committed parish priest, usually your own, upon your vocation.

Not long ago I had a visitor from my first parish assignment. I could hardly recall her. She proceeds to show me the picture of her two-year-old grandson, and tells me that his name is "Timothy Michael," after me, because her daughter, the little boy's mother, remembered me so gratefully from a very difficult time when she was in seventh grade. I can't even remember who she was! I never even knew I had done anything! There's the power of parish priesthood.

We are the dispensers of God's grace; others look to us to be men of God, to remind them of God. As the Holy Father wrote in *Pastores Dabo Vobis*, "The priest must be a man of God, the one who himself belongs to God and makes people think of God. People expect to find in their priest . . . a man who will help them turn to God . . . and so, the priest must have a deep intimacy with the Lord."

Nemo dat quod non habet . . . that's why the sacred enterprise of the seminary is to develop a rich interior life protected by habits of holiness, to foster a strong sense of self-confidence, call, and priestly identity that will see you through tough times, and to gain theological depth and effective pastoral skills precisely so you can bring the life of God to your people and your people to the life of God.

Let one of "our people," a woman in the pew, conclude. Here is a poem she wrote to her parish priest written Father's Day, published in *The Priest*:

> Who are you, man of Mystery, our Father?
> By what arrogance do you approach the Holy —
> offering your manliness to mate with Sacred Spouse,
> and vowing with such singular abandonment
> to wed yourself to Holy Mother Church
> and sow with her, in promiscuity divine, the seeds of Life?

Or can it be that, led by ceaseless calling,
summoned by the Matchmaker who serves the cause of Love,
pursued by the Relentless One, you have succumbed —
and so it is submission which, to unholy eyes, appears
    presumption?

How is it that, child-free, you are our Father?

Is it that you daily bear God's children?
Is it that, with human voice, you speak a Father's Word?
Is it that you, fasting and breaking fasts, call us to supper
and gather us at table for meal of Bread and Wine?
Or that you celebrate our rites of passage,
advising, chastising, baptizing us with water and with fire?

Is it that you lift us in your prayer, holding,
embracing and blessing as only a Father might?
Or that you hear our calling in the dark
and come to take our hand and light a light —
Or, in your priestly parenting,
you come anointing, pointing the way past death to life?

Who are you, man of Mystery, our Father?
You've wed yourself to Holy Mother Church and, everywhere,
you sow with her, in promiscuity divine, the seeds of Life.
You bear and speak and feed, you shape and renew
and heal and bless as only a Father can do.
And so we, on this Father's Day, your untold children,
    grateful, pray,
"May life and Holy Spouse and God bless you."

21

Priestly Zeal

(Scripture selection — 2 Timothy 1:6-12)

Each of us, I suppose, had priests we looked up to when we were growing up. One of my models was the pastor of my home parish, Father Schilly. To me he was an exemplary priest: in love with his priesthood, confident in his priestly identity, a respected leader in the parish, a man who would open the church way before the six o'clock morning Mass so he could pray and then remain afterwards for his thanksgiving.

But I smile now as I recall some of the things that initially attracted me to the priesthood through him: he drove a big new Buick; he knew very fine restaurants; he could get box seats at a Cardinal baseball game; he went on great vacations; he was held in awe by the parishioners; no one would question his authority; people would seek his help and counsel; if he visited a home, everyone knew it and these people were thought special. In a word, he was a leader, a man with clout, respected by people, a man of power and prestige who enjoyed the good things of life and was very happy in his priesthood. It was easy for me to want to be like him! This is the priesthood I found attractive!

One Christmas Eve morning, when I was a senior in the high school seminary, he asked me to accompany him on his Communion calls to the local nursing home. The thought of driving the Buick, with people waving as we passed, impressing some of the neighborhood girls, was exciting. Of course I went! Plus I knew it would merit at least a twenty, since Father Schilly was very generous, and probably a steak at lunch at the Coach House Restaurant, where all the waitresses snapped to attention at the pastor's entrance, and where I could even drink a beer with no questions asked, since I was under the protection of such a *pezzo grosso* ("big shot").

Our first stop was the local nursing home. I had passed it all my life but never been in, an old three-story house on a hill in town.

Father Schilly explained to me that he came here weekly to visit the residents and bring the sacraments to the half-dozen or so Catholic patients. Never will I forget the smell as I walked in — the odor of human waste, the dirt, the dinginess — I almost suggested I wait in the Buick.

Father smiled and greeted the people in wheelchairs, and we went to the room of the first Catholic resident. I gasped as we entered, for there she was, yellow, skeletal, probably ninety pounds, lying on the floor beside her bed in a puddle of her own urine, her soiled nightgown almost twisted off her. This hardly seemed the proper place for this distinguished gentleman pastor! I froze, not knowing what to do.

And Father Schilly? He bent over her, consoled her, got her to smile, and directed me to help him lift her to bed. He then took a wet towel and soothed her face, went and got a mop — he was obviously used to this — and cleaned up the urine. He settled her in bed, calmed her down, prayed with her, gave her Holy Communion, chatted with her, gave her a little bottle of lotion as a Christmas gift, and we left her. His tender love for her was so evident! And on we went to each patient, as he lit up with care for each of these forgotten, dying, neglected, unattractive people! Now, this was a part of priesthood I had not thought of!

I share this recollection with you because it was a turning point in my life regarding my own appreciation of priesthood. What really happened is that I made the step from priestly identity to priestly zeal.

Ordination reconfigures us to Christ at the core of our being, that we are priests before God and his Church, that priesthood is forever and faithful, that what we do as priests must flow from who we are, from our priestly identity. Now let's take the next logical step: our priestly identity is not some cozy, comfortable possession we keep to ourselves and hold over others. It is a gift, an identity, all right, but one that by its nature constantly compels us to selfless, sacrificial love and service of God's people!

In Father Schilly I saw priestly identity; that Christmas Eve I also saw his priestly zeal. Priestly identity without zeal is clericalism; zeal without confident and sustained identity will not last.

Our mission at the North American College is to form zealous priests: that means priests on fire with love for God and his people, priests whose greatest privilege is to serve their people, at the cost of sacrifice and even maybe life itself. Their motive is the salvation of the people entrusted to their care, to bring people into living contact with Jesus the Savior through his Word, his Church, his sacraments. We are excited about this, indefatigable in our efforts, enthusiastic in our ministry, men driven by a supernatural task that has captivated us. That's zeal.

The inspiring Jesuit preacher and author Walter Burghardt speaks eloquently about the words we use at every Eucharist, "He took the bread, he blessed it, broke it, and gave it to his disciples." He then applies them to us as priests: Jesus also takes us — he has chosen us as his priests. Jesus blesses us — as he configures us to him in holy orders. Now, these two, taking and blessing, are pleasant concepts. Then — are you ready? He breaks us — as we are broken, wounded, poured out, drained — even as he gives us in sacrificial service to his people.

Are you ready to spend your life giving to others? Are you prepared for at times unrewarding service, constant inconvenience, continual giving, radical availability — to be taken, blessed, broken, and given? If you are approaching the priesthood as a life of ease, comfort, convenience, advancement — and it can be — get out! We do not need any more lazy, whining, self-serving, lethargic priests. Their name is legion!

When I was a deacon here I took a summer assignment in Liverpool, England. The pastor was one of the most colorful men I ever met. The first evening I reported to the presbytery I said, "Father, what would you like me to do?" He replied, "I do nothing and you assist me!" I thought he was joking until the next morning. The first Mass wasn't until noon; he came for breakfast at ten o'clock, read the paper leisurely over a hearty breakfast, went to church about 11:15 to read the entire office, said Mass at noon, and, at 12:15, back in the sacristy, said to me, "Phew . . . I can finally relax!"

I hear some of our seminarians say to me after their summer apostolates that they are somewhat scandalized by the priest they work under, not because he drank, chased women — or men — or lived an opulent lifestyle, but because he did nothing. If you want it to be, the priesthood can be one of the most comfortable, cozy lives around, and you have all seen priests who have made it so.

One of my priest-friends said, "The major health problem of priests today is not burnout but bed sores." A very effective bishop at home observed to me, "If I could get my priests to put in an eight-hour day, forty-hour week, I'd have the most vibrant, evangelized diocese around. The problem is not priest-shortage but zeal-shortage." This scandal of lazy, listless, lethargic priests can only be corrected with a strong dose of the virtue of zeal.

We need, not tired, scared, pampered priests who are only concerned about their time off, their rooms, their cars, their clothes, their comfort, their rights, but priests whose hearts are so on fire with love for Jesus and the salvation of his people that, as St. Paul said, "all is rubbish save my knowledge of Jesus Christ."

Now, you know as well as I do that most priests work hard and are selfless servants of Christ and his Church. Odds are you would not be here had it not been for the example of such a zealous priest. We know too that misguided zeal can destroy a priest if he does not care for his own spiritual, personal, and physical life. All I am asking is that we hold up the ideal of a priest who is so in love with Jesus and his Church that he is bursting to bring that to others, not sit in the rectory and watch soaps; who is not afraid of plain hard work, instead of spending hours in his health club; who is available in service to his people, not protected by ironclad office hours; who expects inconvenience and does not pout if his tee-off time is occasionally delayed; who tells his fellow priests in the parish and his people he's at their service and willing to try his best to do what they ask instead of listing the things he will not do; who meets his pastor by saying, "What can I do to help?" instead of "Here's what I won't do" — that's zeal. Remember my favorite quote from Pope John Paul, his words to priests and seminarians: "Love for Jesus and his Church must be the passion of your lives!"

Passion! That's what zeal is about! We're excited! We're eager! We're raring to go! We've got the chutzpa, nerve, energy, drive, and zest of the apostles that first Pentecost morning. Do you have it? Are you itching to get out and help Jesus deliver his Kingdom to his Father? If not, I'd head elsewhere, because we've passed our quota of tepid, lackluster, couch-potato padres.

One of the greatest revivalists in colonial America, George Whitefield, said, "The reason why congregations have been so dead is because dead men preach to them."

We're talking about a vocation that entails, as St. Paul wrote, "being poured out like a libation."

We're being configured to the One who said:

- "I've come to light a fire."
- "Don't put anyone or anything ahead of me!"
- "Don't follow me unless you turn your back on every other interest and attraction."

That to me hardly sounds like a lackluster, halfhearted, mediocre style of life. That sounds like a life to be embraced with zeal.

Let me be candid: I worry that all the scandals, all the problems, all the cases of priests who have left, all the studies on the crisis in the priesthood, all the talk about shortage and burnout, all this has robbed us of our zeal. We are tempted to run, to hide; we become tired, cautious men who prefer to speak of limitations instead of possibilities, who begin by stating what we can't do rather than what we can, who husband our resources instead of risking all for Christ. Where is the daring, the energy, the zeal? You know what image comes to mind? The dry, lifeless, scattered bones, over which Ezekiel prophesied, injecting them with God's power and forming them into a living, breathing, strong person. That's what the priesthood needs today!

Let me get more specific in observations about priestly zeal.

Our zeal is not directed to earthly success — our zeal is directed to the salvation of souls. "Give me souls — keep all the rest," as Don Bosco said. Jesus saw to the core of a person, to the person's soul. Do you recall when the paralytic was lowered through the roof in front of Jesus? What did he heal first, body or soul? "Your sins are forgiven!" In other words, he saw beyond the twisted, powerless body and into the soul.

So do we see with the eyes of Christ in developing a zeal, a thirst for souls. "I became a priest to save my own soul and to help other people save theirs," an old priest once told me: not a bad motive at all. We are driven to win souls for Christ, to help people come in contact with the saving grace of Jesus so they can reach heaven. Remember when St. John Vianney was lost on the way to his new assignment in Ars? He asked a little boy if he knew where the village was. When the boy responded yes, Father Vianney said, "You show me how to get to Ars, and I'll spend the rest of my life showing Ars how to get to heaven." The hunger for souls!

We will do many things as priests, from coaching basketball to flipping pancakes, from directing plays to barbecuing hamburgers at a picnic, from hospitals to funeral homes, from the parlor to the pulpit — but it is all done for the salvation of souls.

Priestly zeal for souls is especially evident in our love of the sacraments. Our greatest privilege as priests is to administer the sacraments with joy and reverence, for it is in the sacraments that souls come into contact with the Savior. "All the visible realities of our Redeemer have passed over into the sacraments," as Pope St. Leo the Great said.

I remember once when one of the ladies in our quilt club at the parish passed out and they called over to the rectory. I went over as the ambulance was arriving and accompanied her to the hospital. When I returned, the pastor asked how it went. I explained, rather proudly, how I had gone with her in the ambulance, stayed in the emergency room, called her family, accompanied her to her room, and stayed with her while the doctor gave his analysis.

"Did you anoint her?" he asked. Was I embarrassed! To have given her the sacrament of the sick would have been the most effective way I could have helped her as a priest, and I had overlooked it! To baptize, to hear confessions, to celebrate the Eucharist, to prepare couples for marriage and then witness it, to get our young people ready for confirmation, to console the sick with the sacrament of anointing — this is the meat and potatoes of priestly life, and we do it with zeal in our thirst for souls.

Likewise does our priestly zeal for souls urge us to invite people into the Church. My first pastor in St. Louis said, "The two happiest questions a priest can hear from someone are, 'Father, will you hear my confession?' and 'Father, how can I become a Catholic?' " We are zealous for souls for Christ and his Church, and are eager to present the richness of our Catholic faith with conviction and cogency. We are not afraid to invite someone personally to become a Catholic, and we will always have time to give someone instructions in the faith.

We priests can never claim someone as a natural son or daughter, but we beam when we can say of someone, "He's a convert of mine." The Fundamentalists have stolen our zeal on this one and it's time we recaptured our zeal for winning converts to the Church. Another group that has a claim on our priestly zeal are fallen-away Catholics. As a mother and father of a family with a special child can be expected to show unique tenderness and give exceptional time and patience to such a child, so can the zealous priest be expected to seek out those who have wandered from the family just as the Good Shepherd went after the lost one.

Zeal for souls. "Give me souls — keep all the rest!" As the Curé of Ars said, "If a priest has died as a result of trial and trouble undergone for the glory of God and the salvation of souls, that would not be such a bad thing."

A second observation on priestly zeal: the greatest arena for the fight for souls is the parish. Bishop after bishop tells me this: I need good parish priests. It's the greatest life in the world with challenges of every type. Is there drudgery, frustration? You bet! But the zealous priest is happiest in a parish.

In a parish we are general practitioners. Our pastor, our bishop, our people have a right to expect us to do almost everything. A pastor was telling me about his assistant who showed up and began the conversation by saying, "Well, I'm no good in school or with old people. Don't expect me to do that!" People don't want us at everything because we're good at it but because we're priests. Yes, we know our limits; yes, we know when to refer; but as parish priests our zeal is for all people in all circumstances and we close the door on none.

A spiritual director I had in my first years of priesthood said, "Pinpoint the two or three things you most dislike and are least effective at, and make sure you force yourself to do that. The stuff you like and that you're good at you'll do naturally; contract with yourself to do the stuff you most dislike."

Another comment about priestly zeal in a parish: learn to be a self-starter. You know what that means? You don't wait for work, you initiate it; what the pastor assigns you to do is not the extent of your ministry but only the starting point. You are self-motivated and self-starting.

You know if you only do the minimum asked of you by the pastor or expected of your people you're on easy street. Say your Mass, give a decent short sermon, smile at the folks, take your share of baptisms, weddings, and funerals — you're fine. A lot of pastors are happy if you do no more than hand them the channel selector and go get the ice. So we don't sit around whining, "There's nothing to do." Are you kidding?

There's no end to what a creative, energetic, zealous self-starter can do in a parish. A few years ago when I spoke to one of our alumni about his summer work in the parish, he mentioned how the parish was a sprawling one that was growing rapidly. The pastor kept commenting how, on the average, three to four new families were moving in each week. So, our man simply asked the secretary for the names and addresses of the families who had moved in since the first of the year and began to visit them. Excellent!

I recall another alumnus recounting how, during his second summer in the parish, the pastor really gave him not much to do, but kept saying how he wished he was there all year so he could do something about the CCD program, which the pastor admitted was ineffective. This man began to visit each of the CCD teachers just to talk to them, encourage them, and see if he could be of any help in their preparations for class, and actually lined up a presentation on the *Catechism of the Catholic Church* for them.

Priestly zeal prompts us to be self-starters, not passive, tepid men waiting for people to tell us what to do but self-starters who never find an end to their work. The days of waiting in a rectory for people to come knocking on our door seeking us out are over — we now have to go after them, and that takes zeal. One pastor told me, "If my associate spent one fourth the time on the streets going after the unchurched as he does on the computer devising programs on evangelization, we'd have them out in the aisles on Sunday."

Another remark on the zeal required of a parish priest: there is no replacement for priestly presence. Our zeal prompts us to be present to our people! One hopes the parish to which you are assigned is blessed with Eucharistic ministers, but that should never keep a parish priest from helping to distribute Holy Communion at every Sunday Mass and from regularly bringing the Lord to the housebound and sick; one hopes the parish has a bereaved support group or a Martha and Mary society, but that can never replace the visit a priest makes to the funeral home; you have trained catechists in your school, CCD, and RCIA, but the priest still has an active presence.

One savvy priest told me, "Lay ministry has now made clerical laziness a virtue, as now we can sit at home and let the people do our work and justify it as being 'collaborative' and 'encouraging lay ministry.'" The zealous, effective parish priest is very visible and present to his people: at meetings, on the playground, in homes, at the hospital, in the sick room, on the street — never do we pass up the chance to preach the Gospel by our priestly presence.

We need priests who are zealous but not zealots. By zealous I mean a priest whose heart burns with love for Jesus and his people and who is eager and effective in generously bringing that flame to others; by a zealot I mean a single-minded, obsessed priest who thinks that the answer to everything is by excessive attention to one cause. Our cause is Christ and his Church — every other cause is secondary. Be careful about excessive absorption in one single cause, however good that one cause might be. Causes such as the pro-life movement, Medjugorje, perpetual Eucharistic Adoration, Divine Mercy, RCIA, peace and justice, the environment — all are worth careful attention and zealous care, but do not become a zealot over any one cause except Jesus and his Church.

You will find priests who have almost a "cause of the year" — Renew, marriage encounter, Bible Study, Stephen ministry; every year there's a new program, new movement, new plan that is the be-all and end-all. We need priests who are zealous but not zealots, because zealots usually end up destroying the very goals they set out to promote. "There are few catastrophes so great and irremediable as those that follow an excess of zeal," wrote the convert-priest Robert Benson.

Now, I've tried to speak of specifics about priestly zeal, some of the ways we demonstrate it; now let me consider the ways we foster and protect it. You recall that I opened this chapter with a reference to the Scripture passage 2 Timothy 1:6-12, which is St. Paul's injunction to Timothy to "fan into a flame the gift that God gave you." The virtue of zeal is often pictured as fire, a flame, such as the tongues of fire that came upon the apostles that first Pentecost and transformed them from timid weaklings to zealous witnesses. What an apt image fire is for zeal, as we picture our priesthood being consumed with a burning love for Jesus, his Church, the souls of his people!

Yet, fires can fade, can decay into cold ashes; fires can burn out. So can zeal. How do we fan it into a flame?

We cannot, but He who gave it in the first place can. That's why it will hardly surprise you that I list prayer as the most effective way to maintain and foster zeal. Let's get more inclusive: the cultivation of a strong interior life, a daily recognition that the life of God dwells in my soul, and a daily nurturing of that spiritual life, are essential. Daily to feed that fire with our meditation, the divine office, our celebration of the Eucharist, our quiet time before the Blessed Sacrament, frequent confession — feeding that fire with these proven ways will keep the flame alive. When we find it wavering, when we discover our zeal flagging and our ministry becoming lazy and torpid, admit it to the Lord, and simply and humbly ask him for an increase of the zeal that should color the life of his priests.

The wise priest will orchestrate times to fan the flame. An annual retreat is so very important, so essential, that Canon Law mandates it for every priest; occasions such as the Mass of Chrism on or near Holy Thursday, when priests gather with their bishop to renew their promises of ordination, is so special; attending the ordination of new priests and deacons always rekindles one's ideals and vigor — all practical ways to pray for zeal.

May I share with you a particular mode of prayer I find helpful in fostering zeal? That is prayer to the Most Sacred Heart of Jesus. To meditate on our Lord's heart, literally on fire with passionate love for his people, surrounded with a crown of thorns, so much did he sacrifice for the salvation of his people, beating with his precious blood poured out for us — that prayer before the Sacred Heart never fails to rekindle my priestly zeal.

Pope John Paul II closed his 1986 Holy Thursday Letter to Priests by exhorting, "As the Curé of Ars uttered: 'The priesthood is the love of the heart of Jesus.' . . . Let us join St. John Vianney and seek the dynamism of our pastoral zeal in the heart of Jesus, in his love for souls. If we do not draw from the same source, our ministry risks bearing little fruit."

I also find using the lives of the saints as my spiritual reading to be most helpful, as I marvel at the remarkable zeal that has characterized such saints a Philip Neri, Ignatius Loyola, Dominic, Francis, Catherine of Siena, Teresa of Ávila, Don Bosco, John Neumann, just to name a few.

While I am discussing the cultivation of the interior life as *sine qua non* for priestly zeal, let me mention how important time in the seminary is in this regard. Realizing that the life of a priest is one of ongoing, selfless, sacrificial service, the wisdom of the Church prescribes that intense, prolonged preparation is essential. That's called a seminary. I trust all seminarians are itching to be priests, eager to serve, longing to "get out of here." Rightly so! However, the zeal you have as a priest is in proportion to the habits of prayer, study, and pastoral skill you develop here. In a way you are investing in spiritual capital from which you will draw interest the rest of your priestly life.

In the old days the month of February was dedicated to the "Hidden Life" of Jesus. You ever heard of that? For three years of intense ministry — his public life — the Son of God, the First Priest, spent thirty years of quiet preparation. What a powerful example! Our days as priests are filled with unending activity that we tackle with relish and zeal, a very active life — but there must be a "hidden life" as well, to keep that flame alive. This time of seminary allows you somewhat of a "hidden life" and encourages you to develop habits of the heart that will lure you to moments of "hiding with the Lord" throughout a very active priesthood. The first word our Lord said to his apostles was "Come!" The last word, "Go!" No use going if we haven't first come to him.

A second way to guard our priestly zeal: watch for danger signals, hints that the flame is flickering and the zeal is fading. What are some of these "surgeon general warnings"? Let me mention a few common ones:

• Too much sleep — devotion to Our Lady of the Pillow is very popular among priests.

• Missing appointments, not returning our calls, postponing obligations — another sign something is wrong.

• Becoming reclusive, staying in our rooms behind closed doors, avoiding others lest they bother us, fleeing from people and responsibilities — I knew of a priest who every day after breakfast told the secretary he was going on calls, got in his car, drove up the block and parked it, then snuck back to the rectory to his room where he locked the door and holed up until supper.

• Getting crabby and cynical with our people.

• Becoming too wrapped up in books, TV, a hobby, or — two popular ones today which, if taken to extremes, can sap zeal — computers and cooking. Nothing wrong with either as long as they enhance our priestly zeal and make us more effective. One priest at home tells his people how simply he lives by not having a house-keeper, and then reminds them that he cannot be disturbed be-tween 4:00 and 7:00 p.m. daily, since he's cooking — something's wrong!

• Extended cocktail hours, drinking more than usual, and too many lunches and dinners out.

These are just a few practical danger signals that tell us the flame is flickering. Good spiritual directors, confessors, and friends can help us detect these and deal with them.

A third way to fan the flame of priestly zeal: constantly cleans-ing our lives of whatever diminishes our evangelical effectiveness. You see, a fire can create, but a fire can also burn away; the fire of priestly zeal constantly burns away from our lives anything that makes us less a priest after the heart and mind of Christ!

A humble self-knowledge reveals shortcomings we have that need to be worked on — maybe a bad temper; perhaps a lack of promptness; could be an arrogant attitude; might be a shyness and aloofness that keep people from approaching us; maybe it's exter-nal, like sloppy dress or an unkempt appearance, or lack of proper hygiene; perhaps it's an inappropriate sense of humor or a habit of talking too much. We all have such traits that can hinder our evan-gelical effectiveness and threaten our zeal.

Thus we should be grateful when a pastor, brother priest, pas-toral collaborator, good friend, bishop, diocesan official, or one of our people, points something out to us that is hindering our effec-tiveness as a priest.

"O good Jesus, make me a priest, like with your own heart, filled with zeal for your people."

Are you excited about that? Are you eager to enter a life of selfless, generous, sometimes inconvenient service to God's people? Are you prepared to be configured to a man who was nailed to a cross as he offered every ounce of blood he possessed as an oblation to his Father for the salvation of his people?

I remember our spiritual director at the college, Father David Donovan, saying: "Don't become a priest if you're not excited about it." Yes, if we drift into the priesthood, we'll drift through it. We need priests on fire with zeal. As Pope John Paul II wrote to priests on Holy Thursday, 1979:

> The only priest who will always prove necessary to people is the priest who is conscious of the meaning of his priesthood:
> The Priest
> who believes profoundly,
> who professes his faith with courage,
> who prays fervently,
> who teaches with deep conviction,
> who serves with zeal,
> who puts into practice in his own life the program of the beatitudes,
> who knows how to love disinterestedly,
> who is close to everyone, and especially to those who are most in need.

As St. Vincent de Paul ended his Common Rule: "When we have carried out all we have been asked to do, we should, following Christ's advice, say to ourselves that we are useless servants, that we have only done what we were supposed to do, and that, in fact, we could not have done anything at all without him."

22

Preaching

(Scripture selection — Romans 10:14-19)

In the chapter on the parish priesthood, while making the point that a parish priest has as his principal duty the administration of the sacraments, I referred to the frieze surrounding the former main altar of our Chapel of the Immaculate Conception at the North American College, which beautifully depicts a priest celebrating each of the sacraments. However, something else immediately jumps out: while there are seven sacraments of the Church, there are eight scenes on the frieze! What's the eighth one? In the lower corner to the left is a scene of a priest preaching! It is almost as if the artist was telling future priests that there was an eighth sacrament, preaching!

The sculptor of that frieze was somewhat of a prophet, because, in the last thirty-five years, the duty of the priest to preach the Word of God has been highly emphasized. Theologically, the Second Vatican Council recovered and reemphasized this ancient office of the priest as preacher. Listen again to the clear teaching from *Presbyterorum Ordinis*: "The People of God finds its unity first of all through the Word of the living God, which is quite properly sought from the lips of priests. Since no one can be saved who has not first believed, priests, as co-workers with their bishops, have as their primary duty the proclamation of the Gospel to all" (No. 4).

This emphasis, as you are aware, has been elaborated upon by subsequent documents of the magisterium, and by abundant scholarly research, all dwelling upon the theological basis of the primacy of preaching in the life of a priest.

But this stress on preaching is not just a theoretical one. Pastorally, we know that the Church expects her priests to be skilled preachers. Our people want — no, demand — that we be good preachers. Let's cut through all the verbiage: when you listen to thoughtful Catholic people discuss what's wrong with the Church, it's not the hot-button issues like women's ordination, married clergy, sexual immorality, or divorce that they mention. For them, the major flaw in the Church today is that our sermons stink! Like him or not, Andrew Greeley is right: his studies show that people most fault their priests not for sexual indiscretion, laziness, or drunkenness, but for our lousy homilies!

We must wake up! Any man who loves the Church, who has a hunger for souls, who feels called by Christ to holy orders, and who desires to be a good priest must long to be an effective preacher, because our people are telling us that's what they most need. We ignore this at our peril. Our people are leaving the Church, the "Faith of our Fathers" — which "dungeon, fire, and sword" could not force them to do — because they can't stand our preaching! I'm not saying that's right, believe me . . . but it's a fact!

An ancient Christian principle tells us that "grace builds on nature." Thus, I want to make some remarks on some human, natural aspects of preaching. As already mentioned, our people are very critical of our preaching. But, very often, the faultfinding is not with doctrinal, moral, biblical, or spiritual matters — no, they don't get that far! They find fault with the more natural, human imperfections:

- "I can't even hear him!"
- "He speaks so fast!"
- "He never shuts up!"
- "He speaks so garbled!"
- "He keeps repeating himself!"
- "He is so boring!"
- "He never looks up at the people!"
- "He stares out in space!"
- "He exhales ether!"
- "He talks way over my head!"
- "He treats us like kids!"
- "He is so unorganized!"

Am I not correct? We're talking here about common, human, natural defects! Nothing here about doctrine, exegesis, or spiritual depth. We're talking "Speech I" in high school or college! But yet, this is where so many priests fail.

And, ironically, we've all been victims of this! For fifteen, twenty,

thirty years or more, all of us have wanted to stand up and scream:
- "Would you please use the microphone properly?"
- "Would you please speak up so I can hear?"
- "For God's sake, shut up — you've made your point!"
- "Do you mind looking at me every once in a while?"
- "Could you maybe wrap this up before I have to shave again?"

We've all been victims of "homily abuse"! And then when we get up there, we repeat the mistakes that drove us nuts! There's not one of us who has not railed against poor speaking habits in the pulpit, and then we get up and do the same thing!

Never, ever, subject your people to what you have had to go through! Make a list — I'm serious — make a list of the bad pulpit habits that drive you wild. Again, I'm talking natural, human flaws: the mumbling, the slavery to a text, the voice you can barely hear, the auctioneer pace, the homilies where we check not our watch but our calendar, all the things that have often made homilies unbearable — and, for God's sake, don't do them! Because, odds are, you will.

That's why I'm so grateful we have Sister Benedicta to help our students in public speaking at the North American College. She couldn't care less if they quote from Bossuet or Bob Hope; she cares if we can hear you, if you're clear, distinct, lively, engaging, and understandable.

Because you might have a masterpiece that is structurally perfect, doctrinally sound, morally compelling, and spiritually rich — but you might as well line the bottom of the bird cage with it if nobody can hear you, or understand you, or if you are so lifeless that the folks start showing videos on the inside of their eyelids within thirty seconds of your droning.

In November, 1998, I hosted an all-day meeting with a dozen specialists in preaching to help me plan a new "Carl J. Peter Chair of Homiletics" here at the college in Rome. Excellent insights surfaced.

Effective preachers need to work on the human, natural, basic skills of communication first. Father Peter Daly, a priest from the archdiocese of Washington, observed, "If a man cannot speak publicly with effectiveness and clarity, he certainly should not be a diocesan priest, and maybe not a priest at all." In other words, the natural ability to speak — I'm not saying to be a great orator, but simply to be a decent public speaker — is necessary to be a priest. If a man lacks chastity, and we know it, we could not recommend him for orders, could we? Well . . . if a man simply can't speak publicly, should he be ordained?

That having been said, we are not training orators, we're preparing preachers, and there's a big difference. The nature is indeed important, but the grace is even more so. "A preacher is like a trumpet which produces no tone unless one blows into it," writes St. Joseph of Cupertino. "So, before preaching, pray to God: 'You are the spirit and I am only the trumpet, and without your breath, I can give no sound.' "

St. Bonaventure, in his classic *Life of St. Francis*, remarks, "When he stood in their midst to present his edifying words, he often went completely blank. . . . This he admitted with true humility, and directed himself to invoke the grace of the Holy Spirit. Suddenly he began to overflow with eloquence."

At the preaching symposium I mentioned above, Dominican Sister Joan Delaplane from Aquinas Institute in St. Louis remarked that preaching for a priest is not a function but an identity. Our preaching arises from who we are. I was reminded of Samuel Wilberforce's observation that "some clergy prepare their sermons; others prepare themselves." Dr. William Graham, from The Catholic University of America, told the symposium that skilled technicians are not enough; good preachers are much more than good speakers, for good preaching comes from the soul and heart, not just from the mind and vocal chords.

And so all the experts agree and our people can sense — that it is impossible to be a good preacher unless you are a man of prayer. At the meeting I chaired on preaching in D.C., there was a real smorgasbord of opinions about homilies and how a seminary should prepare priests to preach well. But one point all agreed upon was that a vibrant interior life was essential to effective sermons. Monsignor Peter Vaghi, a pastor from the archdiocese of Washington, stated that in the seminary homiletics must be part of spiritual formation, since a priest's prayer life is the foundation of his preaching.

Now, of course, this means that an effective preacher must

have an intimate, personal relationship with Jesus Christ. Another participant in our symposium, Sister Barbara Reid, insisted that, for the preacher, "Jesus is not just someone he knows a lot about, but someone he knows."

You have probably heard the famous story about the dinner party attended by both Fulton Sheen and Richard Burton. The host, at the end of the meal, drew attention to both guests, observing that both were distinguished public speakers. He then asked if both would read Psalm 23, "The Lord Is My Shepherd." Richard Burton did so with the precision, cadence, and drama one would expect from a Shakespearean actor, and the guests applauded vigorously; Fulton Sheen then read the psalm with obvious devotion, meaning, and depth, and the guests remained in reverential silence.

The host commented, "The actor knew the psalm, the preacher knew the Shepherd."

Father Peter Daly also observed at the meeting that "I love Jesus, and I love my people. My goal in a sermon is to introduce the two of them to each other." Isn't that moving? So, in our sermons we preach Jesus. Billy Graham says, "Wherever the name of Jesus is preached, no matter how crudely, there are bound to be results." And we preach the Jesus whom we personally know, love, and serve.

Thus, it should not surprise us to learn that the Holy Father usually writes his homilies from a little desk he sets up in the chapel; it should not astonish us that Fulton Sheen claimed he spent an hour on his knees before the Blessed Sacrament for every minute he spent standing in the pulpit; that most good preachers tell you their sermons are usually composed mentally during their meditation before they put it on paper. The question is never what are we going to preach on, but who are we going to preach — and that "who" is always Jesus, whom we personally know, love, and serve, and with whom we frequently commune in prayer.

Father Thomas Kane, a Paulist, observed that we should let the universities form you as theologians, while we form you as preachers, which is broader than (while inclusive of) your theological training. I like that. I also nodded in agreement with a remark by Father John Burke that what we preach, how we preach, and why we preach, should be a frequent topic with our spiritual director, for, again, a good sermon flows from our soul, our heart, and our personal relationship with Jesus Christ.

Recalling my favorite quote from the Holy Father to priests and seminarians that "love for Jesus and his Church must be the passion of your lives" and, agreeing that our homilies flow from our interior love for Jesus, then our sermons will be passionate. Where is the passion? In the famous words of Father Walter Burghardt, another participant in our meeting: "Where is the fire in the belly?" Some of us read the Gospel and preach with all the passion of the radio announcer giving the sow-belly prices at the 5:00 a.m. farm news! Where is the passion? I'm not talking about cheap theatrics or foaming-at-the-mouth shouting that is thankfully not part of our Catholic heritage — I'm talking about a preacher whose love for Jesus and enthusiasm for his saving message are evident and come through in the pulpit.

Now, you can't have "fire in the belly" unless you're confident. Father Al McBride noted at our meeting that the major obstacle he discovers in his seminarians is a lack of self-confidence. There is a human side to this, methods we can use to develop a sense of comfort and confidence in the pulpit. But ultimately the self-confidence necessary for passion in preaching comes not just from taking a deep breath to calm our stomach but from breathing in the Holy Spirit, and acknowledging that, as long as our sermons flow from our prayer and our relationship with Jesus, we cannot fail! We have divine insurance, his guarantee that he will help us. Preach as if you really believe that! Be confident! Be passionate! Have "fire in the belly"! Prepare long, hard, and diligently, and then entrust it to the Lord, approaching the pulpit with confidence in the Lord's power, in the grace of holy orders, and in your conviction that you are acting in his person.

Preaching Jesus also necessarily means preaching the cross. There is no way around that. St. Paul tells us: "Yes, Jews demand signs, Greeks look for wisdom, but we preach Christ crucified — a stumbling block to Jews, an absurdity to Gentiles, but to those who are called . . . Christ the power of God and the wisdom of God . . . I determined that while I was with you I would speak of nothing but Jesus Christ and him crucified."

It is very convenient today to avoid preaching the cross, because therapeutic, feel-good, affirming, self-help, New Age, self-fulfillment themes are the new orthodoxy. After completing a study recently for the Lilly Foundation on contemporary trends in religion, Craig Dystra concluded, "We are not seeking anything like the radical care for others and obedience to God that mark authentic religious communities. Instead, we crave a community of confirmation, one that acknowledges neither the necessity of discipline nor sufferings shared. Our search seems not for salvation but for cosmic affirmation."

I'm afraid Professor Dystra has a point! To that culture looking for ease, convenience, affirmation, and comfort, we need priests who, like St. Paul, are not afraid to hold up the cross, the *splendor veritatis* in all its integrity.

If you need further evidence of this, look no farther than the relatively recent cover of the *New York Times* magazine, noting an article therein, entitled, "The New American Consensus," which displayed a take-off on the Preamble of our Constitution:

> We, the relatively unbothered and well off, hold these truths to be self-evident: That Big Government, Big Deficits and Big Tobacco are bad, but that big bathrooms and 4-by-4's are not; that American overseas involvement should be restricted to trade agreements, mutual funds and the visiting of certain beachfront resorts; that markets can take care of themselves as long as they take care of us; that an individual's sex life is nobody's business, though highly entertaining; and that the only rights that really matter are those which indulge the Self.

This is the culture that needs to be confronted with the cross. To preach pro-life in a suburban parish today is to preach the cross! To preach chastity on a college campus is to preach the cross! To preach on the danger of riches and the demands of social justice to an affluent congregation is to preach the cross! To preach the preference for dialogue, patience, and diplomacy over military action at an army base is to preach the cross! But preach Christ crucified we must!

Which, of course, means that, as Father Al McBride observed, every sermon, rather than finger-wagging condemnation or Pelagian moralizing, is rather an invitation to ongoing conversion! And here is the delicacy of preaching, because a sermon can never be a tract on what we must do for God to win his favor but rather a proclamation of what God has done for us in Christ to inspire our love and obedience!

As Norman Pittenger remarks, "A sermon is a proclamation of the generous love of God in Christ, or it simply is not a Christian sermon!" Never do we have the right to preach so as to send our hearers away on flat tires! A discouraged listener is not an asset but a liability. John Newton made this observation: "My grand point in preaching is to break the hard heart and to heal the broken one."

Therefore, our invitation to conversion is never delivered so as to make our listeners feel bad about themselves, but to help them see the overwhelming graciousness of God, which then sparks them to respond to God's call to conversion of life! Father Jared Wicks was recently telling me that the word he hears most in sermons here is *"Dobbiamo"* ("We must")! — or *"Dovete"* ("You have to")! Avoid the *"dovete* heresy."

Yes, every sermon inspires us to take a long, hard look at ourselves to see where we need conversion, but that hard look at ourselves is prompted not by the preacher railing against his congregation, but by telling of God's loving designs and generous offer of salvation which then inspires people to reform their lives.

Let's get practical. Five "S's," five tips on a good homily: it is short, simple, sincere, succinct, and substantial.

A good sermon is short: KISS — "Keep it short, stupid." This is the major complaint our people have against us — we are too windy. I will get in trouble from some, but anything longer than three minutes on a weekday or ten minutes on a Sunday is counterproductive. Fulton Sheen said, "The three parts of a good sermon are a catchy beginning, an emotional conclusion, and keeping the two as close together as possible." Or, as the old saying goes, "Be prepared, be clear, and be seated!"

The great fallacy, of course, is to equate substance with length. The opposite is true. Fulton Sheen observed, "If you want me to preach for an hour, give me a week's notice; if you want me to preach for five minutes, I need a month to prepare." The better prepared, the shorter; the more substance, the more compact.

Nowhere is "homiletic abuse" more obvious than in having to listen to sermons that are too long. You know that! A good sermon is short!

A good sermon is simple. When I was a deacon here, a priest on the faculty said: "Learn to preach well to fourth graders. Say it so they can comprehend it well. Perfect your style of preaching to the fourth grade — and, if you're smart, you'll preach that way to everyone!" Now, be careful! Never do we want to become patronizing or condescending, because our people today expect quality, and are in many areas far better educated than we are. Yet, St. Alphonsus Liguori wrote, "I must preach so that the most illiterate laborer can understand me." A good sermon is simple.

A good sermon is sincere. Now, this is closely allied to conviction. Our people can quickly detect if we really believe what we're saying. Of course, for a parish priest, this means that our sermons have no credibility at all if they do not see us model what we preach in our own life. As the old saying goes, "It's one thing to love to preach; it's another to love those to whom we preach."

St. Peter Canisius remarked, "If you are traveling somewhere to preach, you better preach while you are traveling," meaning, of course, that our lives are the best sermon of all. Pope Paul VI observed shrewdly that today's world prefers to learn from witness rather than preaching, reminding us of Don Quixote's maxim that "he who lives well is the best preacher."

The picture on the cover of *Time* magazine of Pope John Paul II embracing his would-be assassin in jail was more effective than a thousand sermons on forgiveness. "If preaching is your job," St. Charles Borromeo wrote to his clergy in Milan, "then prepare diligently and study well. But be sure that you first preach by the way you live. If you do not, people will notice that you preach one thing, but live otherwise, and your words will bring only cynical laughter and a derisive shake of the head."

Sincerity, of course, requires that we must be ourselves in the pulpit. Gimmicks, or imposed recipes for model sermons, or trying to be someone we are not, or depending upon homily notes, backfire. Margaret Melady did her doctoral dissertation on an analysis of the communication style of John Paul II. She found that for all his talks — audiences, public events, addresses to heads of state, visits around the world — for all his talks but one, he depended upon the help of his advisers. The one style of communication he personally wrote all alone was a homily. That should not surprise us, because how else could a sermon be sincere?

At our symposium, Father Jim Wallace told how he taped his seminarians preaching, and then, when they finished their practice homily, had them remain at the pulpit to discuss the sermon, and kept the camera running. When he replayed it, the men immediately noticed how, when they were preaching, they were stiff, formal, uncomfortable, but, once they finished, they became themselves, relaxed, informal, and more effective. . . . In other words, they had not been themselves in the pulpit.

A good sermon is succinct. Father Virgilio Elizondo suggested that, in preparing our sermons, we develop "sound bites," colorfully expressing our message in one or two pithy, catchy phrases, since, for better or worse, our listeners are conditioned to receive knowledge that way. Father Al McBride urges that we be able to write out the point of our sermon in one, brief declarative sentence, or to list succinctly the two or three points we want to cover. Robert Schuler recommends that the preacher first tell the people what he is going to say, then says it, and then tells him what he said.

If you're going to keep the sermon succinct, you can't do everything. The experts tell us that we are obliged to have a story; then we have to do exegesis; then we have to cover every reading, and show how they blend together, and then tie it all into the Eucharist. . . . If we do everything the experts tell us in every homily, we'll never be succinct! The best compliment you can receive as a preacher is, "Father, I wish you had gone on longer!" The worst was given a friend of mine by a man after Mass who said, "Father, you had a great ending to that homily. . . . unfortunately, it came about ten minutes before you actually concluded!"

As Cardinal Newman noted, "Keep your idea in view, and write sentences over and over again until you have expressed your meaning accurately, forcibly, and in a few words."

Finally, a good sermon is substantial. Our people need solid content, doctrinal meat, scriptural lessons, and moral instruction.

Father Gene Hemrick spoke at our D.C. symposium of the need to know our congregation well, to realize what they need to hear, what Father Val Peter called "audience analysis." The temptation today is toward "fluff," cute gimmicks, jargon, trickery, silly stories that take up more time than the message, and excessive use of the "I" pronoun instead of speaking of the Lord. Raw, basic evangelization; primitive, fundamental kerygma; solid, faithful catechesis; sound biblical teaching — this is what our people need. You will know you are giving them this when they say to you, "Father, I can always bring something home with me from your sermons." There's a nugget there, something worth savoring . . . a good sermon is substantial.

The five "S's": a good sermon is short, simple, sincere, succinct, and substantial.

It's a real matter of justice, my brothers: the Church expects her priests to be careful, competent preachers. Our people are demanding it; if we don't provide it, more and more go elsewhere, even, sadly, to other denominations.

Develop a "homiletic sense," what Father Robert Wozniak calls "theological reflection." In your prayer, in your study, in your friendships, in your daily experiences, in your travel, in your reading, in art, drama, literature, movies, history . . . in all things, glean lessons, examples, and images that can be used in the pulpit. We are so in love with Jesus, so committed to his truth, that we are forever looking for ways to preach him and his truth with enthusiasm and cogency.

A priest is always asking, "How can I share this with my people in an attractive, interesting way?" A "homiletic sense" can be the unifying factor in our priestly formation.

Like so many things in priestly life, it is never a finished task: we are always being formed as better preachers. Noted preachers, such as Walter Burghardt, John Burke, and Peter Cameron, still admit trepidation as they approach the ambo, realizing their awesome, sacred task, as the words from the ordination rite ring in their ears:

> My son, apply your energies to the duty of teaching in the name of Christ. . . . Share with all the Word of God you have

received. Meditate on the law or God, believe what you read, teach what you believe, and put into practice what you teach.

Let the doctrine you teach be true nourishment for the people of God. Let the example of your life attract the followers of Christ, so that by word and action you may build up . . . God's Church.

23

Celibacy and Chastity

(Scripture selection — 1 Corinthians 6:15-20)

Perhaps you are already familiar with the true story involving the Church in Japan. At the end of the sixteenth century, all foreign missionaries were expelled from Japan, where the seeds of the faith had just been planted and were beginning to sprout. Vicious persecutions followed, leading, for instance, to the gruesome martyrdom of St. Paul Miki and his companions. The light of the faith seemed extinguished.

Two hundred sixty years later, missionaries returned. In a remote corner in the northeastern part of the country, Jesuit missionaries were flabbergasted to discover a tiny village where the hundred or so inhabitants gathered every Sunday to pray the Apostles' Creed, Our Father, Hail Mary, Glory Be, Acts of Faith, Hope, Charity, and Contrition, and recite the ten commandments and eight beatitudes.

Shocked, they asked the people where this custom came from, only to be told by the Japanese villagers that, sometime in the distant past, men whom they called "fathers" had taught those words to the people, and, anticipating their martyrdom, instructed the people to memorize those formulas and gather every Sunday to recite them together.

The "fathers" had also assured them that, one day, other "fathers" would return to teach them more about Jesus and his way. Ecstatic, the new missionaries blurted out, "We are those fathers," only to be met by a stony, suspicious silence. The village leader came forward. "It has been passed down, too, that, when men come back claiming to be those 'fathers,' we must ask them four questions to be sure they are from the true Church."

A bit nervous, the newly arrived priests responded, "Go ahead, ask us the questions." The village leader came forward:

"When you enter your Churches, what do you do?" The Jesuits

replied by demonstrating a genuflection, which was met by excited gasps from the crowd.

"Second, does your Lord have a Mother?" "Yes," assured the priests, "and her name is Mary," whereupon more electricity spread through the people.

"Where does the earthly leader of your Church live?" continued the village elder. "In Rome," answered the missionaries, as the crowd neared unrestrained joy.

"Finally," anxiously inquired the chieftain, "do you 'fathers' have wives?" And, as the priests smiled and responded, "No," the villagers broke into a tumult, hoisted the missionaries on their shoulders, and led them into the little church that had not seen a priest for over two-and-a-half centuries.

True story. Now, at this point, I could present material on the Real Presence of Christ in the Eucharist, or on our Blessed Mother, the Holy Father, or priestly celibacy, since those were obviously the four marks of authenticity the old missionaries had instructed their flock to look for when new preachers arrived. It is the last I will address.

Now, in a way, those courageous missionaries were not completely correct, were they, since all of us know that celibacy is not essential to the priesthood. It is a discipline of the Church cherished in priests from the beginning, common from the fourth century, and obligatory in the West for the last nine hundred years.

While not of the essence of the priesthood, a few observations at the start are called for: for one, there is no indication that it is going to change, and — I trust this goes without saying, but we can take nothing for granted — if you are expecting it to change in your priestly life you are gravely mistaken. No one should enter the diaconate believing this sacred requirement will be mitigated in the future.

Two, whether essential or not, celibacy has become such a respected, cherished sign associated with priestly identity that it is part of our charism, mystique, and apostolic effectiveness. Fulton J. Sheen in his book *Those Mysterious Priests*, still worth reading after nearly four decades, credits celibacy with giving the priest a credibility, a mystery, an aura that makes him almost an icon inviting people to enter into the beyond and look into eternity.

You see what I am saying? Those missionaries may have been lacking theological precision in placing clerical celibacy on a par with the other unique marks of the Church, but they were right on target in realizing that celibacy is a treasure celebrated and embraced as a rich blessing to the Church that has ensured the identity, love, and zeal of her priests.

Now, I am not going to give a lengthy theological exposé on priestly celibacy. This is not to say such is not most important in your priestly formation. It is only to presume that such a rational consideration of this virtue is part of your theological study, your own personal research, input on retreats, and frequent conversation with your spiritual director and formation adviser. We must understand fully the why of priestly celibacy. As the old saying goes, "A man can do almost anything as long as he knows there is a reason." Lord knows, if you do not understand the why of celibacy, its faithful living-out will be tough.

The best "why" I've come across is found in Pope Paul VI's encyclical on priestly celibacy, *Sacerdotalis Caelibatus*, where, in the midst of a storm of doubt and loud calls for change, he, in 1967, taught warmly, calmly, and firmly the supreme value of this ancient charism.

He eloquently speaks of the Christological reason for celibacy, in the example of Christ's own virginity, and in the invitation to follow Jesus with an intimacy so profound that it is not shared with another human person; he describes the ecclesial value of celibacy, as the priest is so united to Jesus in his love of the Church that he is actually betrothed to her in a bond so strong it is exclusive; Paul VI describes the eschatological rationale for celibacy, as it powerfully reminds people of a bond, a love, an attachment beyond this life; and he discusses the pastoral value of celibacy, as it allows the priest to serve God and his people with a love undistracted and undiluted.

There's the why in a nutshell. All I can do is exhort you to understand the why as clearly as you can because we need a reason for what we do, and the Church's reason for celibacy is cogent, rich, and persuasive.

I can perhaps bring all of these whys together in a word that I think powerfully explains our acceptance of celibacy, and that word is purity. As priests, we totally, exclusively, radically, profoundly, completely — purely — belong to the Lord. He shares us with no one, and thus is able to share us with everyone. Every ounce of our strength, every urge of our affection, every drive of our libido, we freely hand over to Jesus and his Church. We are purely his, from our brain cells to our sperm cells — all belong to him. We are purely his, *totus tuus*. Thus, purity has come to mean that virtue where all thoughts, words, and deeds flow from a heart totally committed in love to Christ.

Perhaps another word for purity is integrity. As a matter of fact, the *Catechism of the Catholic Church* speaks of chastity in terms of integrity. The challenge to live chastity in our culture is a challenge very often to be heroic. But it is our challenge, and we must not shrink from it. Our bodies and souls have been purchased by the precious blood of Christ, with eternal value. We are called at this moment to what the *Catechism* calls "a vocation to chastity." And the *Catechism* talks about chastity in terms of integrity: first, the successful integration of sexuality within the person (the inner unity of the bodily and spiritual person), and, second, the successful integration of myself, a sexual/spiritual person, into the community.

Now, I want to dwell on this notion of purity, integrity, chastity, call it what you will, as I consider celibacy. You, of course, know that celibacy is traditionally approached from a negative and a positive way, both important. With the choice of celibacy, the priest freely renounces something, and enthusiastically embraces something. Let us look at both.

From a negative point of view, by choosing celibacy, we freely give up the beauty of a wife and children, one of life's greatest treasures. Since the Lord has revealed that genital sexual pleasure is a gift so sacred that it is to be enjoyed only between a man and a woman united in marriage, our choice of celibacy means as well that, in freely giving up a wife, we freely give up all genital sexual activity and pleasure, hetero- or homosexual, alone or with others, in thought, word, and deed. Such is the bluntness, the finality, the realism of celibacy.

Now, purity, integrity, and chastity are the virtues that guard our celibacy.

The Church, as is her right, insists that celibacy is a prerequisite for the transitional diaconate and priesthood. However, we are acting foolishly if we accept celibacy only because it is required. In other words, you must be confident that you are personally called to celibacy. We just don't say, "Well, I guess I'll have to be celibate if I want to be ordained." I have heard Archbishop Harry Flynn remark that celibacy is not "spray-painted" on, as something that just happens to come along with priesthood, like an AM/FM radio might happen to come along with a new car. As he said at the 1990 Synod of Bishops, "Celibacy is not simply a condition necessary for priestly ordination; no, celibacy and priesthood are two distinct though related vocations. Those who feel God is calling them to priesthood must also detect a call to celibacy."

You must then think and pray long and hard, and seek counsel from those you trust, especially your spiritual director and formation adviser, to discern a call to celibacy. Do not just put it off and say, "No use thinking much about it because, if I want to be a priest I just have to accept celibacy as part of the package." No — your choice for a life of perpetual celibacy must be free, sincere, and personal.

A corollary to this: if you as seminarians are unable to live a chaste life right now, that is a rather clear indication that you cannot embrace celibacy, which means that you are not called to the priesthood. We are called to chastity now; if, in this period of vocational discernment leading us from clarity to certitude, we experience constant, glaring lapses in chastity, we should interpret such as a clear sign we are not meant to be priests. Can I get specific? I hope I do not offend with this candor:

• if you now find yourself in a genital relationship with a woman or a man . . .

• if you are purchasing pornography, viewing pornographic films, or using pornography on the Internet . . .

• if you visit prostitutes, female or male, or are into "cruising," that is, frequenting bars, parks, or areas of town in the hopes of making sexual contact of any kind . . .

• if you bury or ignore questions of sexual behavior or orientation, or cannot even calmly discuss such matters without becoming tongue-tied or snickering like a sophomore in high school . . .

- if you are uncomfortable around women, unable to enjoy their company and collaborate with them as equals . . .
- if you are leaving open as a real possibility the chance of a genital relationship or sustained romantic involvement in the future . . .
- if you look forward to periods of sexual experimentation, or count on periodic genital encounters . . .
- if you are involved in a very possessive friendship with a woman or man, demanding all her or his time, attention, and affection . . .
- if you detect any genital attraction to children . . .
- if you have an uncontrollable habit of frequent masturbation . . .
- if you find yourself constantly viewing women — or men — as sex objects, existing to satisfy your lustful desires . . .
- if you find it impossible to be alone or to live without the constant company of another person . . .

If one or more of the above apply to you, then you should seek the time, space, and counsel necessary to control whatever pertains to you before continuing on the path toward the priesthood. If you already are ordained you should seek the help necessary to recommit yourself to the purity of life you promised the Church.

Now, I am not talking about periodic falls, ongoing temptations, or the struggles to live chastely that every healthy person faces. I am speaking about serious, continual, sustained lapses or uncontrollable urges.

In this area of chastity I urge you never to make a decision without proper counsel. In struggling with chastity we always think we are the only person so struggling. Do not despair! You are not the first person to deal with this. But I'm telling you: you have an obligation to deal with it. The best way to deal with it is to get it into the open, in an appropriate way, with your spiritual director, a professional, your formation adviser, or any trusted, wise friend.

Healthy integration is helped tremendously by receiving good information and having the assurance that you are not isolated as you deal with issues of sexuality. In the area of chastity it is never good to trust our own counsel. We tend either to be too strict or too lax, and need the guidance and assessment of trusted people. Satan is masterful at using our sexuality to ruin us, either by coaxing us to ignore serious problems by denying them and rationalizing our way out of them, or by burdening us with such guilt and turmoil that we despair. These are very personal matters, yes, but they are matters of supreme importance to the Church. If you have any serious problems with chastity, in justice to yourself and to the Church, settle them before you are ordained, and do not settle them alone.

Chastity must be integrated. What do I mean by that? For seminarians the main task now, in preparation for priesthood, is integration, that is, putting the pieces together, with a great deal of help from the Holy Spirit, to form one man, free and faithful. We incorporate who we are, what we know, the wisdom of the Church and the person of Jesus into one healthy life. It is essential that you work at integrating your sexuality, that is, desires, thoughts, temptations, actions, impulses, as well as past sins and experiences into your understanding of yourself as one ready to embrace a life of celibate chastity with freedom, maturity, and sincerity.

Have any of us been untouched by the tragedy of priests who have been unchaste and have ruined their lives, their ministry, have hurt innocent people, and have shamed the Church? We have seen these poor men on TV and, while the cameras rolled, it seemed as if their lives were disintegrating right before our eyes. But that disintegration was long in coming. They had kept a compartment of their lives hidden, where the lights of faith and truth were never turned on. Problem is, you can never live your life for long in separate compartments. When you enter the part of your life that is dishonest or immoral, you bring your body, your soul, your reputation, and your priesthood with you. At that point, you are gambling with everything, and you risk losing everything.

I recall the insights of two professionals who presented a weekend on chastity to our seminarians. They noted that one thing characterized all the priests who were sent for treatment after scandalous sexual abuse: none had ever owned up to it, dealt with it honestly, sought help; none had integrated their sexuality! It had remained closed, hidden, denied, in a dark closet, apart from the light of faith, truth, grace.

So, there can be no double lives; no "Sunday celibacy"; no "time off for good behavior"; no hidden compartment of our behavior that is exempt from Christ and his continual invitation to conversion. Know yourself well, and let someone trusted who loves Jesus and his Church as passionately as you do, know you, too. As St. Philip Neri said, "Humility is the best safeguard of chastity."

But, I have dwelt too long on the negative-side of celibacy — what we give up — and we must, for our own good, turn to the positive side: what we embrace, what we choose, what we gain.

We often see celibacy in the solely negative terms of self-denial, whereas St. Paul saw it as a virtue in which the unmarried person "can devote himself to the Lord's affairs" and worry only about pleasing the Lord (1 Corinthians 7:32). If celibacy is a way of devoting oneself "to the affairs of the Lord," then it must be a way of loving, a love that knows no rivals and provides a joyous disposition of heart for pastoral service. Defining celibacy only as giving up sex is just as unrealistic as a groom seeing marriage as giving up all other women.

Neither marriage nor celibacy is livable without a commitment of love so deep as to cause one to want to give up all else. As Dietrich Bonhoeffer said, "The essence of chastity is not the suppression of lust, but the total orientation of one's life toward a goal. Without such a goal, chastity is bound to become ridiculous."

Monsignor Daniel Thomas, one of our spiritual directors at the college, shared a powerful quote with me from a Protestant minister who writes to priests encouraging them in their celibacy. He asks, "Is celibacy crazy?" He answers, "Yes, about as crazy as a soldier jumping on a live grenade to save his buddies." Both are done only out of sacrificial love.

Thus it is necessary to state that celibacy and bachelorhood are two different things. Both are similar in what they give up — a wife; but they are different in the motive: the bachelor forgoes a wife for freedom, convenience, and comfort; the celibate for generosity and love toward Christ and his Church.

A close friend of mine at home, a woman religious, recalls how years ago, in her first years as a sister, while teaching first grade, she experienced grave doubts about the value of her celibate commitment. One day one of her seven-year-olds, whom she knew came from a broken family and an abusive father, said to her, "Sister, are you married?"

"No," my friend replied.

"Do you have any kids?" asked the little girl.

"No," Sister answered.

"Oh, good," smiled the first grader, relieved, " 'cause now you belong to all of us."

Yes, we do, and our celibacy allows us to do that. You see, we have fallen hopelessly in love, head over heels, with Jesus and his Spouse, the Church. Our love is pure, total, true. To die for our love we would, but, even more, we will live for our love, live with integrity and chastity.

The purpose of celibacy is to provide the freedom for an unlimited love to blossom in joy and generosity. In the moving words of *Pastores Dabo Vobis*, "The Church, as the Spouse of Jesus Christ, wishes to be loved by the priest in the total and exclusive manner in which Jesus Christ her head and spouse loved her. Priestly celibacy, then, is the gift of self in and with Christ to his Church and expresses the priest's service to the Church in and with the Lord" (No. 29).

May I mention some practical safeguards to fostering and protecting this "pearl of great price," our celibate chastity? Perhaps it is best to use the same categories, negative and positive.

The negative — things to avoid:

• Abuse of alcohol. Listen to any veteran of lapses in chastity and, more often than not, you will find that excessive drinking was involved. Firm control of the passions is difficult enough when we have our wits about us; when we've been drinking, it becomes nigh onto impossible.

• Suggestive television, movies, and magazines. Gentlemen, our culture has deliberately lured us into thinking that we can handle all the suggestive images we see on TV, in movies and magazines, on the Internet. As one crusty old priest told me, "Suggestive, hell — they don't 'suggest' anything — they just come right out and do it." We are foolish if we think we can look at some of this stuff and not be affected. We need to insert a V-chip! The primary sex organ is the brain, the oldest VCR around, and when we spend our waking hours taking in scenes that would arouse an Egyptian mummy, should we be surprised we cannot shake lustful thoughts? Is that old-fashioned? You're darn right it is!

• Lewd talk. St. Alphonsus Liguori wrote, "We must mortify our tongue by abstaining from obscenity. An impure word spoken in jest may prove a scandal to others, and sometimes a word of double meaning, said in a witty way, does more harm than a word openly impure." We priests and future priests sometimes use language that would make a sailor blush, characteristic of a high school locker room. We need to encourage one another to purity, not drag one another down. The way we speak about something usually indicates the way we treat it. If we speak of sexuality with awe and reverence, we'll be inclined to treat it as such; if our language is more flippant and trashy, don't be surprised that temptations to impurity are more frequent.

• Failure to set proper boundaries. We would never allow ourselves to be alone with people to whom we are powerfully attracted, or never go any place where temptation is high, whether that be certain areas of town, or bars, or even restaurants known for sexual immorality. We are so aware of our weakness, so prudent in setting boundaries, that we would not — as we used to say in the old days — place ourselves in an occasion of sin.

• Boundaries . . . we know ourselves well. We don't ask for trouble by putting ourselves in situations with people to whom we are attracted that could go beyond chaste propriety.

I would hope we could have genuine friendships with women, enjoy their company, benefit from their counsel, seek their collaboration. I would also hope this would always be pure. As Hans Urs von Balthasar wrote, "In their relationships with women, priests take as their model the nobility and naturalness of Jesus." Just as a married man is spoken for, so are we. A married man can enjoy friendships with other women, but must never let it jeopardize his primary love relationship with his wife.

We, too, can, and should, enjoy friendships with women, but never can it jeopardize our celibate commitment. As a married man must always ask, "Can I explain this relationship to my wife with honesty and at peace?" so must we ask about a relationship with a woman, "Can I explain this relationship to the spouse, to my bride, the Church?" I hope we can, most of the time. But there will be times we must say, "This should not progress any further."

• Avoid using the standards of this world as your guide. This world will tell you: "Everyone needs a fling now and then!" "Chastity is unnatural and impossible!" "Even your brother priests are ignoring their vows . . . why are you still serious?" "These silly laws of the Church are based on some medieval, outmoded ideals. Get with it!" "Chastity is no more a virtue than malnutrition."

Nowhere is the urge to conform ourselves to the ways of the world stronger than in the area of sexuality. We conform ourselves instead only to God's designs, the example of Jesus, the teachings of his Church, and the implications of a free choice made on a well-formed conscience, and nothing else! As the Holy Father has written, "From the cross the Lord Jesus speaks to all his priests, inviting them to be, with him, signs of contradiction before the world."

The positive helps — to be embraced:

• Prayer. Why are we embarrassed to take our sexuality to prayer? Why are we afraid to admit our weaknesses, own up to our falls, and ask his grace? Is chastity and celibacy a gift? Well, then, ask for it in prayer! Father Dominic Maruca says, "You are committing psychic suicide if you think you can be genuinely celibate without a strong ongoing relationship with the Lord."

Celibacy has its moments of loneliness, frustration, intense struggle with temptation. That's when we need to be united with Jesus in his agony in the garden, in his pouring out on the cross. Von Balthasar again: "Ready for a possibly lifelong struggle, priests regard the unsatisfied longing for completion and the loneliness in an often unsuccessful priestly ministry as a grace of participation in the cross of the Lord." Celibacy has its moments of joy and fulfillment. That's when we need to be close to Jesus in his risen glory.

Listen again to Archbishop Flynn:

> The commitment to celibacy can only be sustained in prayer. The noise of the world must be regularly shut out so as to create an island of silence where the priest or seminarian can hear the Lord speak. [We] must learn the absolute necessity of sustained and solitary prayer. . . . In those times. . . , the Lord will chasten and he will affirm, but without it the light of celibacy is gradually extinguished.

Look at it this way: our celibate chastity is the outward sign of our interior love of Jesus and his Church. If that inner life is morbid, the outward sign is a lie! As a husband finds chastity difficult unless he has a strong relationship with his wife, we find celibacy difficult if we do not sustain a vibrant interior companionship with the Divine Lover.

Struggles with chastity move us to prayer: prayer of petition, yes, as we seek strength from our Lord; prayers for mercy, as we ask the Lord's pardon for falls; and, paradoxically, prayers of gratitude, as we thank the Lord for our frailty, our sexuality, since it leads us to him and reminds us of our need for him and our need for the love of others. A particularly effective prayer strengthening our celibate promise is the sacrament of penance.

• An enjoyment of solitude. Do we enjoy our own company, happy to pray, read, write, listen to music, exercise, or do some constructive hobby or labor? Or are we gadflies constantly running around in search for new thrills, fads, and company? Healthy celibacy requires an enjoyment of solitude.

• A disciplined, balanced way of life. This entails choreographing prayer, work, rest, recreation, and friendship, with a disciplined approach to eating, drinking, spending money, buying new gadgets, and entertainment. We used to call it an "ascetical" approach to life. Now we call it establishing a healthy rhythm of life. The psychologist Richard Sipe, who has written extensively on priestly celibacy, says that the elements essential to preserving this "healthy rhythm of life" are work, prayer, community, service, care for one's health, ordered and balanced living, continuous learning, and an appreciation of beauty.

• Good priest-friends. These are men whom we can trust, with whom we can share joys, frustrations, and let off steam, men who are so secure in their relationship with us, and vice versa, that they can speak bluntly to us when we are deceiving ourselves about our priestly ideals and commitments.

• And good married friends. Celibacy is built upon a profound appreciation of marriage. As Cardinal O'Connor said, "Good celibates are those who would also make good husbands and fathers." Good relationships with married couples ground our celibate love in common sense, and powerfully remind us that we are called to

318

love the Church as tenderly as this man loves his wife and to love our people as sacrificially as this couple care for their children. They can also knock sense into our hard heads when we start longing for marriage as a paradise!

I close by confessing that I have barely scratched the surface. And I conclude with one final observation: it is possible to live a happy, wholesome, fruitful life, faithful to one's commitment of celibate chastity. The world will tell you it is not — they will deny celibacy's value, contend it is unhealthy, unnatural, and impossible. They will tease you and say, "Come on, you're getting it somewhere." And, let's face it, enough priests have acted in such a manner as to provide them ammo.

But, with the grace of God, it is possible, and, not only possible, but downright wholesome and happy. Is it difficult? You bet it is, at times, but so is the chastity and sacrifice of marriage. Is it tough at times? You bet it is, and, not just the lack of conjugal love, but the absence of the tender, understanding, affirming companionship of a woman whose world revolves around you and who has given you living, breathing results of your love, namely children.

But realistically facing those admitted challenges drives us into the arms of the most infinite, satisfying love of all, and frees us for a life of sacrificial service to the most enchanting Bride ever, the Church. And those same people who taunt us that celibacy is impossible and harmful are deep down fascinated that a man has found a love that satisfies and excites even more than that of a spouse; and then those cynics turn into searchers as, in our stumbling yet sincere attempts to love Jesus and his Church purely, we hint to them that there is more to this life than meets the eye.

So we embrace celibate chastity sincerely, realistically, sanely, joyfully, freely. Fear, holding back, or lack of honesty has no place in this romance. As St. Francis de Sales wrote:

> Be Not Afraid . . .
> Do not look forward to the changes and chances of this life
> in fear; rather look to them with full hope that, as they arise,
> God will deliver you out of them. He has kept you up to now, do

you but hold fast to his dear hand, and he will lead you safely through all things; and, when you cannot stand, he will carry you in his arms. Do not look forward to what may happen tomorrow; the same everlasting Father who cares for you today will take care of you tomorrow and every day. Either he will shield you from suffering, or he will give you unfailing strength to bear it. Be at peace then, and put aside all anxious thoughts and imaginations.

Let us pray . . . as Pope John Paul II concluded his Holy Thursday Letter to Priests:

Thank you, O God, for the gift of the Priesthood.
"Te Deum laudamus, Te Dominum confitemur. . . ."
We praise you and we thank you, O God: all the earth adores you. We, your ministers, with the voices of the prophets and the chorus of the apostles, proclaim you as Father and Lord of life, of every form of life which comes from you alone. We recognize you, O most Holy Trinity, as the birthplace and beginning of our vocation; you, the Father, from eternity have thought of us, wanted us and loved us; you, the Son, have chosen us and called us to share in your unique and eternal priesthood; you, the Holy Spirit, have filled us with your gifts and have consecrated us with your holy anointing. You, the Lord of time and history, have placed us on the threshold of the Third Christian Millennium, in order to be witnesses to the salvation which you have accomplished for all humanity. We, the Church which proclaims your glory, implore you: let there never be lacking holy priests to serve the Gospel; let there solemnly resound in every Cathedral and in every corner of the world the hymn *"Veni, Creator Spiritus"* — Come, O Creator Spirit! Come to raise up new generations of young people, ready to work in the Lord's vineyard, to spread the Kingdom of God to the furthermost ends of the earth. And you, Mary, Mother of Christ, who at the foot of the cross accepted us as beloved sons with the Apostle John, continue to watch over our vocation. To you we entrust the years of ministry that Providence will grant us yet to live. Be near us to guide us along the paths of the world, to meet the men and

women whom your Son redeemed with his blood. Help us to fulfill completely the will of Jesus, born of you for the salvation of humanity. O Christ, you are our hope! *"In te, Domine, speravi, non confundar in aeternum."*

24

Devotion to Our Lady

(Scripture selection — Acts 1:12-14)

Nine times out of ten, I sit on the pulpit side of the sanctuary for morning prayer and Mass in our chapel at the North American College. The reason I do so is simple. At that time of the day I need all the help I can get in concentrating and focusing. From this side I can look straight at the mural of the Annunciation that dominates the opposite wall, and, for me, that early concentration on Mary and the Archangel Gabriel supplies the "first aid," the focus I need. According to art scholar Kenneth Clark the Annunciation is the most re-created scene in the history of painting, so apparently I am not alone in finding it magnetic.

When I asked three of our students who had just returned from the Holy Land what place most moved them during their pilgrimage, they each replied separately, "The Church of the Annunciation in Nazareth," and, specifically, the seal in the floor, *Hic Verbum caro factum est* ("Here the Word was made Flesh").

So, again, I find myself in good company being attracted by the Annunciation. "The Annunciation," wrote Martin Luther, "when the angel came to Mary and brought her the message from God, may be fitly called the Feast of Christ's humanity, for then began our deliverance."

> The angel of the Lord announced unto Mary.
> And she conceived by the Holy Spirit.
> Behold the handmaid of the Lord.
> Be it done unto me according to the Will.
> And the Word became flesh.
> And dwelt among us.

The Incarnation; the pivotal mystery of Christianity; the "good news" — that God became man, the Word became flesh, the second

323

Person of the Blessed Trinity took upon himself human nature in the womb of a virgin. It is that truth that provides me a focus each morning, it is that scene of the Virgin that reminds me, as I start the day, of my identity, my vocation, my mission.

For, as Fulton Sheen has so eloquently preached, the real good news is that the Incarnation continues, as the Word of God is enfleshed each day in the heart and mind, speech and actions, of his disciples. So do priests identify most closely with Mary, for the fundamental question posed to them, the answer to which gives them identity, vocation, and mission is the same one posed to her at the Annunciation: Will you give flesh to the Son of God? Will the divine become human through you? Will you provide God the Son with a human nature? As I sit in one of those chairs and look at Mary, my mission, identity, and vocation as a priest are reaffirmed; I am reminded that in a matter of minutes, at the altar, I will sacramentally provide God flesh, and I resolve that throughout the day, with his help, the Lord will become again incarnate for his people in and through me.

Is it any wonder that, ever since the first priests took Mary with them after the Ascension to await the coming of the Paraclete in the cenacle, so have the priests of the new covenant always enjoyed a special relationship with the Mother of the Eternal High Priest? It is this devotion to our Lady in the life of the priest I wish to address.

This exhortation to love our Blessed Mother will hardly be ethereal or theoretical. I propose a deep, filial love of Mary as a very sound and pragmatic way to be and to remain faithful, effective priests. I can say in all honesty that I soon discover that every priest who has been a model for me has an unshakable trust in her; and I must admit that, when I ask the "giants" among my priestly heroes to tell me the reason for their ministry's success, they list a reliance upon her near the top.

I once attended a day of prayer for priests led by Sister Bridge McKenna, and she urged us to love Mary as sons. "No wonder you priests are so close to her," she said, "for you both look at Jesus — she on earth and now in heaven, you, in the Eucharist — and you both say, as no one else can, 'This is my body; this is my blood.' "

When I survey the North American College, I see many reasons to thank God, and one of the top ones is our vibrant devotion to our Lady. This has been noted of our seminary since its founding at the corner of the Via dell'Umiltà and the Via della Vergine on the Feast of her Immaculate Conception in 1859. I am so happy when I see seminarians praying the rosary together, celebrating our Blessed Mother's feasts, enthusiastic about pilgrimages to her shrines, and initiating such helpful endeavors as the act of total consecration to her. As I mention to each class of new men on their first full day at the college, Mary's role in our house is as dominant and visible as the mosaic behind our altar, and sincere devotion to her has been a feature of college life from day one.

Likewise does the Eternal City foster a love of her; from the ancient frescoes at the catacombs to St. Mary Major and Santa Maria in Trastevere; from the *Salus Populi Romani* to Our Lady of Perpetual Help at St. Alphonsus; from the charming parochial and neighborhood feasts to her image that adorns almost every *angolo* ("corner") of this city —she is there.

And then, of course, there is the powerful example of the Bishop of Rome, who, probably more than anyone is responsible for the current renaissance in Marian piety. His manly, genuine, evangelical love of her has animated every address, encyclical, word, travel, and pastoral initiative of his extraordinary pontificate. His conclusion to *Gift and Mystery* could well serve as a commentary on his whole pastorate: "May the Virgin Mary accept this testimony of mine as a filial homage, for the glory of the Blessed Trinity. May she make it fruitful in the hearts of my brothers in the priesthood and of all the members of the Church. May she make it a leaven of solidarity for the many good people who, although they do not share the same faith, often listen to my words and engage me in sincere dialogue."

We can testify that this hope of the Holy Father has certainly been fulfilled.

Again, I thank God for the vibrant devotion to our Lady that blesses our college. And, since the seminary is so very often a microcosm of the Church universal, we are not surprised that the Church — in fact, the world — is experiencing a tremendous renewal of attention and dedication to her. You can hardly find a more popular barometer of world trends than *Life* magazine, and, as you probably know, that publication had her on its cover in their December, 1996, issue. In a well-done article they tried to discover what they termed "the mystery of Mary," concluding that attraction to her is one of the world's most potent forces, luring not only Catholics and the Orthodox, as it always has, but Muslims, Protestants, Jews, and people of no creed whatever.

Allow the historian in me to take over for a minute to observe that, within recent memory of many, devotion to Mary was not always as popular as it is now. In the heady, difficult, cleansing years after the providential Second Vatican Council, many felt the Reformation discomfort with her had finally reached even Rome, and that she had been at last relegated to the storage rooms and museums. There were calls for a more rational, calm, theologically proper, cerebral attention to Mary. Some even began to ridicule Marian piety. As I will explain shortly, perhaps some of this reform was necessary and even beneficial, but we do know now that a tender love of the Mother of Jesus is so strong and so ingrained in the Christian psyche that it could not be erased. As Cardinal Carlo Martini recently commented to his priests in Milan: "I believe the time has come to take a new look at Marian devotion, to find an equilibrium between theological clarity and the spiritual yearnings of the Christian people. Otherwise, we may face a dangerous loss of warmth and feeling in our faith, our prayer, our life. . . . We have arrived at a point where this cold, scientific attitude no longer responds to an obvious emotional need for an attachment to Mary."

As I hinted, there were unfortunate excesses in the postconciliar renewal of Marian devotion, but, then again, there were excesses in the piety itself prior to the council. I hope I am not being naïve in agreeing with the archbishop of Milan that perhaps now, having seen extremes on both sides, we can benefit from the renewed, sound devotion to our Lady that seems to be sweeping the Church today.

A valuable catechesis in genuine love of our Lady came from Pope Paul VI in his apostolic letter of 1974, *Marialis Cultis*, on the right ordering of veneration to Mary. Rejecting both the saccharine, overly sentimental, and doctrinally questionable devotion to her that characterized some circles prior to the council, and the dry, rationalistic downplaying of her central role indicative of some in the late sixties and the seventies, Paul VI called for a genuine, reinvigorated veneration to Mary, a *cultus* purified of any taint of so-called Mariolatry, but emphatic about her indispensable role in the economy of salvation.

He proposed four checks to make sure our devotion to the Mother of God was pure, sound, and mature: that it be Christological, scriptural, liturgical and ecclesial, and ecumenically sensitive. I submit these are worth reviewing now in our ongoing desire to ensure that our devotion to the Blessed Mother is with the Church.

Christological: as the old maxim goes, *"Ad Jesum per Mariam"* ("To Jesus through Mary"). The only goal of attention to Mary, as it is the only goal of anything we do, is to reach Jesus. It is simple Catholic wisdom that one of the more effective, reliable, enjoyable, and tender ways of growing closer to Jesus is by holding the hand of his Mother. The woman whose last recorded words in the Gospel are, "Do whatever he tells you," resists and disdains more than anyone else any attempt to place her above or in front of her Son.

Can there ever be an excess of Marian piety? Well, there can certainly be an excess of wrong Marian piety! However, there can hardly ever be an overabundance of genuine, properly ordered devotion to her. As St. Bernard preached, "Let us not imagine that we obscure the glory of the Son by the honor we lavish on the Mother, for the more she is honored, the greater is the glory of her Son." Listen to Pope John Paul describe his early veneration of Mary in his memoir, *Gift and Mystery*:

> At the time when my priestly vocation was developing . . . a change took place in my understanding of devotion to the Mother of God. I was already convinced that Mary leads us to Christ, but at that time I began to realize also that Christ leads us to his Mother. At one point I began to question my devotion to Mary, believing that, if it became too great, it might end up compromising the supremacy of the worship owed to Christ. At that time I was greatly helped by a book by St. Louis Marie Grignion de Montfort, *Treatise of True Devotion to the Blessed Virgin*. There I found the answers to my questions. Yes, Mary does bring us closer to Christ; she does lead us to him, provided we live her mystery in Christ. . . . This is the origin of the motto *Totus Tuus*, an abbreviation of the more complete form of en-

trustment which reads: *Totus tuus ego sum et omnia mea Tua sunt. Accipio Te in mea omnia. Praebe mihi cor Tuum, Maria.* (I belong to you entirely, and all that I possess is yours. I take you into everything that is mine. Give me your heart, O Mary.)

If our attention to Mary stops with her, it is wrong. She loves being a means to an end, the end being her Son. True, genuine, orthodox veneration of Mary is always Christological.

Likewise it is scriptural, says Paul VI. All we need for a rich, sustaining Marian piety is found in the Bible. This does not mean that the Church's tantalizing array of feasts, titles, apparitions, prayers, songs, poetry, and traditions are misguided. No, they are so welcome, so helpful, because they flow from, enhance, and enliven God's revelation about his chosen daughter contained in Scripture, passed on in Tradition, and guarded by the magisterium. A pure and genuine devotion to her is not dependent upon the more exotic features of apparitions, secrets, miracles, and new revelations. Thomas Merton said it well: "Since God has revealed very little to us about Mary, people who know nothing of who and what she was only reveal themselves when they try to add something to what God has already told us about her."

Genuine veneration of Mary is Scripture-based.

Thirdly, it is liturgical and ecclesial. The richest way the Church honors Mary is in the Church's official public prayer, celebrating her feasts and content with the liturgical prayers we are blessed with. Again, private devotions and prayers are laudable, as long as they flow from and lead us to the corporate praise of the Church, the liturgy. The term used by Pope Paul is ecclesial, for we are wary of an excessively individualistic Marian devotion.

Finally, says Paul VI, we should be mindful of the ecumenical dimensions of our attention to Mary. Positively, this means we are eager to share with our separated brethren the richness of true devotion to her; negatively, this means we are sensitive about reformed and evangelical uneasiness caused by past errors and excesses.

By the way, a most welcome ecumenical development, as you probably know, is that reformed and evangelical Christians are slowly gaining an appreciation of Mary's role. One of the most powerful

328

contemporary studies on her, as you may have seen, is that of the great Lutheran scholar Jaroslav Pelikan, *Mary Through the Centuries*. I remember a few years ago after the terrible TWA flight 800 tragedy hearing Dr. Forrest Church, pastor of the Unitarian All Souls Church in New York, remark: "People were asking, 'How can God allow such a thing?' But then they'd turn around and pray for the victims, and I watched many pray to Mary . . . for support and nurturing. And I mean nurturing in a strong, not a weak way. She would put their tough questions to God on their behalf! She would lift them up and help them move forward! I envy Catholicism its Mary."

Yes, you heard me! This from a Unitarian!

So, a genuine devotion to her is Christological, scriptural, liturgical and ecclesial, and ecumenically mature.

Now let's take this treasure of Christian life, our love of the Mother of Christ, and see how she can be of particular aid to the priest. Observes St. Bernardine of Siena, " 'Behold thy mother.' By these words, Mary, by reason of the love she bore them, became the Mother, not only of St. John, but of everyone."

But it is not selfish or exclusive, my brothers, to claim that her maternal love applies in a particular way to her priests. She loves Jesus more than anyone. It only makes sense to conclude that those configured to her Son through holy orders, those who act in his person, have a special claim on her universal motherhood.

It goes without saying that the most obvious way she helps us is through her intercession. "There is no more excellent way to obtain graces from God," concludes St. Philip Neri, "than to seek them through Mary, because her divine Son cannot refuse her anything."

Priests can never go wrong in turning to her, as did her Son, the first priest of the new covenant. Especially in trial, temptation, and loneliness can we find in her an attentive ear and a soft shoulder — and, believe me, I know that from experience. You will find that priests who struggle with chastity, temperance, doubt, despair, and illness have a very warm and intimate relationship with her. So, most obviously, she helps us because she is a powerful intercessor. Our patron saint, the Curé of Ars, preached, "It is enough to turn to Mary to be heard. 'My Mother,' our Lord said to her, 'I cannot refuse you anything.' "

The French have a wonderful saying: If you want to find the secret to a man's success, *Cherchez la femme* ("Look for the woman"). Well, we sure hope our priestly ministry is fruitful and successful. If it is, "look for the woman" who caused it, and that woman in a priest's life is Mary. As a husband returns home from work and pours out his troubles to his wife, so do we find attentive ears and loving eyes as we confide in Mary. I don't want to get maudlin here. All I know is that it works, and that Jesus knew what he was doing when from the altar of the cross he entrusted his first priests to his own Mother.

One of my best friends as a priest was very close to his mom, especially after the death of his dad. After the passing of her husband, his mother had struggled with bouts of depression, and even had to be hospitalized. It was so moving to watch my friend so lovingly care for his mom. On one of his days off, he showed up at home to spend the day with her, only to discover that she had taken her own life. You can imagine his devastation.

A few weeks after the funeral he went through with the plans he had made a year before and came here to Rome for the international retreat for priests. He was at a real low point in his life. Never had he felt so alone, so orphaned. A turning point, he tells me, came during a prayer service in the Audience Hall when an icon of the Mother and Child was carried in. At that moment, gazing at the icon, surrounded by thousands of his brother priests in prayer, he realized that Mary was truly his Mother. He joined her at the foot of the cross. He broke down in tears, and two of the priests near him took him outside and listened as he told them the tragedy of his mother's suicide and his own discovery of Mary just moments before in the prayer service. He marks that episode as the beginning of spiritual rebirth for him.

Thus is she there for every priest.

But I contend that she can also assist us by her example, and I have some specifics in mind, one of them being that she teaches us, as no other person can, about the earthiness of the Church. "Mary is our only savior from an abstract Christ," observes Coventry Patmore. The God who was conceived and carried in her womb, born in a stable, nursed at her breasts, cried on her shoulder, and grew under her care, can hardly be abstract and unreal. Neither he

— nor his Mystical Body, the Church — is always neat, tidy, predictable, and clean.

Yet we expect that of the Church at times, don't we? Our pastor should be perfect, our parishioners adulating, our bishop ever attentive, the Curia efficient, our assignments thrilling, the schedules predictable, and the Church so pristine and pure. Good God, wake up, my brothers! Mary will set you straight! You're working for a God who couldn't even get a proper room for the birth of his only-begotten Son, and you want a Church where every assignment is ideal?

I've quoted before what Walker Percy wrote to the novelist Mary Lee Settle when she became a Catholic, "It's a very untidy outfit you're hooking up with." As a priest told me once when I was in the seminary, "If you want it all nice, clean, presentable, and neat, join the Anglicans." Something tells me that, about the time of the flight into Egypt, Mary was ready to get in touch with Gabriel and call it all off. Nothing comfortable and cozy about any of it — it can be messy, untidy, earthy — all synonyms for "incarnational," and woe to the priest who forgets that.

Mary teaches us that discipleship, serving her Son, brings uncertainty. Priests can become proud of résumés, and have a career path all charted out. Our Lady smiles and says that when you say *fiat* to the Lord you are surrendering your most prized commodity — your future and your security to plan your life. Get ready for surprises, some plums, some prunes, some Bethlehems, some lost-in-the-temple episodes. In other words, be prepared for uncertainty.

Our Blessed Mother shows us the necessity of fidelity in both the joys and the sorrows of priestly discipleship. She was there at the happiest moment ever — the first Christmas. And she was there at the saddest event ever — the foot of the cross. Likewise will our priesthood have its Bethlehems and its Calvarys. Her lesson is that what is happening to us is not as significant as with whom it is happening, for what is of the essence is that, at both the crib and the cross, she is close to Jesus. That is fidelity.

Mary's impact would be much less had we only the account of her at Christmas and not at Calvary, had we only the Madonna with Child and not the Pietà. So are we faithful to the Church when it is fresh, full of life and promise, alive and bouncy — as was the Infant of Bethlehem; and we are faithful to Christ and his Church when it is dead, lifeless, bleeding and torn — as on Calvary.

As the old saying goes, "God may not have favorites, but his Mother does." Our Lady exemplifies a special care for certain people, namely the sick, forgotten, poor, sinful, and troubled, and she models such a solicitude for the true pastor. We call her "comforter of the afflicted," "refuge of sinners," "health of the sick," "help of Christians." As a good mother will display a special love for whichever of her children might be sick, troubled, or ignored by the others, so does Mary for her spiritual children. Go to Lourdes, for instance: do not expect to find the wealthy, the strong, the sleek, or the elite, but watch the twisted, battered, tired, and sick in mind, soul, and body bask in a mother's care.

So does the good priest have a heart that goes out to those in need. We have our favorites, and they are the sick, the poor, the forgotten, the sinners. Watch the effective pastor: at a dinner party for parishioners, he will spend the most time with the one there who has fallen away from the Church; he will drive down a block where ten of the homes are Catholic and stop to visit the one where the housebound person lives. Invited to all twenty parties after First Communion, he will make sure he attends the one of the child who has no father; of all the kids on the basketball team after the game he makes sure the one who sat on the bench during the entire game is the first one he invites to go out for a hamburger or pizza. Our Lady teaches us to show a special concern to those in need — they, the sick, poor, the sinners, and the troubled are her favorites, as they should be ours.

I was inspired by the recent example of Father Juan Julio Wicht, the priest in Lima, Peru, who was one of the hostages in the Japanese Embassy a few years ago. The terrorists wanted to let him go; they told him he was free to leave whenever he wanted. He did not; he chose to stay with the people, to support them, comfort them, pray with and for them. Now there's a great priest, knowing his vocation is to be close to people who need him.

Mary can teach us a dignity and respect for women. She is strong, confident, and has a pivotal role in God's plan. God honored her more than any human being, and, in so doing, as the Holy

Father reminds us in *Mulieris Dignitatem*, put to rest the notion that women are inferior and have fewer rights than men. John Ruskin observes, "There has probably not been an innocent home throughout Europe during the period of Christianity in which the imagined presence of the Madonna has not given sanctity to the duties and comfort to the trials and the lives of women."

You see, any religion which holds that the second Person of the Blessed Trinity took flesh in the womb of a woman, that God himself waited upon the free consent of a woman before proceeding with his plans, that the only human person in heaven, body and soul, is a woman, then that religion, that Church, knows the dignity of women, a true feminism, and that Church is a defender of women's rights in their most elementary sense. Comments Pelikan on the Annunciation, "The entire plan of salvation hung in the balance. So if God does not rape, God woos, then it had to be a free and independent source of action in Mary that made this happen. This makes her not just some passive receptacle."

And as the novelist Mary Gordon mentions, "Devotion to Mary is the objective correlative of all the primitive desires that lead human beings to the life of faith. She embodies our desire to be fully human yet to transcend death. The hatred of women is the legacy of death; in Mary, Mother and Queen, we see, enfleshed in a human form that touches our most ancient longings, the promise of salvation. . . ."

You want a model of how to treat women? Look at how God treated Mary.

I would like to mention one final way our Lady helps her priests. She reminds them of their identity.

The author-psychologist Robert Coles has observed that usually the first moment of self-identity a baby has is when the infant, held up by its mother, stares into its mother's eyes and sees there its own reflection. For the first time ever, in the eyes of its mom, the baby realizes it is someone different, that it has an identity.

May I propose that an effective way we discover our priestly identity is by gazing into the eyes of our Blessed Mother? Therein we see the reflection of Jesus, and therein we see ourselves.

She literally carried the Word-made-flesh inside her. She sensed the movement, growth, and life of the God-man within her. So must we imitate her in allowing Jesus to move, grow, and come to life within us. Such is our identity as priests.

In June of 1996 I visited the Shrine of Our Lady of Guadalupe. Reading up on it beforehand, I was fascinated by the story of Mary's eyes. Under scientific, microscopic examination of the *tilma* on which, as you know, the image of Mary was imprinted, the scholars had discovered that in the eyes of the Virgin they detected a reflection of another person, and that person fit the description of Juan Diego.

The day I went to the shrine was a time of pilgrimage for priests. I stood on the platform in front of Mary's image, observing, praying, and watching as dozens, hundreds of priests, old and young, sick and strong, white, brown, and black, processed in front of her, looking into her eyes. And I imagined the reflection of each individual priest in the eyes of the Virgin, as she looks at each one of us with the same intensity, passion, and motherly love as she did Jesus, as she did Juan Diego. She helps us discover, deepen, and persevere in our identity, our vocation, and our mission.

Vergine Immacolata! Aiutateci!
("Immaculate Virgin! Help us!")

Our Sunday Visitor. . .

Your Source for Discovering the Riches of the Catholic Faith

Our Sunday Visitor has an extensive line of materials for young children, teens, and adults. Our books, Bibles, booklets, CD-ROMs, audios, and videos are available in bookstores worldwide.

To receive a FREE full-line catalog or for more information, call **Our Sunday Visitor** at **1-800-348-2440**. Or write, **Our Sunday Visitor** / 200 Noll Plaza / Huntington, IN 46750.

- -

Please send me: ___A catalog
Please send me materials on:
___Apologetics and catechetics   ___Reference works
___Prayer books   ___Heritage and the saints
___The family   ___The parish

Name_____

Address_____Apt._____

City_____State____Zip_____

Telephone (   ) _____

A09BBABP

- -

Please send a friend: ___A catalog
Please send a friend materials on:
___Apologetics and catechetics   ___Reference works
___Prayer books   ___Heritage and the saints
___The family   ___The parish

Name_____

Address_____Apt._____

City_____State____Zip_____

Telephone (   ) _____

A09BBABP

- -

Our Sunday Visitor
200 Noll Plaza
Huntington, IN 46750
Toll free: 1-800-348-2440
E-mail: osvbooks@osv.com
Website: www.osv.com

Your Source for Discovering the Riches of the Catholic Faith